The YADA YADA Prayer Group

Book One

Neta Jackson

THOMAS NELSON
Since 1798

NASHVILLE   DALLAS   MEXICO CITY   RIO DE JANEIRO

Published in Nashville, Tennessee, by Thomas Nelson. Thomas Nelson is a registered trademark of Thomas Nelson, Inc.

The Yada Yada Prayer Group® is a registered trademark of Thomas Nelson, Inc.

Published in association with the literary agency of Alive Communications, Inc., 7680 Goddard Street, Suite 200, Colorado Springs, CO 80920

Thomas Nelson, Inc. titles may be purchased in bulk for educational, business, fund-raising, or sales promotional use. For information, please e-mail SpecialMarkets@ThomasNelson.com.

Scripture quotations are taken from the following:
> The Contemporary English Version © 1991 by the American Bible Society. Used by permission.
> The Holy Bible, New International Version. © 1973, 1978, 1984, International Bible Society. Used by permission of Zondervan Bible Publishers.
> King James Version of the Bible.
> The New King James Version, © 1979, 1980, 1982, 1990 by Thomas Nelson, Inc., Publishers.

"If Not for Grace," written by Clint Brown. © 2000 Tribe Music Group (administered by PYPO Publishing) BMI.

This novel is a work of fiction. Any references to real events, businesses, organizations, and locales are intended only to give the fiction a sense of reality and authenticity. Any resemblance to actual persons, living or dead, is entirely coincidental.

ISBN 978-1-4016-8533-1 (Value Edition)

ISBN 978-1-40168-983-4 (2013 repackage)

Library of Congress Cataloging-in-Publication Data

Jackson, Neta.
The yada yada prayer group / by Neta Jackson.
  p. cm.

ISBN 978-1-59145-074-0 (trade paper)
ISBN 978-1-59554-439-1 (repack)

1. Women—Illinois—Fiction. 2. Christian women—Fiction. 3. Female friendship—Fiction. 4. Prayer groups—Fiction. 5. Chicago (Ill.)—Fiction. I. Title.
PS3560.A2415Y33 2003
813'.54—dc21   2003010588

Printed in the United States of America
13 14 15 16 17 RRD 5 4 3 2 1

To my sisters in the women's Bible study

of Reba Place Church

—you know who you are!—

who loved me anyway and stretched my faith.

And to Dave

—best friend, husband, writing partner—

who had the vision for this book in the first place

and believed in me in the process.

Prologue

CHICAGO'S NORTH SIDE—1990

A soft mist clouded the windshield of the Toyota wagon, playing catch-me-if-you-can with the intermittent wipers. Apartment buildings and three-storied six-flats crowded the wet narrow street like great brick cliffs. The woman behind the wheel of the Toyota drove cautiously through the Rogers Park neighborhood of north Chicago, looking for Morse Avenue.

At least it wasn't the typical macho Chicago thunderstorm: blowing in on big winds, shaking the trees, darkening the skies. *Boom! Crash! Flash!* Sheets and sheets of rain . . . and then just as quickly rolling away, leaving puddles and sunshine. A midwestern girl at heart, she usually enjoyed a good storm.

But not today. She hated driving in a heavy rain, especially on unfamiliar city streets with her kids in the car.

Mist . . . swipe . . . mist . . . the gentle rain softened even the rough edges of this Chicago neighborhood as she peered past the wipers looking for street signs—

A dark blur rose up suddenly in front of the car through the thin film of mist. Startled, she stomped on the brake. *Swipe.* The clear windshield showed a dark bedraggled shape—man? woman?— banging a fist on her hood. Heart pounding in her chest, the driver fumbled for the door locks. *Oh God, Oh God, what's happening?*—

"Mom-meee!" A frightened wail from the car seat behind her stifled the woman's first instinct to pound on the horn.

"Shh. Shh. It's okay." She forced her voice to be calm for the children's sake. "Someone walked in front of the car, but I didn't hit him. Shh. It's okay." But she gripped the steering wheel to stop her hands from shaking.

With one final bang on the hood, the figure shoved its fists into the pockets of a frayed army jacket and shuffled toward the driver's-side window. The driver steeled herself, heart still racing. Now she was going to get yelled at. Or mugged.

But the person hunched down, tapped gently at the window, and whined, "Change, lady? Got any change?"

Anger and relief shredded her anxiety. Just a panhandler. A woman at that, surprisingly small and bony beneath the bulky army jacket and layers of scarves. But the nerve! Stopping her car like that!

The driver rolled down her window a mere crack.

"Mom! Don't!" commanded her five-year-old man-child in the backseat.

"It's okay. Give Blanky to your little sister." She peered at the woman now standing just inches from her face. Dark-skinned, bug-eyed, the army jacket damp and limp, buttoned askew . . . the mist clung to the woman's uncombed nappy hair like shimmering glass beads.

"Got any change?" the panhandler repeated.

The driver channeled her voice into assertive disapproval. "You shouldn't jump in front of my car! I could have hit you."

"Need food for my baby. And diapers," said the woman stubbornly. She peered though the crack in the window into the backseat. Her voice changed. "You got kids?"

The driver was tempted to roll up the window and move on. Her family had made it a rule not to give money to panhandlers. Even a suburban mom from Downers Grove knew a dollar was more likely to find its way to the corner liquor store than be spent for bread and diapers.

But she hesitated, thinking of her two preschoolers in the backseat. What if the woman really *did* have kids who needed food and diapers?

Still she hesitated. Then an idea popped into her head. "Uh . . . I was just headed for Uptown Community Church on Morse Avenue." *To pick up my husband,* she could have added. Uptown had invited men from several suburban churches to volunteer once a month in an "urban outreach" to homeless men and drug addicts. "If you stop in there, I'm sure somebody will help you."

The woman, damp and glistening, shook her head. "Been there b'fore. Don't wanna wear out my welcome. Just a little change, lady? A dollar will do."

If you do it unto the least of these, you do it unto Me.

The driver sighed. Life would sometimes be a lot simpler if years of Sunday school lessons didn't follow her around like Jiminy Cricket sitting on her shoulder. What would her husband do? After all, he came to this "outreach" today because he wanted to help people like this woman.

On impulse, she leaned over and pulled up the lock on the passenger side of the car. "Get in," she said to the woman standing in the mist. "I'll take you to a grocery store."

"*Mom!*"

The panhandler scurried around and got in the car. She didn't put on the seat belt, and the driver tightened her mouth. She couldn't be this woman's keeper about *everything*. She turned and glared at her five-year-old before he opened his mouth again.

Now what? She had no idea where a grocery store was in this neighborhood! She'd passed the Rogers Park Fruit Market a few blocks back, but it probably didn't carry stuff like diapers. What she needed was a Jewel or Dominick's.

Or maybe her son was right—this was crazy, picking up this woman!

Then she saw it: Morse Avenue. She could ask at the church where to find a grocery store. Turning onto the busier street, full of small stores with security grids on the windows, she watched the door numbers slide by. There. She slowed beside the old two-story brick storefront that housed Uptown Community Church and turned off the ignition. The wipers died.

The woman in the passenger seat narrowed her eyes. "Thought we was goin' t' the store."

"We are," the driver chirped brightly, hopping out of the car. "I just have to let my husband know that I'll be a little late. Be right back." She opened the back door. "Come on, kids." Another encouraging look at the woman in the front seat. "I'll only take a minute."

With her daughter's legs wrapped tightly around her waist and the boy plodding along in sulky silence, the mother pulled hopefully on the handle of the glass door. *Oh, please open.* Relieved when it swung outward, she hustled up the narrow stairs to the second floor that had been remodeled into a large open meeting room. She stood uncertainly at the top of the stairs, looking for her husband among the small groups of volunteers scattered around the room who were talking, some praying. There he was. She caught his eye, and he acknowledged her with a smile. *Could I see you a moment?* she mouthed as she motioned at him.

The kids hugged their daddy as she explained the situation. But instead of being pleased, his voice rose. "You picked up a panhandler? In the car? Of all the—"

A tall thin man with wispy gray hair and wearing a Mr. Rogers sweater suddenly appeared beside them, smiling warmly. Her husband shook his head, still incredulous. "Uh, Pastor, this is my wife . . . honey, you tell him."

Feeling foolish now, she described the woman who had stopped her in the street and her intention to get the woman some groceries. "She said she's been here before. But I've got the kids . . . do you think it's okay?"

Uptown's pastor nodded, his large Adam's apple bobbing. "I know the lady. Last time she was here, I tried to get her into a detox program, but she didn't follow through. Probably not too anxious to see me again." His warm hazel eyes hinted at the compassion he no doubt handed out as freely as meals and good advice. "She can be a nuisance but is probably harmless. Sure, get her a bag of groceries . . . but as a general rule? Don't pick up panhandlers."

Relieved, she got directions to the nearest supermarket and ruffled her son's hair. "Okay, kids. We'll just help this lady out then come back and pick up Daddy." She picked up her daughter and reached out for her son. The boy pulled away from his mother's hand but allowed himself to be guided back down the stairs and out the door.

"Now be nice," she muttered under her breath as they approached the Toyota. "We're supposed to help people, even when it's inconvenient." Right.

"Hey, Mom, look!" Her son pointed an accusing finger at the car. The woman was gone.

CHICAGO, ILLINOIS—2002

I didn't really want to go to the "women's conference" the first weekend of May. Spending two hundred bucks to stay in a *hotel* for two nights only forty-five minutes from home? Totally out of our budget, even if it did include "two continental breakfasts, Saturday night banquet, and all conference materials."

Now if it had been just Denny and me, that'd be different. A romantic getaway, a second honeymoon . . . no teenagers tying up the phone, no dog poop to clean up in the yard, no third grade lesson plans, no driving around and around the block trying to find a parking place. Just Denny and me sleeping late, ordering croissants, fruit plates, and hot coffee for breakfast, letting someone else make the bed (hallelujah!), swimming in the pool . . . now *that* would be worth two hundred bucks, no question.

I'm not generally a conference-type person. I don't like big crowds. We've lived in the Chicago area for almost twenty years now, and I still haven't seen Venetian Nights at the lakefront, even though Denny takes Josh and Amanda almost every year. Wall-to-wall people . . . and standing in line for those pukey Port-a-Potties? Ugh.

Give me a small moms group or a women's Bible study any day—like Moms in Touch, which met at our church in Downers Grove all those years the kids were growing up. We had some retreats, too, but I knew most of the folks from church, and they were held at a camp and retreat center out in the country where you could wear jeans to all the sessions and walk in the woods during free time.

But listening to the cars on I-90 roaring past the hotel's manicured lawn? Laughing like a sound track at jokes told by high-powered speakers in tailored suits and matching heels? Having to take "after five attire" for a banquet on Saturday night? (Why would a bunch of women *do* that with no men around to admire how gorgeous we look?)

Uh-uh. Was not looking forward to it.

Still, Avis Johnson, my boss—she's the principal at the Chicago public school where I teach third grade this year—asked if I'd like to go with her, and that counts for something. Maybe everything. I've admired Avis ever since I first met her at Uptown Community Church but never thought we'd be pals or anything. Not just because she's African American and I'm white, either. She's so calm and poised—a classy lady. Her skin is a smooth, rich, milk-chocolate color, and she gets her hair done every week at a salon. Couldn't believe it when I found out she was fifty and a *grandmother*. (I should be so lucky to look like that when Josh and Amanda have kids.) I feel like a country bumpkin when I'm around her. My nondescript dark brown hair never could hold a "style," so I just wear it at shoulder level with bangs and hope for the best.

Not only that, but when we moved from suburban Downers Grove into the city last summer, I applied to teach in one of the public schools in the Rogers Park neighborhood of Chicago, where we live now, and ended up at Mary McLeod Bethune Elementary, where Avis Johnson just happened to be the *principal*. Weird calling her "Avis" on Sunday and "Ms. Johnson" on Monday.

Avis is one of Uptown Community's worship leaders and has tried to wean its motley congregation of former Presbyterians, Baptists, "Evee-Frees," Methodists, Brethren, and No-Churchers from the hymnbook and "order of service" to actually participating in *worship*. I love the way she quotes Scripture, too, not only from the New Testament, but also from those mysterious Minor Prophets, and Job, and the Pentateuch. I mean, I know a lot of Scripture, but for some reason I have a hard time remembering those pesky references, even though I've been in Sunday school since singing "Climb, Climb Up Sunshine Mountain" in the toddler class.

People at Uptown want to be "relevant" in an urban setting, which means cultivating a diverse congregation, but most of us, including yours truly, aren't too comfortable shouting in church and start to fidget when the service goes past twelve o'clock—both of which seem par for Sunday morning in black churches. Don't know why Avis stays at Uptown sometimes. Pastor Clark, bless him, has a vision, but for most of us transplants, our good intentions come with all the presumptions we brought from suburbia. But she says God called her to Uptown, and Pastor Clark preaches the Word. She'll stay until God tells her to go.

Denny and me—we've only been at the church since last summer. That's when Honorable Husband decided it was time white folks—meaning us, as it turned out—moved back into the city rather than doing good deeds from our safe little enclaves in the suburbs. Denny had been volunteering with Uptown's "outreach" program for over ten years, ever since the kids were little, driving into the city about once a month from Downers Grove. It was so hard for me to leave the church and people we've known most of our married life. But Denny said we couldn't hide forever in our comfort zone. So . . . we packed up the dog, the teenagers, and the Plymouth Voyager, exchanged our big yard for a postage stamp, and shoehorned ourselves into a two-flat—Chicago's version of a duplex—on Chicago's north side.

But frankly? I don't really know what we're doing here. Uptown Community Church has a few black members and one old Chinese lady who comes from time to time . . . but we're still mostly white in one of the most diverse neighborhoods in the U.S.—Rogers Park, Chicago. Josh says at his high school cafeteria, the black kids sit with the black kids, Latino kids sit with Latinos, nerds sit with nerds, whites with whites, Asians with Asians.

Not exactly a melting pot. And the churches aren't much better. Maybe worse.

In Des Moines, Iowa, where my family lives, I grew up on missionary stories from around the world—the drumbeats of Africa . . . the rickshaws of China . . . the forests of Ecuador. Somehow it was so easy to imagine myself one day sitting on a stool in the African veld, surrounded by eager black faces, telling Bible stories with flannel-graph figures. Once, when I told Denny about my fantasy, he snorted and said we better learn how to relate across cultures in our own city before winging across the ocean to "save the natives."

He's right, of course. But it's not so easy. Most of the people I've met in the neighborhood are friendly—friendly, but not friends. Not the kick-back, laugh-with-your-girlfriends, be-crazy, cry-when-you're-sad, talk-on-the-phone-five-times-a-week kind of friends I had in Downers Grove. And the black couple who lived upstairs? (DINKS, Josh called them: Double-Income-No Kids.) They barely give us the time of day unless something goes wrong with the furnace.

So when Avis asked if I'd like to go to this women's conference sponsored by a coalition of Chicago area churches, I said yes. I felt flattered that she thought I'd fit in, since I generally felt like sport socks with high heels. I determined to go. At worst I'd waste a weekend (and two hundred bucks). At best, I might make a friend—or at least get to know Avis better.

THE LOBBY OF THE EMBASSY SUITES HOTEL in Chicago's northwest suburbs was packed with women. An intense hum rose and fell, like a tree full of cicadas. "Girl! I didn't know *you* were coming!" . . . "Where's Shirlese? I'm supposed to be roomin' with her." . . . "*Look* at you! That outfit is *fine!*" . . . "Pool? Not after spending forty-five dollars at the salon this morning, honey. Who you kiddin'?"

Avis and I wiggled our Mutt and Jeff selves through the throng of perfumed bodies and presented our reservations at the desk.

"Jodi Baxter? And . . . Avis Johnson. You're in Suite 206." The clerk handed over two plastic key cards. "If you're here for the Chicago Women's Conference"—she added with a knowing smile—"you can pick up your registration packet at that table right over there."

Avis let me forge a path back through the cicada convention to a long table with boxes of packets marked A–D, E–H, all the way to W–Z. As we were handed our packets emblazoned with CWC in curlicue calligraphy, I noticed a bright gold sticker in the right-hand corner of mine with the number 26 written in black marker. I glanced at the packet being given to the woman standing next to me at the A-D box who gave her name as "Adams, Paulette"—but her gold sticker had the number 12.

"What's this?" I asked the plump girl behind the registration table, pointing to the number.

"Oh, that." Miss Helpful smiled sweetly. "They'll explain the numbers at the first session. Don't worry about it . . . Can I help you?" She turned to the next person in line.

Humph. I didn't want to wait till the first session. I was nervous enough surrounded by women who seemed as comfortable in a crowd of strangers as if it were Thanksgiving at Grandma's. I didn't want any "surprises." Avis waved her packet at me over the heads of five women crowding up to the table between us and nodded toward the elevators. We met just as the door to Elevator Two pinged open, and we wheeled our suitcases inside.

"What number did you get?"

"Number?"

"On your packet, right-hand corner, gold sticker."

"Oh." Avis turned over the packet she was clutching in one hand, along with her plastic key card, purse strap, and travel-pack of tissues. "Twenty-six. What's it for?"

I smiled big and relaxed. "I don't know. They'll tell us the first session." Whatever it was, I was with Avis.

As it turned out, we didn't need our key cards. The door to Suite 206 stood ajar. Avis and I looked at each other and stole inside like the Three Bears coming home after their walk in the woods. The sitting room part of the suite was empty. However, through the French doors leading into the bedroom, we could see "Goldilocks" sitting on the king-size bed painting her toenails while WGCI gospel music blared from the bedside radio.

The stranger looked up. "Oh, hi!" She waved the tiny polish brush in our direction. "Don't mind me. Make yourselves at home."

We stood and stared. The woman was average height, dark-skinned, and lean, with a crown of little black braids sporting a rainbow of beads falling down all around her head. Thirties, maybe forties; it was hard to tell. Her smile revealed a row of perfect teeth, but a scar down the side of her face belied an easy life.

Avis was braver than I was and said what I was thinking. "Uh, are we in the right room? We didn't know we had another room-mate."

The woman cocked her head. "Oh! They didn't tell you at registration? Suite 206, right?" She capped the nail polish and bounced off the bed. "Florida Hickman—call me Flo." She stuck out her hand. "Avis and Jodi, right? That's what they tol' me downstairs. Anyway, I was going to room with this sister, see, but she had to cancel, and I didn't want to pay for a whole suite all by myself. Had to sell the kids just to get here as it is." She laughed heartily. Then her smile faded and she cocked her head. "You don't mind, do you? I mean . . . I don't need this whole king-size football field to myself. Unless . . ." Her forehead wrinkled. "You want me to sleep on the fold-out couch?"

My good-girl training rushed to my mouth before I knew what I was saying. "Oh, no, no, that's okay. We don't mind." *Do we, Avis?* I was afraid to look in Avis's direction. We had pretty much agreed driving out that since it was a suite, we could each have a "room" to ourselves. Avis was definitely not the stay-up-late, sleepover type.

"Oh. Well, sure," Avis said. "It's just that no one told us." I didn't know Avis all that well, but that wasn't enthusiasm in her voice. "I'll sleep on the fold-out," she added, wheeling her suitcase over to the luggage stand.

I noticed that she didn't say "we." I stood uncertainly. But our new friend had generously offered the other side of the mammoth bed, so I dragged my suitcase into the bedroom and plopped it on the floor on the other side of Florida's nail salon.

Well, this was going to be interesting. I had thought it would be quite an adventure to get to know Avis as my roommate for the weekend. As members of the same church, this was a chance to get beyond the niceties of Sunday morning and brush our teeth in the same sink. But I hadn't counted on a third party. God knows I wanted to broaden my horizons, but this was moving a little faster than I felt ready for.

As I hung up the dress I hoped would pass for "after five" in the narrow closet, I suddenly had a thought. "Florida, what number is on your registration packet?"

Florida finished her big toe and looked at it critically. "Number? . . . Oh, you mean that gold sticker thing on the front?" She looked over the side of the bed where she'd dumped her things. "Um . . . twenty-six. Why?"

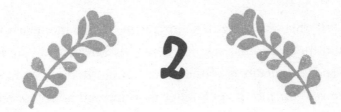

2

*A*s I walked between Avis and Florida toward the ballroom where the Friday night session was going to be held—feeling rather like the white stuff in an Oreo cookie—I could hear keyboard, drums, and bass guitar already pelting out some contemporary praise song I wasn't familiar with. As loud as the instruments were, however, I could hear a woman shouting, "Glory! Glory!" amid similar repetitions from other powerful female voices.

I cringed. Were we late? The schedule said the first session was at seven o'clock, and my watch said only six-fifty. No way did I want to walk in after the thing had started and have people stare at me. On the other hand, maybe it was a good excuse to just slip into the back and observe from afar.

But I guess we weren't late because there were still quite a few people milling around, finding seats, and greeting each other with enthusiastic hugs. I needn't have worried about people staring at me because no one seemed to care a spit. In fact, several women squealed when they saw Florida, as if they could hardly believe their eyes that she was here, but she didn't introduce me to any of her friends.

Meantime, I gave up any hope of sitting in the back because Avis was moving steadily toward the front, where people were already walking back and forth in the space between the front row and the platform, waving one arm and praying out loud over the music. *Oh, please God,* I groaned, *not the front row.* No telling what was going to happen during the meeting, and I didn't want to be a target for some well-meaning prophecy or someone who decided I needed to be slain in the Spirit.

Fortunately Avis turned into the fifth row back—still too close to the front to my way of thinking—and went all the way to the end of the row next to an aisle. Same as she does at Uptown Community, because she likes to move about during worship. I sighed. *Relax, Jodi. Don't be so nervous.* After all, I knew Avis—not very well, but still—and trusted her to be rock solid when it came to the Christian gospel. Whatever was going to happen at this confer-ence, Avis thought it was going to be good and had invited me to experience it too. Like I said before, that counted for something.

There was no actual "beginning" to the first session. But right about seven o'clock the worship band swung into another thump-ing contemporary song and a lady with mocha-cream skin and a red suit came onto the stage with a hand-held mike and revved us up like a cheerleader at a football game. "Come on! Come on! Let's hear you praise the Lord!" We all stood, and everybody was moving to the music in one way or another—stepping, clapping, waving hands. Five hundred female voices tackled that song like a powder-puff football team: "Cel-e-brate . . . Je-sus . . . Celebrate!"

I clapped and sang along with everyone else and started to enjoy myself. This was good. If only Amanda and Josh could see me. Denny too. My family thinks I'm too stiff. The kids love to go to Cornerstone in the summer—the music festival out in the corn-fields of Illinois sponsored by an aging group of Jesus People—and they come home pumped. We tried it as a family when Josh was in middle school, camping on the grounds, choosing from vari-ous sessions by the likes of Tony Campolo, Ron Sider, and John Perkins, and listening to all the Christian bands. I tried not to walk around with my mouth open staring at the kids with green spiked hair and dog collars sporting Jesus T-shirts. "I Broke the Rules—I Prayed in School" . . . "He Blew My Mind When He Saved My Soul" . . . "He Who Dies with the Most Toys—Still Dies." But by the time we got home, my ears were ringing and I wanted a T-shirt that said, "I Survived Cornerstone!"

We'd been singing in the ballroom about twenty minutes when I realized we were only into the second song. At forty minutes I wondered if we were ever going to get to sit down. Didn't these women ever get tired? But Avis and Florida were still going strong at sixty minutes.

Finally the speaker for the evening was introduced: Evangelist Olivia Mitchell, from right here in Chicago, though I hadn't heard of her before. She was about my age—in her forties—and very attractive. Not just her looks, which were fine enough. But she moved and talked like she was comfortable in her own skin.

Whew! She laid it on thick, coming off the platform, speaking directly to this woman or that one, about needing to be "women of purpose" and "living into our destiny."

I scrunched down in my seat, hiding behind the women in front of me. Destiny? Who had time to think about destiny! Trying to keep up with a classroom of thirty third-graders, half of whom could barely speak English, much less read it, two teens with raging hormones, a happy-go-lucky husband who was more generous than thrifty, and a full schedule of church meetings at Uptown Community, I felt lucky to wake up each morning knowing what day it was.

But listening to her challenge us to "be the woman God created you to be" started me thinking. Who *did* God create me to be? Did God have a particular purpose for Jodi Baxter? If so, I couldn't put words around it. I grew up in a solid Christian home—well, after my dad got "saved" when I was still in preschool. We not only went to church on Sunday, prayer meeting on Wednesday, and Pioneer Girls Club on Saturday morning (Boys Brigade for my brothers), but we had family devotions every night after supper, which I didn't mind if they were short, but we always prayed "from the youngest to the oldest," and my dad tended toward long-winded prayers. Every Sunday morning we had to say a Bible verse from memory at breakfast, and John 3:16 wasn't allowed as a fallback. I knew the Ten Commandments and the nine "Blesseds" of the Sermon on the Mount, and even though we were "no longer under the law but under grace," I definitely knew what was expected of a good Christian girl from Des Moines.

But who was that little girl, really? Baby of the family (a fact I shamelessly milked to my advantage whenever possible) . . . nuts about teddy bears (I'd collected one hundred stuffed bears by the time I went to college, a feat that impressed no one) . . . a scaredy-cat about bugs and big dogs (giving my two big brothers plenty of fuel for driving me crazy) . . . dreamy and romantic (of *course* I would get married to a dark-haired, handsome man and live happily ever after) . . . told everyone I was going to be a missionary to Africa when I grew up (which I never put together with big bugs and scary animals).

What did that safe, protected, idealistic little girl have to do with—

The voice of the lady in the red suit broke into my thoughts. "—the number in the little gold dot on your registration packet," she was saying. *Aha!* I thought. *The mystery is about to be revealed.* I felt around under my padded chair for my registration packet, even though I knew my number by heart: twenty-six. "This is the number of the prayer group you have been assigned to for the weekend," she went on, waving a packet. "Each group will have ten to twelve women. Roommates will be together in the same group; otherwise we have mixed up people from different churches and different parts of the city. After all, ladies, a major purpose for this Chicago Women's Conference is to break down the walls and link hands with our sisters . . ."

The red suit with the hand-held mike went on giving instructions, but my mind was already leaping ahead. A small group—now that might be more my speed than a huge crowd. On the other hand, I backpedaled; a small group was a pretty intimate setting for a group of strangers. I craned my neck and looked around the ballroom. Pretty diverse all right—if 80 percent black and 20 percent "other" counted as diverse. If this conference was supposed to draw together women from a broad spectrum of Chicago-area churches, where were all the white churches from Elmhurst and Downers Grove and Wilmette?

The worship band and singers struck up a thunderous chorus of "Awesome God" as the rest of us began to file out of the ballroom to our "prayer groups," presumably, though I'd missed where we were supposed to go. But Avis and Florida were "twenty-sixers," too, so all I had to do was follow along—

"Mmm. Getting on toward my bedtime," Avis's voice murmured behind me. "Maybe I'll just go back up to our room."

I turned, opening my mouth in protest. But before I could say anything, Florida jumped in. "Now I *know* these touchy-feely groups aren't my thang." A touch of street slang slipped in, making me realize I didn't know cucumbers about this woman. "Though it ain't my bedtime, that's for sure." She laughed, her beaded braids shaking around her head. "But I sure could do with a cup of coffee and a—"

"Whoa, whoa! Just a minute." I was surprised to hear my own voice throw a block on the deserters. I looked at Avis, who was stifling a yawn. "You got me into this, girlfriend." (Whoops. The moment the handle slipped out of my mouth, I was sure I'd gone too far using the familiar tag I'd heard all around me that night. But I rushed on.) "The prayer groups sound like a major part of the weekend, so I'd like to go." (Yikes! Was that true?) "But I don't want to go alone." (*That* part was certainly true.) "Come on. Let's go together. It's for prayer, after all." Now I was getting shameless. The Avis I knew on Sunday had a big thing about prayer. But just in case, I looked at both women and added hopefully, "Please?"

Florida crinkled her eyes at me and her mouth broke in an open grin. "Girl, you are so funny! You beggin' me to come to this prayer group thang?" She wagged her head, setting the little beads to dancing again. "Okay, okay, I'll come. Just give me a moment to get some coffee and a cig. Meet you in ten minutes in . . ." She looked at something she'd scribbled on her packet. " . . . Room 7."

I watched her bounce through the crowd and disappear toward the general direction of the coffee shop. "Think she'll show up?" I asked Avis, who now looked resigned. I took that as a good sign and steered us toward the bank of meeting rooms that circled the ballroom. "Maybe that's why God put Flo in our suite," I blabbered on, "so we could be in this prayer group thing together. She could use some deliverance from those cigarettes, for one thing." Obligation and guilt—I was good at laying it on thick.

"Ten o'clock," Avis announced as we fought our way through a river of women in the hallway, hunting for their meeting rooms. "I'll stay till ten o'clock. Then I turn into a pumpkin."

I smiled to myself as we sidled into Room 7. The clock on the wall said 9:05. Ten o'clock was fine with me. I couldn't imagine praying longer than an hour with a bunch of strangers anyway.

Four circles of chairs filled the four corners of the hotel meeting room, with a large printed number hanging on the back of one chair in each circle. Avis and I headed for number twenty-six, where several women of differing ages, sizes, and colors were already beginning to fill the twelve chairs.

Twelve chairs. Twelve women.

I had no idea.

3

*A*vis and I sat down on two of the folding chairs beside each other. I tried to save a seat for Florida, but a large black woman with close-cropped reddish hair and big gold earrings handed me my tote bag that I'd put on the seat and sat down with a *whumph*. I shrugged and tried a smile. "Hi. My name is Jodi."

"Adele." The woman gave a short nod.

O . . . kay. That was a ragged start. Almost all the seats were filled now, with just a couple vacant. Well, if Florida showed, she'd have to fend for herself.

For a few minutes, everyone just sat silently or talked to the person next to them—their friend or roomie, I presumed. But by now the clock said 9:15. If someone didn't get this thing rolling soon, we wouldn't have any time for prayer or whatever it was we were supposed to do.

I took a big breath. "Well, I'm not sure what we're supposed to do, but I don't know most of you so maybe we could just go around the circle and introduce ourselves."

"We've got nametags," said Adele, voice flat.

She might just as well have sat on me. I felt my face go hot.

Just then Florida slipped into the vacant chair on the other side of the circle. She looked around curiously, taking in the awkward silence. "Y'all didn't wait for me, did you? What are we doin'?"

"Uh . . . introducing ourselves, I think," said the woman next to her. Hispanic-looking. Slightly plump, but pleasant face, her dark wavy hair pulled back into a ponytail at the nape of her neck. She grinned at Florida. "Why don't you start?"

I could have kissed the lady. The ball had been dribbled to the other side of the circle, giving my face time to return to its normal pasty hue.

"Who, me?" Florida shrugged. "Oh well, why not. My name is Florida Hickman. I'm five years saved and five years sober, thank the *Lord.* Got three kids. Two are living with me right now; the oldest one is ADD, otherwise they doin' good. My husband works full time"—she gave a little laugh—"lookin' for work."

"Uh-huh. Kick the loser out," muttered Adele.

I nearly fell off my chair. The nerve! I imagined myself Walter Mitty-like telling the woman to shut up. But no one else must have heard her, and Flo just carried on. "But thank God, I got my GED, passed the civil service exam last year, and got a job at the Chicago post office that puts food on the table. So I can't complain. I'm blessed!" She smiled sweetly at the Hispanic lady. "Now you."

I wanted to snort. Florida let drop more in sixty seconds than

I would in a month of Sundays, given the same situation. What kind of precedent did *that* set?

"*Sí.* No problem." The woman next to Flo gestured with every sentence. "I am Delores Enriquez from Iglesia del Espíritu Santo, and I work as a pediatric nurse at Cook County Hospital." I couldn't speak Spanish, but I was pretty sure she said "Church of the Holy Spirit." Delores's eyes rolled up, as though searching her brain for more information. "Um, my husband, Ricardo, drives truck, and we have five kids, from five to fourteen." She shrugged. "Guess that's it—oh!" She turned to the slim young black woman on her other side. "This is Edesa, from my church. She babysits for my kids, and she's good—but don't nobody steal her!" Delores gave the young woman a squeeze.

Well, it was rolling now. Edesa seemed shy, with a trace of an accent. Jamaican? Haitian? Didn't Haitians speak French? Why would she end up at a Spanish-speaking church? Edesa didn't say much, just that she was a student at some community college, but I didn't catch which one.

I hadn't really noticed the woman next to Edesa. But when she spoke, her voice was soft, cultured, almost European—which startled me because she was black. Not black-black, like some Africans I'd met, but rich brown, like Starbucks coffee beans. And she wore a scarf in an African print tied smartly around her head and wore a matching tunic in orange and black. How could I *not* have noticed her?

"I am Nonyameko Sisulu-Smith. Just Nony is all right," she added, seeing that several of us didn't quite get it. "My homeland is South Africa, but I came to the States to go to the University of Chicago, where I met my husband, and so here we are. I love the Lord, and that's why I'm at this conference." She gave a little shrug as if to say *that's all.* I wanted to say "More! More!" But she had already turned to the tall Asian girl next to her. "This is Hoshi Takahashi. She is a student in my husband's history class at Northwestern University—he's a professor there." Nony's smile now was wide and genuine. "Hoshi just became a Christian!"

The young woman nodded and smiled and nodded. "Yes! My name is Hoshi. I am student from Japan. Like Nony say, she tells me about Jesus and I am new Christian." She beamed. "Glad to be here. Glad to know all of you. Glad to practice my English!"

Okay, I was impressed. Prayer Group Twenty-Six was practically a mini–United Nations.

Silence reigned. I leaned forward slightly to see if there was someone hiding between Hoshi and Adele. Nope. It was Adele's turn.

The big woman sighed. "Adele Skuggs, just like it *says* here on my name tag. 'Adele's Hair and Nails' on Clark Street in Rogers Park, if any of y'all want a makeover." Her voice seemed to take on a smile at the mention of her beauty shop, and I glanced at her. She had a small gap between her two front teeth I hadn't noticed before. I quickly looked back at my lap. "Oh, yeah," Adele added, "I've been a member of the Paul and Silas Apostlic Church on Kedzie since I was in the children's choir. Me and Chanda over there." She nodded at another woman we hadn't got to yet. She folded her arms. She was done.

21

My turn. I suddenly felt about as interesting as an economics textbook. But I couldn't invent an exciting persona on the spot— besides, Avis was sitting next to me—so I stuck to the truth. "My name is Jodi Baxter. I'm married, have two teenagers, and I teach third grade at Bethune Elementary in Rogers Park." I skipped the born-in-Iowa-recently-moved-from-the-suburbs part. I was sure everybody would automatically think *Hick Chick.* "I'm a member of Uptown Community Church in Rogers Park, and Avis Johnson, who is the principal of the school where I teach, invited me to this conference . . . so, here I am!"

"What kind of church is Up-town Com-mun-ity?"

I was startled by Adele's question. No one else had gotten questions. And the way she pronounced every syllable of the church name made it seem like a challenge.

"Uh, it's nondenominational. Just . . . Christian. You know." It sounded lame.

The big shoulders next to me shrugged. "Just asking. All sorts of *unitys* and *communitys* out there. Just 'cause you put the name *church* on somethin' don't mean anything these days."

I didn't trust myself to speak. What *was* this woman's problem?

Avis came to the rescue. "I think it's my turn. My name is Avis Johnson, and as Jodi said, we both attend Uptown Community Church in Rogers Park. I grew up Church of God in Christ but began attending Uptown a couple years ago because I like the emphasis on bringing people to Jesus, not bringing them to a denomination. Like this conference. We're about Jesus, right? Unless you tell me different, I assume that's why we're all here."

Thank you, Avis, I breathed inwardly. I kept my eyes riveted on my friend's face, not daring to look at Adele on the other side of me.

"And I'm glad to have us introduce ourselves," Avis continued, "but I think the whole idea is to spend some time praying. So maybe we can move along and share some prayer needs. Or pray for the conference itself. Speakers . . . praise team . . . women who need healing in their lives."

With that admonition, the remaining women in the group quickly introduced themselves:

Chanda George, Adele's friend, had a Jamaican accent that was a little hard to understand. I wondered why she and Adele weren't sitting together. Maybe they just attended the same church so they got put in the same prayer group.

Leslie Stuart ("Just call me Stu," she said) was in her mid-thirties, long and shapely, with big eyes and long blonde hair with dark roots. Didn't say what church she came from, just that she was a real estate broker in Oak Park, Chicago's first suburb to the west. "I think we should pray for the peace of Jerusalem," she announced.

The peace of Jerusalem? Seemed a little off the mark at the moment, though the Middle East was a hotbed in the news. But the middle-aged white lady on the other side of her immediately said, "Amen! As Jerusalem goes, so goes the world. And as long as we're praying for peace, pray that I don't knock off my husband. I won't go into details. Details, shmetails. If you're married and human, you know what I mean." She rolled her eyes and sighed.

Chuckles around the group broke the crust of awkwardness and seemed to let in a breath of fresh air.

"Oh. My name is Ruth . . . Ruth Garfield. I'm new to this Christian thing, too. Popular in my family, I'm not. And if I knock off my husband, they'll definitely blame it on being a lapsed Jew."

The chuckles burst into outright laughter. "You are a cool lady!" Florida said, wagging her forefinger at Ruth. "Maybe we could knock off our husbands together." She simpered at the rest of the group. "Just kidding. Just kidding."

"*Sure* you are, honey," muttered Adele next to me.

There was still one person to go. Another white girl—woman, rather. At first glance she looked young, her short hair bleached blonde on the tips and combed in the spiky look popular in those big Calvin Klein ads on the sides of buses. She wore denim overalls, which, I had to admit, looked youthful and cool but out of place among the carefully dressed women in pantsuits and business dresses, and Nony in her exotic African garb. But as she pursed her lips, as though considering what to say, I realized her eyes betrayed hardships beyond her years.

She shrugged. "I'm just . . . Yolanda. They call me Yo-Yo. Don't know why I'm here. I'm not really into this Jesus thing you talk about. But you guys are all right. I'm cool with that." She shrugged again. "I'm with her"—she jerked a thumb in Ruth's direction.

"A cook she is, at the Bagel Bakery in my neighborhood." Ruth winked. "She makes pastry to die for."

That's interesting, I thought. "Where'd you learn to cook, Yolan—uh, Yo-Yo? Professionally, I mean."

Yo-Yo's lips tightened, and for a brief second her eyes took on a wary look, like a cat in a corner. Then the shrug again. "Lincoln

Correctional Center." She let it hang in the air. "Prison," she added.

Lincoln? The new Illinois women's prison? I could have slapped my mouth. I'd only meant it as a friendly question.

Yo-Yo glanced around the quiet circle. "What'd I do—punch everybody's bozo button?"

"Don't you worry about it, honey," Adele spoke up. "We all got skeletons in our closet of one kind or another . . . *all* of us."

I didn't dare glance at Adele. Did she mean that for me?

Yo-Yo leaned forward, elbows on her knees, worn athletic shoes planted widely on the floor. "I'm not ashamed of it. Not like I axed anybody or anything. Served eighteen months for forgery. Had my reasons. But I did the crime, served my time. It's behind me now." She sat back, casually hooking one arm over the back of the chair. "Ruth, here, put in a good word for me at the bakery, helped me get a job. Ain't easy to get work after you've done time."

Gosh. I felt like I'd opened Pandora's box. Obviously there was a lot more history to Ruth and Yo-Yo's relationship than met the eye. And what did Yo-Yo mean, "had my reasons"?

"I'm sure it hasn't been easy." Avis's voice broke into my thoughts. "I'd like to pray for Yo-Yo, if that's all right with the rest of you—and you, Yo-Yo?"

Once more Yo-Yo shrugged. "Hey, if it makes you feel good. Just . . . you know. Don't get all hyper."

Avis stood up, moved to the outside of the circle behind Yo-Yo, and began to pray. "Thank You, Lord. Thank You, Jesus," she began.

That was smooth. Avis had a kind of authority—not bossy, just firm, confident—that gathered up the loose ends and knotted them so they wouldn't fray any further. At least we were finally praying—which was the point, after all.

"Others of you, feel free to pray," Avis invited a few moments later. To my surprise, Florida knelt down in front of Yo-Yo, laid a hand on her denim knee, and began to pray in a loud voice, praising God for new beginnings. I wasn't sure how Yo-Yo reacted to being the focus of attention, because my own eyes misted up, and I had to fumble around in my pockets for a tissue.

After a while, Avis moved behind Ruth, laid a hand on her shoulder, and began to pray for the marriages in the group that were on rocky ground. Ruth and Florida had been pretty blunt about theirs . . . didn't know about any of the others. At least my marriage was solid, thank God.

At one point I glanced at the clock: 10:47 . . . and Avis was still going strong.

4

I t was almost 11:30 by the time Avis and I got back to our
room. Florida said she'd be up in fifteen minutes—probably
stepped out for another cigarette. Told us she'd be real quiet
when she came back. I hoped so. I was *tired*.

"You didn't leave at ten," I teased as Avis pulled out the sofa
bed in the "sitting room" part of the suite. I found two puffy pillows on a shelf in the closet and tossed them in her direction.

"I *knew* it would go late," she grumbled, unzipping her suitcase
and pulling out a black-and-gold caftan. Man, it looked comfy—
and a whole sight more elegant than Denny's Chicago Bulls
T-shirt that I usually wore.

"Sorry you stayed?"

"Hmm. No." Avis carefully wrapped her head with a black
scarf—to preserve her hairdo, I presumed—and knotted it on
her forehead. "Once we got to praying. It was the idea of sitting
around talking with a bunch of strangers that put me off."

I studied her curiously. That was the part I liked, once we escaped the cast of thousands—well, hundreds—in the main session. "Oh. Sorry if I got us off track by asking everybody to introduce themselves." I wasn't *really* sorry; somebody had to get us rolling. But the introductions had gone rather long.

"You surprised me, jumping right in like that. But I think people were glad you did," she said. *(Except Adele,* I thought, but kept that to myself.) "We can spend more time praying the next time we get together," Avis went on, picking up her toilet kit and disappearing into the bathroom. "What time did we agree to?" she called back.

I raised my voice. "Nony suggested 7:00 A.M. Before breakfast. Think anyone will show after going so late tonight?" I was personally hoping we'd all oversleep. At this moment seven o'clock sounded like the crack of dawn. But the water was running in the sink now, and there was no answer.

By the time I used the bathroom and came out, Avis was in bed and the lights were out in the sitting room. I left the bathroom light on and the door open a crack for Florida and crawled between the sheets of the humongous king-size bed on the side next to the window. My body was tired, but my mind still felt all wound up. The main session had been pretty good, even if it was loud. Prayer Group Twenty-Six was going to be interesting. I liked knowing a few more people at this conference by name. Maybe I wouldn't feel so out of place.

The door to the suite clicked open, and two seconds later Florida slipped into the bathroom and shut the door. When she came out, I lay still, hoping she'd think I was asleep. I was too tired to do any more talking. But opening my eyelashes a crack, I noted she had her beaded braids wrapped in a scarf like Avis's. Must be an African-American thing. But her big Chicago Bulls T-shirt? I grinned inwardly. Just like me.

SOMETIME DURING THE MIDDLE OF THE NIGHT, I awoke and went to the bathroom. By the time I came back into the bedroom, my eyes had adjusted to the darkness, and I stopped short. Florida wasn't in the bed. Her side was rumpled, and I was pretty sure I remembered when she'd crawled in. Remembered I'd been glad it was a king, which left lots of room for two people not used to sleeping in the same bed.

But where had Florida gone? Surely she didn't have to have a cigarette in the middle of the night! Curious, I opened the French doors between the bedroom and sitting room and peeked in. Only one lump in the sofa bed. I tiptoed in, shuffling old-lady slow so I wouldn't bang into something. There was another lump on the floor between the sofa bed and the window. The air conditioner— hardly needed in early May—was humming steadily. Florida? Why was she sleeping on the *floor?*

I crawled back into the king-size bed feeling confused. Sure, it felt awkward to sleep in the same bed with a virtual stranger. When it turned out we had three in our room, I would have preferred sharing the bed with Avis. Or sleeping by myself on the sofa bed, lucky Avis. But I hadn't thought about how Florida might feel. Was it just too weird sleeping with a white girl? Nah, I told myself. Couldn't be that. Florida seemed cool with that. No chip on her shoulder—not like that Adele. But a sense of rejection settled over me like the kid who got no Valentines.

Suddenly I missed Denny terribly. Missed reaching out and resting my hand on his arm, feeling the rising and falling of his steady breathing as he lay on his side. Missed snuggling against his bare back and fitting my body into the curve of his legs. Missed the comfort and safety that his mere presence fed into my spirit. Missed knowing that I *belonged*.

I even missed the kids. Missed getting up in the middle of the night to go to the bathroom and peeking into their rooms to be sure everyone was okay. That was when I fell into my deepest sleep, knowing we were all under one roof, safe and sound and together.

Did they miss me? Was anyone losing any sleep at the Baxter house because Mom . . . Jodi . . . wasn't under that roof? Did the house feel incomplete without me?

I sighed. Probably not. Teenagers were too self-centered to even notice Mom was gone. And Denny . . . he would miss me, sure. But once he fell asleep? He wouldn't notice I was gone till morning.

Lying there awake, taking up a miniscule slice of space on the king-size bed, I felt terribly alone . . . and lonely. It wouldn't feel so bad if the conference was over tomorrow—make that today, since it was obviously past midnight already. But I'd paid for two nights. *Two long nights!*

From here, Sunday felt like an invisible speck on the distant horizon.

I WOKE UP TO THE SOUND OF THE SHOWER. Rolling out of bed, I pulled back the "blackout" hotel curtains and was nearly blinded as a wash of sunlight poured into the room. Blue sky . . . sunshine . . . what a great day to go for an early morning walk. Denny and I often walked to Lake Michigan on weekend mornings, only a few blocks from our house. "The lake," as everyone calls it, is Chicago's playground, lapping at the sandy beaches and rocky breakwaters that define miles of parks along the shore, filled with joggers and bikers, in-line skaters and dog-walkers, picnickers and bench sitters, volleyball players and windsurfers, kids and old folks and family reunions. The lake is what made city living bearable for me and a million or so other small-town transplants.

But the steady hum of cars and eighteen-wheelers on I-90 reminded me that on this particular Saturday I was a prisoner in a fancy hotel with undoubtedly *no* place to go walking except the parking lot.

What time was it anyway?

The door to the bathroom opened as I squinted at my watch—six-twenty—and Avis emerged in her caftan with a plastic bonnet over her night scarf. I hadn't seen a plastic bonnet since high school days, when my mother wore one in the shower to protect her monthly permanent. Avis looked at Florida's empty side of the bed, jerked a thumb in the direction of the sitting room, and whispered, "What gives with that?"

I shrugged . . . just as Florida wandered through the French doors in her big T-shirt. She stopped, seeing us both just standing on either side of the king-size bed. "It's not time to get up yet, is it?" She yawned. "Bathroom free?"

"Sure," I said automatically. But I'd been up long enough now that the urge to pee was growing stronger. "On second thought, just let me go and it's yours." I dashed into the bathroom. From the relative anonymity behind the almost-closed bathroom door—like a pink-tiled confessional—I called out, "I was worried about you when I found you missing in the middle of the night. What happened?"

Florida laughed from the other side of the door. "You snore, girl! Had to find me another bed if I was going to get any sleep."

I was so startled I stopped peeing in midstream. "Oh, gosh, Flo. I'm sorry!" I didn't know I snored. Denny never complained. I emerged a moment later feeling both embarrassed and contrite. "It's terrible to pay all this money for a hotel room and end up on the floor. I'll trade tonight, okay?"

"Hey, don't you worry about me. I'm a light sleeper—*anything* wakes me up." Florida disappeared into the bathroom. "Besides," she called back, "those long cushions from the sofa made a great bed—better than the one I've got at home. Turned on a little white noise, and I slept like a baby."

She poked her head back out of the bathroom door. "You guys going to that prayer thang at seven? Don't wait for me. I'll meet you at breakfast."

SOMEHOW AVIS AND I BOTH GOT SHOWERED and dressed and down the elevator just as the lobby clocks ticked past seven. I had even managed to pour three Styrofoam cups of coffee made in the tiny coffeemaker perched on top of the in-room "mini-bar." Avis shook her head, which I translated as No-thanks-I-don't-drink-coffee, but Florida, seizing the moment, simply took a cup in each hand.

Strike one against spontaneous deep sharing with Avis. What did one do with a girlfriend if you couldn't go out and bare your heart over bottomless cups of coffee? Or celebrate with an occasional double mocha latte at Starbucks?

Nony Sisulu-Smith was the only other person from last night's group when we made our appearance in Meeting Room 7. She was on her knees already praying out loud, so we just sat down in nearby chairs and joined her. At least I closed my eyes and tried to concentrate on Nony's prayer. Her cultured voice rose and fell like a piece of classical music. But as I listened, her prayer sure did seem full of a lot of clichés.

" . . .You are the root and the offspring of David, the bright and morning star. The Spirit and the bride say, Come. And let him that heareth say, Come. Let him that is thirsty, come. Thank You, Father! Thank You that You have said, Whosoever will, let him take the water of life freely . . ."

On and on she went, her voice growing stronger. "I will bless the Lord at all times. Your praise shall continually be in my mouth. My soul shall make her boast in the Lord; the humble shall hear and be glad. O magnify the Lord with me! Let us exalt his name together! . . ."

I opened my eyes and peeked. Nony's cheeks glistened with moisture. Avis was on her feet, murmuring, "Yes! Thank You, Father! . . . Thank You, Jesus! . . ." as Nony prayed. I closed my eyes again. Looked like Nony was going for the long haul.

"O God, we know that young lions do lack, and suffer hunger. But if we seek the Lord we shall not want any good thing . . ."

Speaking of hunger, wasn't breakfast at eight o'clock? I took a peek at my watch. Only 7:22. Just then I was aware of a presence behind me, and Avis whispered in my ear. "Psalm thirty-four."

Psalm thirty-four? Did she want me to look it up? I reached in my bag and pulled out my small travel Bible. Psalm thirty-three . . . thirty-four . . . My eyes skimmed over the verses. *Duh.* Of course! Nony was praying Psalm thirty-four. Had probably been "praying Scripture" all along. And Avis, no doubt, knew right where each Scripture verse came from. *Double duh.*

I squeezed my eyes shut. *Okay, God, I feel like a dork. I'm sorry for thinking Nony's prayer was just a bunch of clichés. You gotta help me here. Everything's just so . . . different. But I want to learn whatever You want me to learn this weekend . . . I think.*

5

The line for the breakfast buffet wound clear out of the
hotel café when we arrived at eight, but Avis, Nony,
and I managed to get a table for four by the time we got
through the line about eight-thirty. The line had thinned, and a
few minutes later Florida hustled over with a cup of coffee and
a sweet roll. I waved her into the fourth chair beside Nony. "Someone offered us a hundred bucks for this seat, but . . . we saved it
for you."

Florida chuckled. "You did right." She tore her sweet roll in
half. "So . . . was the prayer group good?"

"You're looking at it," I said.

For a blink Florida stopped chewing. "Well, thank God! At
least I wasn't the only delinquent." She waved her sweet roll at the
rest of us. "Though I'm sure God was pleased that a few of you
showed up to get your praise on."

I stifled a grin. Florida talked about "getting your praise on" like it was a blouse or a pair of shoes. Then her forehead wrinkled up. "It was optional, right? I mean, they'll probably have the prayer groups get together again during the conference, don't you think?"

"I'm sure they will." Nony slipped cream into her tea. "But I was just as glad there were only a few this morning. The prayer time was precious."

I studied the beautiful woman across from me. I'd never met anyone who seemed so totally unself-conscious when she was praying. Besides Avis, I mean. I thought maybe Avis had some special connection to God that was on "high" all the time. But Nony slipped Scripture in and out of her prayers so easily, it was like a second language.

With time slipping away and the first session of the day starting at nine o'clock, we mostly paid attention to our bagels, plastic cups of yogurt, and fruit juice amid small talk. I gave a quick glance around the room to see if I recognized anyone else from the night before. But mostly I saw women in a variety of "casual dress" with an occasional color-coordinated jogging suit. Guessed I was dressed okay in my beige slacks and off-white cotton sweater. Nony was wearing another African-print tunic over black pants, but she'd left off the headgear. Instead, a head full of tiny cornrows met at the top of her head and cascaded in a ponytail of coppery braids down to her shoulders. Gosh, it was gorgeous. I felt slightly cheated. My thin wash-and-wear hair would never do something like that.

"Hellooo, Jodi. I said, do you want to go back to the room with me?" With a start I realized Avis had stood up and was waiting for me. "I want to . . ." She pantomimed brushing her teeth. " . . . Before the session starts."

"If you get on up in there before me, save me a seat!" Florida called after us, still intent on her coffee.

Teeth brushed, a fresh application of lipstick, and Avis and I made our way to the ballroom. Once again the worship band and singers were up and running already by nine o'clock, even though women were still finding their seats. Once more we ended up in row five from the front with Avis next to an aisle. I piled my purse and Bible on the chair beside me to save a seat for Florida. *Unless Adele comes and dumps them back into my lap,* I thought ruefully. But that would mean she'd be choosing to sit beside me in a room with hundreds of chairs, and I was sure *that* wasn't going to happen.

Soon the lady in the red suit—except it was a creamy tan today that complemented her skin to a golden glow—was back on stage with the hand-held mike, song lyrics were up on the screen, and the place was rocking.

We're blessed in the city! We're blessed in the field!
We're blessed when we come and when we go!

After six or seven repeats of the same song—verses, chorus, *and* vamp ("Blessed! Blessed! Blessed! Blessed!")—the ballroom was filled with shouts of "Hallelujah!" and "Praise the Lord!" as the worship band quickly slid into another song. The ballroom doors stood open, and I saw some of the hotel staff peek in from time to time to see what all the ruckus was about. Even a house-maid or two. Later when I looked again, the doors were closed. Guess they didn't want us disturbing the other guests.

Avis was totally focused on worshiping. I tried. I really did. But my mind kept wandering, kept looking over the crowd to see if I recognized any of the other women in Group Twenty-Six. But we were pretty close to the front, so I couldn't really turn around and stare. I tried to clap and step to the music, but it was like patting my head and rubbing my stomach at the same time—I couldn't get coordinated. So I just sang along to the unfamiliar songs as best I could.

But after about an hour of chandelier-shaking music, I needed a break. I caught Avis's eye and mouthed that I was going to the bathroom. At least everyone was standing and moving and shout-ing, so it was pretty easy to slip out of the crowd unnoticed.

In the ladies restroom, I headed for the third stall. Funny. I always picked a stall in a public restroom and kept using that same one (unless it was already in use). Did other people do that? Or was I hopelessly in a rut even about bathroom stalls?

The noisy worship from the ballroom still throbbed in the background, but the peaceful ladies' room was like sitting by Walden Pond with a superhighway somewhere beyond the trees. However, my little oasis of quiet was broken by someone else coming in to use the facilities. While that woman was washing her hands—I heard water running—another person came in.

"Sister Monica!" gushed the newcomer. "I didn't know you were at the conference! How ya doin', girl?"

"All right. All right. I'm blessed. Highly favored by the Lord and coming into my prosperity. You?"

"Saved, sanctified, *and* satisfied. Can't complain."

The two women burbled on, but I closed my eyes and leaned against the industrial-size toilet paper dispenser. What was I *doing* here? These women talked a whole new language! I'd been a baptized Christian for thirty-plus years—forty-two, if I included my childhood years when "Jesus Loves Me" was my favorite good-night song—but when someone asked how I was doing, I usually said, "Great," or "Fair" or "Not so good," depending on how I felt at the moment.

Either these women had cliché buttons that played on automatic, or they had an inside track on God's blessings.

I stayed in my stall until the other women left, then washed my hands with the perfumed hotel soap and hit the button on the hot-air dryer. *So, what is it, God? Am I blessed? Is that the same as being thankful for my blessings?*

I GOT BACK TO THE BALLROOM in time to hear another dynamo speaker who barely needed a microphone, then we were instructed to return to our prayer groups and pray for each other, that God would reveal the obstacles keeping us from living out our destiny.

Here we go again, I thought as the flood of estrogen energy flowed through the doors and into our respective meeting rooms.

My "destiny"? I didn't have a clue. And I wasn't sure I felt that comfortable with the jargon. I mean, we're supposed to do God's will as revealed in the Bible—obeying the commandments and stuff like that. And "bloom where we're planted," to borrow a worn-out cliché. As in, be faithful where God puts you. But living into our destiny? What did that mean?

Florida plopped down in a chair beside me in Group Twenty-Six. "Where were you?" I asked. "I saved you a seat."

"Oh, girl, I got there late and didn't want to walk all the way up to the fifth row." She leaned toward me with a conspiratorial whisper. "We gotta deprogram Avis, you know. The fifth row isn't any more spiritual than the fifteenth."

I chuckled. My sentiments exactly.

To my surprise, everyone from last night's circle showed up for this prayer time. Even Adele. Even Yo-Yo. Maybe Ruth dragged her since they came to the conference together. Again there was a bit of awkward looking at our shoes, wondering who would start this thing. *I* sure wasn't going to jump in again.

Finally Delores Enriquez spoke up. "Why don't you get us started, Avis? You're the senior *señora* here, I think." She looked around the circle. "*Sí?*"

There were murmurs of assent from several in the group. I was sure Avis felt put on the spot. But Delores was right. Avis was the natural spiritual leader in the group as far as I knew.

But the woman with all the earrings—Leslie Stuart—spoke up. "Why do we need a leader?" she said. "Let's just start, whoever wants to."

I wasn't the only one who glared at the woman with the long blonde hair who wanted to be called "Stu." She had a right to her viewpoint, but it felt like a put-down after Delores had suggested Avis.

Avis got off the hot seat. "Well, Stu is right. We can just go right to prayer. We don't need to know specifics in order to pray for each other. We can pray in the Spirit, mention each person by name. God knows better than we do what our destiny is, or the obstacles in our lives."

True, I thought, but I felt disappointed. I liked being able to pray specifically for a person—and sharing was a way to get to know each other.

But Stu wasn't finished. "I didn't mean that. I think whoever wants to should share what they'd like prayer for, and then we can pray for that person. I just don't see that that needs a 'leader.'"

Now I was really irritated—especially since I half-agreed with her about the sharing part and praying specifically. But I felt defensive for Avis.

Adele, on the other side of the circle, was sitting with her arms folded and foot tapping. "Leslie, is it?" she said in a voice that made me think of a teacher with a ruler. "I think I heard most of this group agreeing that we'd like to appoint a leader, and Avis is it. Let's not waste a lot of time here. I think you'll agree." The woman who operated Adele's Hair and Nails nodded at Avis. "Go ahead."

Zingo! Good for Adele, I thought. She had just redeemed herself in my eyes—for the moment anyway. But I sure wouldn't have wanted to be in Stu's shoes.

I felt a poke in my side. "Adele knows how to kick a little butt, don't she?" Florida whispered. Again I wanted to laugh.

"Well, I don't know that we really need a leader either," said Avis graciously. "But why don't we quiet ourselves and get in an attitude of prayer. Then if anyone has something to share that needs prayer, just speak out. No one has to share if they don't want to, but let's try to pray for each person during this time. Let the Holy Spirit be our guide."

She closed her eyes, lifted up her face, and began to murmur, "Thank You, Jesus. Thank You for who You are . . ."

Others around me began to pray in a similar way, all at the same time. Beside me, Florida rocked side to side, her eyes squeezed shut. "Thank ya, *Jesus!*" she said. No murmuring there. *"Thank* ya!"

My heart felt stretched. What had just happened here? I couldn't close my eyes. I just wanted to memorize the faces in this group. Even Stu seemed pacified. For a reason I couldn't fathom, I felt teary. I thought I had just seen spiritual leadership at work—though I'd be hard-pressed to explain it.

As I soaked in the murmured prayers and gazed around the group, I suddenly noticed something.

Nails. Lots of painted fingernails, no two shades of red alike. Not only that, but every dark hand, whether African or Caribbean or American, had painted nails. I glanced on either side of me. Even Avis and Florida. But most of the pale hands—Yo-Yo, for sure, but also Ruth and me and Hoshi—had bald nails, though Hoshi's looked carefully manicured with very white moon-slivers at the tips.

Stu was the exception. Her nails were long, blue, and glittery. *Good grief, Jodi! Stop it!* I squeezed my eyes shut. *Dear God, I'm sorry for getting distracted. Help me to stay focused . . . focused on You.*

6

By the time we stopped for lunch, we'd only prayed for half the group. Edesa asked us to pray for her family back in Honduras. (Honduras! Of course. No wonder she attended a Spanish-speaking church. I wondered what percentage of blacks lived in Honduras. That would be interesting for my third-graders to study.) Edesa's parents were believers, she said, but their town had been devastated by Hurricane Mitch in 1998. She felt guilty being away from home and experiencing so much plenty in the States, when her extended family was still struggling with grinding poverty.

Encouraged by Edesa, who mentioned families, Hoshi spoke up. Her parents were coming to Chicago to visit this summer and would be extremely displeased that she had forsaken the Shinto religion for Christianity. She wanted prayer to be strong to share her new faith.

"As long as we're praying for parents, y'all can pray for my mother. And me. I take care of her. And—you know—it's like having another kid." Adele spoke into the circle then retreated behind arms folded across her ample bosom.

Adele took care of her mother? I knew firsthand that was no picnic. Grandmother Jennings had lived with us for a time when I was a teenager. She had dementia (my brothers called it "demented"— but not in front of my parents, of course), and nothing my mom or dad did for her was right. As the only girl, I had to share my room with Grandma. One time I caught her going through my drawers and throwing out birthday cards and notes I'd saved under my sweaters and underwear. Boy, did I yell! When she died and I got my room back, I felt relieved and guilty at the same time.

I corralled my thoughts and tried to focus on Chanda, the Jamaican woman who said she cleaned houses on the North Shore. Had been doing it for ten years, had a good clientele. But the focus on "living into your destiny" had stirred up feelings of dissatisfaction. "I wan' to be doin' someting else, but I don' know what," she said. "Got tree kids, no mon. It's hard to jump the train."

Whew. I was glad people were opening up. Chanda was somebody you didn't really notice just sitting there. Average height, dowdy skirt and blouse, short black hair, cut but not styled, nothing that stood out. But the idea that God had created plain Chanda to be a "woman of destiny" tickled my fancy. Wished I had the gift of prophecy and could zap her with a "word." Well, not really. People who tried that at Uptown Community made me feel uncomfortable, even though I knew *some* people must have that gift because it was in the Bible.

Noting the time, Avis moved us into praying for Edesa, Hoshi, Adele, and Chanda, even though we hadn't gotten around the circle. Well, there was always the next time.

AT LUNCHTIME, the lines for the pay phones just off the lobby were three and four women deep. Lines probably would have been longer, but I saw a lot of women standing in the line for the lunch buffet holding one hand to their ear talking on their cell phones. I did a double take when one woman came marching through the lobby talking loudly to herself and making emphatic gestures— then I realized she had one of those handsfree cords hanging from her ear.

As I waited for a phone, bits of one-sided conversations merged in space above the pay phones, like little cartoon balloons.

"What color is it? . . . Orange? Sure it wasn't just a hairball? . . . Okay, okay, I know it's yucky . . . No, you *can't* leave it for me to clean up! . . . Just *do it*, Morris."

"I want to cancel my Saturday three o'clock . . . Do you have a two o'clock on Monday? . . . *Friday?* I'll look like my mother by Friday!"

"Of course I miss you, honey . . . You broke what? . . . No, no, Mommy's not mad . . . Why were you using my good— . . . Put Daddy on the phone. *Now.*"

Phones got hung up, and the lines inched forward. A new voice ahead of me sounded familiar, but I couldn't quite place it.

"Tomas? . . . Did ya check me lottery numbers on this morning?
. . . On the refrigerator door, where they always put! . . . Gwan
do it . . . Yes, I wait."

Dying of curiosity, I shifted my position, trying to identify the
woman whose back was to me. Then the woman turned, caught my
eye, and we both gave a slight nod of recognition. Chanda George.

Good grief! Chanda played the *lottery?* On a cleaning woman's
pay? It might be legal, but surely it was unbiblical, or . . . or at
least irresponsible. Didn't she have three kids? I strained my ears
as she turned back to the phone. "Ya sure? . . . Ya double-check?
. . . I was *sartin* I gwan be a winna . . . 'cause I been prayin' 'bout
it all weekend."

Oh, brother. The prayers God had to sort through. I was afraid
Chanda would speak to me when she hung up, and she'd *know* I
was rolling my eyes. But just then one of the pay phones got free,
so I dropped in thirty-five cents and punched in my home number.

The phone picked up. "Yeah?"

"Josh! Don't answer the phone like that!"

A pause on the other end. "Hi, Mom. Whassup?"

"Just calling to see how everybody's doing."

"Fine."

I leaned my forehead against the phone box. Why did talking
with my seventeen-year-old always feel like Chinese water torture? "Where's Amanda and Dad?"

"Out somewhere." I ground my teeth, but Josh added, "I think
they went out for brunch—you know, one of those dad-daughter
things."

"Thank you, Josh," I said, my irritation somewhat pacified by this information. That was Denny, Mr. Spontaneous. A dad-daughter brunch—that was nice.

"Well, I'll be home tomorrow afternoon. Maybe we can go out for pizza tomorrow night. We'll do Gullivers—make it special."

"I think Dad said we're gonna order pizza tonight. Besides, the youth group is having a planning meeting for our summer trip tomorrow night."

"Oh." *Might as well stay another night,* I grumbled to myself. *Baxter household's not planning a big Mom homecoming.* "Well, tell Dad I called, okay? Love you."

"Sure, Mom." *Click.*

Right. I had as much confidence that Denny would get that message as I did that the phone was going to give me my money back. I checked the little slot. Nope.

I went through the lunch line by myself, but the buffet was good: a salad bar with lots of different pasta salads, spinach, and arugula greens (usually $4.99 for eight ounces at Whole Foods), lots of fresh fruit, and crusty bread. The hotel had a women's conference pegged right down to the menu.

"Darn," said a familiar voice behind me at the condiment bar. "Where's the mac 'n' cheese? I need me some greens."

I looked up and grinned. "Hi, Florida." (Well, maybe the hotel didn't have *this* women's conference pegged.) "You eaten already?"

She picked up a grape. "If you call this eating? Think they got a Popeye's nearby?"

"You're kidding, right?"

"Girl, no! I'm hungry. Wish I had some crispy fried chicken right about now. Anyway, gotta run. What time's the next session?"

"Uh . . . two o'clock, I think, followed by the prayer group. Then I think we break to get ready for the banquet tonight."

"Oh, yeah! The banquet." Florida perked up. "Maybe they'll have chicken. We gotta get sharp tonight, right?"

Right. I'd almost forgotten dressing up. Had seemed kind of silly to me at first, but maybe it would be fun after all.

I TURNED ON THE HOTEL SHOWER as hot as I could stand it and let the pulsing jetspray massage my head. Ahhhh. Now this was luxury. At home we barely got the "hot" water temperature in our old frame house past lukewarm. Not to mention that when the family on the second floor of our two-flat was doing laundry in the basement, the water pressure in our shower slowed to a trickle. But I'd paid for two nights in this hotel room, *all utilities included,* and I intended to get my money's worth.

I soaped up, lathered my hair with the hotel's silky shampoo, then just stood under the stinging hot water letting my mind and body relax. The afternoon main session had been again a boisterous burst of praise, but by now some of the songs had begun to feel familiar. After a verse or two of "Lift Him Up!" the cream-suited worship leader had stopped the musicians (except for the keyboardist, who kept up a running background) and talked about a verse in Hebrews 13, about offering a "sacrifice of praise" to God.

"Have you ever stopped to think what a *sacrifice* of praise is?" she'd asked, striding across the portable platform and back again. "If it comes easy, if it doesn't cost you anything . . . it's not a *sacrifice!* Now I know some of you would rather be upstairs on those king-size beds, taking a nap." General laughter. "Good for you. At least you're here. That's a *sacrifice*. Some of you other folks see women dancing and shouting and weeping, and you're thinking, *Uh-uh. No way am I going to make a fool of myself.*"

I squirmed a little. Now she was stepping on *my* toes.

The worship leader stopped at the podium, leaned across it, and lowered her voice—but it still carried loud and clear. "I want you to close your eyes and start thinking about *what Jesus has done for YOU*. Some of you were on drugs, your mind so muddled you had no idea what day it was, much less how many kids you had."

Shouts of "Glory!" and "Thank You, Jesus!" erupted from the crowd.

"Some of you have thought of suicide . . . maybe even tried it, but God stopped you. Some of you have been so broke you were digging through dumpsters, just to find something to eat."

The place was losing it now. But the worship leader just lifted the mike and raised her voice over it. "And *some* of you thought you were pretty good. You kept all the major commandments and managed to avoid the big mistakes. But let me tell you—you were *still* going to hell until Jesus saved you!"

I felt like she was talking right at me. But so must all five hundred other women, because all I could hear now were thunderous shouts of *"Thank* You! Thank You, *Jesus!"* On one side of me, Florida was jumping up and down and clapping her hands; on the other, Avis's eyes were closed and tears were flowing down her cheeks. I closed my own eyes and tried to focus on what I'd been saved from. It was hard, because by most anyone's standards, including my own, I'd had a good life. Intact family, not rich but not poor either, no major tragedies. Theologically, I knew I'd been "saved," but it wasn't something I *felt* very much.

The worship leader was hollering now. "Maybe you don't feel like praising today. Praise anyway. Give God a *sacrifice!* Maybe you don't feel like dancing. Dance anyway! Give God a *sacrifice!*"

That must have been a cue, because the worship band and singers lit into the perfect song: "When I think about Jesus, and what He's done for me . . . I could dance, dance, dance, dance, dance, dance, dance all night!" Women exploded into the aisles in every version of "sanctified dancing" one could imagine. I couldn't help but grin. Josh and Amanda would be horrified at all the middle-aged mamas, some seriously overweight, "gettin' their groove on." But why should they? Teenagers had Cornerstone; the "middle-aged mamas" had the Chicago Women's Conference.

Later, during the message, I looked up the passage in Hebrews 13 that the worship leader had mentioned. Sure enough, verse 15 talked about offering God a "sacrifice of praise." But the next verse went right on to say, "And do not forget to do good and to share with others, for with such sacrifices God is pleased." That was a version of Christianity I was more comfortable with—doing good and sharing with others. But the writer called both praise *and* doing good a sacrifice—

51

"Jodi?" A muffled voice on the other side of the bathroom door broke into my thoughts. "You going to be long?"

Oh, help. How long had I been hogging the bathroom? "Be right out, Avis!" I yelled back, shutting off the shower and grabbing a fresh towel so big and thick it felt like a bathrobe. Darn. I'd intended to shave my legs and pits, but . . . oh, well. Pantyhose and sleeves would cover the damage.

I came out toweled like a toga and grinned sheepishly at Avis, who had shed her clothes and thrown on her caftan. "Sorry I steamed it up in there," I said sheepishly. "I'm a sucker for a hot shower."

"Don't worry." She breezed past with mock unconcern. "I'll just get you later if I get a cold shower."

The hot water must have held out because the shower started up again. By the time Avis came out, I had dried my hair and was trying not to mess it up as I slid into my borrowed dress—a black slinky thing that would have made Denny's eyes bug out. "Mm, nice," she commented, moving into the sitting room to dress. "What did you think of the prayer meeting?" she called back.

"Great. I'm kind of surprised everyone has hung in there. Even Yo-Yo." I took a slim tube of mascara out my makeup kit and unscrewed the lid. "Can you believe she's taking care of her teenage stepbrothers all by herself?"

"Not that strange. Grandparents raise their grandkids, siblings raise siblings—happens all the time."

"Oh. Well, it kinda amazed me." I dabbed at my eyelashes with the mascara, trying to make them look thicker and longer.

"What's amazing," said Avis from the other room, "is that she asked us to pray for them. Kind of a breakthrough, don't you think? Considering what she said last night about not being into the 'Jesus thing.'"

"Uh-huh. Great." I started in on blush and lipstick. "Nony is kind of a mystery. She asked for prayer about whether to go back to South Africa, whether that's her destiny to help her people there. But it sounded like her husband—Mark, isn't it?—is American and wants to raise their kids here."

"Yes, well . . . that's a huge decision. Don't know that I'd want to raise my kids there."

"Mm-mm." I mashed my lips together to blot the lipstick. Kids? Probably grown though, since she had grandkids. "Let's see, who else shared . . . oh, Stu." I rolled my eyes at the closet door mirror. "She's a case."

Avis chuckled on the other side of the French doors. "Is that a pun?"

"Pun? . . . Oh." I laughed. "You mean 'cause she wants to quit real estate and get back into social work? Guess she was a caseworker for DCFS right out of college." The caseload for the Department of Child and Family Services was so huge, a lot of young idealistic social workers crashed and burned.

"Sounded like it from her prayer request—that newspaper story about the little girl who'd been left alone in her apartment for two days? Lord, have mercy!"

The French doors opened, and Avis came into the bedroom. "Wow!" I said. "You look stunning." She did, too. For someone her age—I guessed fifty-four, maybe fifty-five—the principal of Bethune Elementary always looked so elegant and smart. Tonight she was wearing black silky harem pants and a loose silky tunic with wide rag sleeves in a bright rose color, belted with a sequined belt.

She looked me up and down. "You look pretty good yourself, girl. Don't show up at church in that outfit, or Pastor Clark might preach a sermon on being a temptation and a snare."

I gawked at her, then giggled and checked myself in the mirror once more. I did look nice . . . even kind of sexy—which I considered a big waste at a women's convention. Still, it felt good to go toe to toe with the fancy dressers I'd seen. Hair tucked behind my ears, silver earrings, silver necklace, slinky black dress . . . mmm, I felt luscious.

"Mm-hm. You two all that an' a bag o' chips."

Neither Avis nor I had heard Florida come in.

"But, um . . . something has come up. The rest of the group thought it was a good plan, and I was sure you two would be willin' to make the sacrifice—"

I broke in. "Florida! What are you talking about?"

"Yo-Yo. She doesn't have a dress. Only those bib overall thangs she wears. She didn't realize there was a dress-up dinner—don't think she has a dress, even if she did. So she wasn't goin' to go tonight. But we thought—"

"We who, Florida?" Avis asked suspiciously.

"You know, Ruth and Stu and Delores and Edesa—the prayer group!"

"Thought what?"

"That we could *all* wear our jeans or slacks or sweats to the banquet tonight to support our sister. You know, all for one and one for all."

I could not believe my ears. I'd just spent an hour getting myself ready for the banquet. I might even be able to hold my head up among the "glitterati" I was sure would appear tonight. Now Florida was asking us—me—to wear my *jeans?*

I almost couldn't trust myself to speak. But I managed a weak "I need a little time to think about this."

"Sure. Banquet doesn't start for another half-hour. Besides, I gotta go check with a couple more folks in the group." And as quickly as she had come, Florida bopped back out the door, leaving Avis and me staring at each other.

*T*hink about it? I was mad! What I really needed was time to cool down before I said something I regretted. Excusing myself from Avis, I shut myself in the bathroom and plopped on the stool. The *nerve* of Florida . . . or whoever thought of this crazy idea. Committing the whole prayer group—still practically a group of strangers—to something so outrageous as showing up at a fancy banquet in our jeans and sweats. The very thought was ludicrous. Or embarrassing.

That's it, isn't it, Jodi? You don't want to look like a fool.

I wanted to hit something or scream. But given the fact that Avis was just outside the door somewhere, I stuck a washcloth in my mouth and shook it with clenched teeth, like Willie Wonka, our chocolate Lab, playing with one of Denny's socks. Then I caught sight of myself in the big bathroom vanity mirror. I looked so silly I didn't know whether to laugh or cry.

Taking the washcloth out of my mouth, I let out a big sigh. I felt trapped. Damned if I did, damned if I didn't. I could either go with Florida's bright idea and look like a fool in a context where I didn't feel on solid ground to begin with, or I could stay dressed up and be unsympathetic to Yo-Yo's plight.

Why didn't she just go in her overalls, and we'd all sit with her and show her we loved her anyway?

Would I do that if I were Yo-Yo?

No-o.

I sighed again. *You're a big hypocrite, Jodi Baxter. Not twenty-four hours ago you were thinking the idea of five hundred women dressing up like Oscar night was pretty silly. You were pining for the small, casual women's retreats up at Camp Timberlee. Now you have a chance to loosen up at this big women's conference—with a dozen other women willing to be just as casual—and you're having a fit.*

But I realized I didn't *want* to be casual tonight. I looked good. I looked as close to gorgeous as I've ever looked—recently, anyway.

Sacrifice.

The word popped into my head so strongly I looked around, thinking I'd heard a voice. *Sacrifice . . . a sacrifice of praise.* I frowned. What did that have to do with anything? *A sacrifice for Yo-Yo. She's not sure about "this Jesus thing," but she's here. She's in your prayer group. What a little thing to sacrifice to show you care about her.*

The tension slowly drained out of my body. But tears welled up in my eyes, and I swiped at them with the washcloth. The washcloth now had black streaks. *Oh, great, there goes my mascara.* But as I thought about what Florida wanted to do, I began to feel amazed . . . and humbled. Here was a black woman, a former drug addict by her own admission, a Christian only five years . . . willing to put aside people's expectations and do something humbling to show the love of Jesus to a white ex-con who landed in her prayer group.

Sacrifice. Sisterhood.

I felt like someone pulled a cord and opened the blinds on my eyes. Why should I care about impressing or fitting in with four hundred and eighty-some women I didn't even know . . . when I had a chance to be "one in spirit" with a group of twelve women who had been thrown into my life, even if just for this one weekend? We were a drawer of mismatched socks if there ever was one—I wasn't sure we even *liked* each other. But we were Prayer Group Twenty-Six. And we had the chance—I, Jodi Baxter, had the chance—to give God a sacrifice of praise and love a young woman who was fresh out of prison.

What was that scripture in Hebrews? "With such sacrifices God is pleased."

I stood up, glancing in the mirror at the black smudges under my eyes. So much for "all decked out."

I'd almost traded a chance to please God for a black silky dress.

AS IT TURNED OUT, not everyone in the prayer group had brought a pair of jeans, but I did, so I teamed it with my cream-colored cotton sweater and a pair of clogs. Sure enough, Yo-Yo showed up at the banquet in her bib overalls and worn athletic shoes. She would have kept right on going when she saw half the prayer group wearing jeans, too—even Adele—but Florida snagged her, and we pushed amoeba-like through the double doors into the ballroom. Avis, who had no jeans, just wore the harem pants outfit she already had on, and Nony topped off *her* jeans with the African print tunic she'd been wearing all day, but added a matching headscarf wound turban-like around her head.

But to tell the truth, it was fall-down funny. Before Florida came up with her bright idea, I don't think anyone had planned to go to the banquet "as a group." But there we were, all twelve of us squeezing into the ballroom-cum-conference room-cum-banquet hall, asking women to move so we could have one of the large tables. It was only set for ten, so we stole a couple of place settings from another table and crowded everybody in.

A chamber ensemble pouring their hearts into Mozart and Bach—hallelujah!—had replaced the worship band for the banquet. I'm not sure I could eat to the high decibels that had carried the worship sessions the last two days. Seemed like a long time before we actually got served, but at least there were carafes of hot coffee and baskets of rolls on the tables to help quell my rumbling stomach.

When the hotel waiters finally brought our plates of food, Florida caught my eye. "Chicken!" she exclaimed with a big grin. It wasn't deep-fried and crusty—smothered in some kind of creamy sauce, actually—but Florida seemed happy.

Tucked in between Nony and Avis and wondering what to do with my elbows, I picked up Ruth's voice on the other side of the table. "So I'm heading out the door, and Ben says, 'Where's my clean shirts?' And I said, 'Who do you think I am? A laundry service?'"

Florida's beads bobbed in agreement. "Uh huh. Housekeeper, fry cook, lover . . . and ATM machine."

Adele rolled her eyes. "Ain't that the truth."

Chanda snorted. "The mon only *say* they got no money. Last week? Took the kids to the library, who there but my baby's daddy. Cooin' and cuddlin' with his new girlfriend while they plannin' some cruise they takin'. 'Im who always say, 'I ain't got no money, honey.' So I'm 'fraid I lay down my religion for a minit and—"

Florida and Adele started hooting with laughter.

"They off on that cruise now," Chanda sighed. "I'm praying for a 'spirit of boredom' to follow them from stem to stern." She grinned at the rest of us. "Sorry. Guess that's not very sanctified."

By now our laughter was so loud we almost didn't hear someone at the microphone saying, "—an emergency telephone call. Is there a Delores Enriquez in the house? You have an emergency telephone call."

"Quiet! Quiet!" I waved the others down. "Did you hear that?" I turned to Delores, who was sitting two seats away from me. "Delores, you have an emergency phone call."

Immediately eleven pairs of eyes turned to the Cook County nurse. Her dark eyes suddenly filled with fear.

"I'll go with you," Edesa said, scooting back her chair and helping Delores to her feet. The younger woman escorted her friend toward the ballroom doors.

The rest of us looked at each other, concern passing from face to face. Avis stood up. "I'll go see what's happening," she said quietly, leaving her napkin in her plate. "The rest of you—pray."

I watched her thread quickly toward the doors. What did Avis mean? Pray silently to ourselves? Obviously not, because at that instant Adele launched into a loud prayer for divine protection, "whatever this emergency is about."

Nony picked up the prayer. "O God, Your Word says that we who dwell in the secret place of the Most High will abide under the shadow of the Almighty. You are our refuge and our fortress. We trust in You. Spread Your wings over Delores; let her find refuge there."

The scripture was comforting. Maybe it wasn't a real emergency. Maybe just a kid with the flu or an injured dog. Didn't Delores say she had five kids? Could be anything.

Hoshi reached across Avis's empty seat and grasped my hand, and I reached out to Nony. The prayers passed around the table like a gift—Chanda . . . Florida . . . Ruth—each in turn. I noticed several women at other tables glancing at us from time to time. No wonder. One minute we were laughing uproariously, the next praying out loud.

I don't know how long our table had been praying—maybe only five minutes—when I felt a touch on my shoulder. I looked up at Avis. She was not smiling.

I cleared my throat. "Everybody? Avis is back."

All eyes opened. Avis leaned in to close out the hubbub all around us. "Delores's oldest son, José, was shot tonight. He's only fourteen. They don't know how bad—he's been taken to Cook County."

Amid a chorus of "Oh, no!" Yo-Yo asked, "Drive-by? Gang hit?"

Avis shook her head. "I don't know. But I'm going up to Delores's room to pray with her before she leaves, if anyone else wants to—"

The whole table stood.

AS IT TURNED OUT, someone wisely pointed out that all of us crowding into Delores's hotel room might be overwhelming. Nony went with Avis, and the rest of us piled into Meeting Room 7 to pray for the Enriquez family. Somewhere far away we could still hear the general hubbub from the ballroom, sounding like someone had left the TV on in another room. How ironic. The banquet had shrunk from big deal to background noise.

Delores . . . I could only imagine the terror she must be feeling. José was fourteen? The same age as my Amanda. My heart squeezed as prayers poured out all around me. *O God! I've only known Delores for twenty-four hours, but . . . she's a mom, like me. Don't let her son die! Save him, Lord! Save him!*

About ten minutes later, Avis came back. "Sorry to barge in, sisters, but if Delores waits for her husband to pick her up, it might be another hour. A taxi would cost twenty-five, thirty dollars from here. She wouldn't take it from me. But if we all pitched in a few dollars—"

"Of course!" I said, joining the chorus as several of us fished for our wallets. Something we could *do.*

Stu stood up. "Never mind. I've got my car. I'll take her."

We all stopped with our purses hanging open.

"Are you sure, Stu?" said Avis. "You'll miss out on the last part of the conference."

Stu shrugged. "Doesn't matter. This is more important."

I should have been glad Stu volunteered to drive Delores to the hospital. But I felt cheated—like Miss-Fix-It-All had robbed the rest of us of a chance to help our friend. But . . . how petty was that? Getting Delores there was the important thing.

We all gathered in the hotel foyer to see Delores and Edesa off. Delores clung to each one of us. *"Gracias,"* she whispered, her dark eyes bright with tears. Beyond the revolving doors a sporty silver Celica pulled up with Stu in the driver's seat. Figured. Just the kind of car a real estate agent would drive. But she'd better think twice about driving that car into the 'hood if she got back into social work. We watched as Edesa squeezed into the tiny backseat of the two-door and Delores eased into the low-slung bucket seat in the front, while Stu stowed their luggage in the trunk. And then they were gone.

We looked at each other, unsure what to do. "Don't really feel like going back to the banquet, but . . ." Ruth shrugged. "Maybe we should eat." Several others nodded and moved halfheartedly toward the ballroom.

"I think I'll go back to the prayer room," Avis said. "Maybe some of the rest of you could come later. We could keep up a prayer chain for José tonight, then all meet in the morning at seven."

Florida jumped on the idea. "I'll take ten to eleven."

I opened my mouth to volunteer for eleven o'clock when Adele jumped in. "I'll cover eleven to midnight." I wanted to groan. The prayer chain was a good idea, but I sure didn't want to end up trying to keep awake in the wee hours of the night.

Seeing my mouth close, Ruth said helpfully, "We could always double up."

I hesitated. I didn't think I was quite ready to go one on one with Adele. Maybe I'd go with Avis now, or with Florida at ten. "Look," I said, digging in my tote bag for my notebook, delaying for time, "we can make a list." I quickly jotted down the hours from now till 7:00 A.M. and filled in the names of Avis, Florida, and Adele. Then I handed it to Ruth. "Just pass it around."

Florida snorted. "Girl, you are too funny."

I had no idea what she meant, but as it turned out, I got to sign up for 6:00 A.M. Not a bad time for me—especially if I could get six or seven hours of sleep first. Nony, Hoshi, Chanda, and Ruth volunteered for the other nighttime hours. But there were still a few gaps. Who hadn't signed up? I looked down the list, then up at Yo-Yo.

"Hey. Don't look at me," she protested. "I don't do chain prayers or whatever you guys call it."

8

*A*vis went to the prayer room while the rest of us returned to the banquet. But I think we'd all lost our momentum and couldn't get it back. The waiters had already cleared the tables—I couldn't even remember if I'd finished my food—and the program had started. They were giving out gift bags to the oldest woman present . . . the mom with the most kids (some brave soul had eleven) . . . the most outrageous outfit (the skinny leather skirt with leopard-print silk blouse and leopard-print shoes got it hands-down) . . . the first one to register . . . two somebodies who had birthdays today . . . and a few other things that brought squeals of giddy laughter.

I kept thinking about Delores's boy. Shot. Maybe dead and Delores didn't know yet. Was he in a gang? The Latin Kings or one of the other Hispanic gangs? Delores was such a nice lady—a Christian, too. How terrible if her son had ended up in a gang.

Whenever I'd read stories in the *Chicago Tribune* about another gang shooting, it always seemed so far away, like another universe. I'd look at my Josh, whooping it up with his dad watching the Bulls or the Bears, and feel relief that I didn't have to worry about gangs. And then I'd close the paper and forget.

But this time I'd met a mother, a mother like me . . . and I couldn't forget.

I sighed. To tell the truth, I wasn't enjoying the banquet anymore. Maybe I should go join Avis in the prayer room . . . or just go up to our suite. *That* appealed to me a lot. I needed some time alone.

Catching Florida's eye I mouthed, *I'm going up to the room*, got up, and threaded my jeans between tables of sprayed, gelled, braided, and sequined ladies till I reached the ballroom doors. Behind me, the bold notes of a brass trio—all women—playing "Shout to the Lord" brought the assembly to its feet, clapping and singing along. On the other side of the double doors I hesitated. Should I go pray with Avis? But instead I headed for the elevator.

I AWOKE WITH A START, struggling for breath, sweat soaking my sleep shirt.

The bedside digital said 3:30. The bathroom light I'd left on was off. A dream . . . thank God it was only a dream!

I'd been running, running through the streets of my neighborhood . . . calling for my boy, "Josh! Josh!" . . . but I couldn't find him! . . . It was night, dark . . . nothing looked the same . . . the shadowy buildings loomed cold, unfriendly . . . streetlights peered like dim eyes through the black, scrawny branches of trees on the parkway . . . parked cars fenced in the sidewalks . . . until I got to Sheridan Road, suddenly bright with winking neon signs and sodium vapor streetlights along the strip of video stores, corner groceries, art galleries, movie theaters . . . Sheridan, as bright as day. I'll look here, *I'd thought in my dream . . . but I still couldn't find him.*

Awake now, I forced my breathing to slow, to picture Josh . . . safe at home in bed, his clothes dumped in blessed piles on the floor, his radio on low just off the dial so that the music scratched like an old record player. Even at seventeen, he had a midnight curfew on weekends. Yes, Josh was safe. It was only a dream.

But José . . . José wasn't safe at home in bed. Neither was Delores Enriquez. *Her* son had been shot. What was happening at Cook County Hospital right now, at three-thirty in the morning? Was Delores still there, sitting by the hospital bed of her son? Holding his hand? Praying that he would be all right? Weeping for her son?

I rolled out of the king-size bed and got down on my knees in the dark. I couldn't remember the last time I had prayed on my knees—maybe not since family devotions when I was a child. But prayer for a boy with a bullet in his body—a boy whose mother I knew by name—needed more from me than a quick prayer from beneath warm covers.

God, I'm sorry. I'm sorry I didn't take one of the nighttime hours to pray. I can't believe how selfish I am—worried about my sleep and signing up on the prayer chain only at a convenient time. Did You wake me up to pray? I'm here now . . . but I don't know how to pray for José! I don't know what happened, or how he is, or even if he's alive. Oh God, help him . . . he's only fourteen . . . help Delores . . .

"Jodi? Are you okay?"

I looked up with a start. Avis was dimly silhouetted in the open French doors between the bedroom and sitting room of the suite, her voice a stage whisper.

"Yeah . . . yeah. I was just . . . you know, praying for José."

"Oh. I heard a moan and just wanted to be sure you're all right."

"Yeah, I'm okay. Just, you know, worried . . ."

Avis came over to my side of the bed and sat down. I was still on my knees. "We don't have to worry," she said quietly. "God is in control. He's bigger than this. He's bigger than the enemy. He's already won this battle."

I frowned in the dark. How could she say that? What if José died—or was already dead? I mean, sure, God was "in control"— but bad things still happened.

I felt Avis's hand close on top of mine. "Jesus! Thank You for what You're going to do in this situation. We know the battle is already won, no matter what the enemy tries to throw at us. Don't let us sink into worry and despair. Satan wants us to cower and whimper. But we're thanking You, Lord. We don't know what happened, or why. But we're thanking You!"

She was using "we," so I whispered, "Yes, please, God." But I didn't know if my faith was that strong. My prayer had been more of the begging variety: "Please, Lord, don't let him die. Please, Lord, help . . ."

After praying awhile Avis left me, still on my knees, used the bathroom, and tiptoed back to bed. I could tell the other side of the king-size bed had not been slept in, though the pillows were gone. "Is Florida in there?" I whispered loudly into the other room.

"Yes," came the reply. "On the floor with the sofa cushions. Go figure."

MY TRAVEL ALARM WENT OFF under my pillow. 5:50 a.m. Parting the blackout curtains, I could tell the sun was already up. Trying to be as quiet as possible, I pulled on my jeans and sweater from last night, splashed water on my face—a shower would have to wait—and slipped out the door of our suite.

Meeting Room 7—an interior room created with expandable walls—was dark when I pulled open the door. I'd forgotten the list and couldn't remember if anyone had signed up for the five-to-six time slot. Guess not. I felt around until I found a light switch, but the light was so bright with only me in the room, I felt like a captured spy about to be interrogated. I turned it off and propped the door open.

Part of me wasn't sure I knew how to pray for a whole hour—especially without my morning cup of coffee. But maybe this was a chance to practice praying like some of the other women in the prayer group. For a while I walked around the circle of chairs in the dim room, silently praising God. Florida or Nony or Avis would've been saying, "Praise You, Jesus!" or "You are God Almighty from whom all blessings flow!" out loud, but I was chicken. Some hotel employee going past might hear me and think I was weird.

Remembering how Nony "prayed Scripture," though, gave me another idea—but I hadn't brought my Bible downstairs. I checked out the room by the light from the hallway and spied a Bible someone had left in one of the other prayer circles, a Contemporary English Version—I hadn't seen that one before. Dragging a chair near the open door—I still wasn't ready to "pray big" in a lighted room all by myself—I turned to the Psalms and began reading out loud. "The wicked try to trap and kill good people, but the Lord is on their side, and he will defend them when they are on trial." Oh, that was a good verse. Right on the money. I skimmed the psalm. "The Lord protects his people, and they can come to him in times of trouble."

What if I turned Psalm 37 into a prayer for Delores and her family? I tried it out loud. "Oh God, the wicked are trying to trap and kill Delores's son, but I know You are on their side, and You're going to defend them during this trial . . . You protect Your people, Lord, and Delores can come to You in this time of trouble." Goosebumps tickled the back of my neck. The words rang in my ear in a new way. Not third person but first person. *I* know *You are on their side . . . You protect Your people . . .* Did I *know* this—really? Could I declare it in faith?

I tried out several other psalms this way—and nearly jumped out of my skin when the lights suddenly flooded the room.

"Jodi! What are you doing in the dark?" Nony and Hoshi had come into the room. Both had sweats on.

"Uh, I was praying for Delores and her son . . . what time is it?"

"Seven. We came for the group prayer."

Seven already? I could hardly believe it. An hour ago I wasn't sure how I was going to fill up the time.

Within a few minutes, nearly the whole group showed up in various stages of morning dress—minus Delores, Edesa, and Stu, of course. Even Yo-Yo, though she sat off to the side, arms folded like a principal doing classroom observations. Yesterday morning, no one had shown up except Nony and Avis—plus me, tagging after Avis. But this morning, it was full house.

I'd always thought of "group prayer" as taking turns praying. But I was about to be introduced to no-holds-barred, every-woman-for-herself prayer. Avis, Adele, and Chanda moved around, praying out loud, all at the same time. Florida and Nony held forth on their knees. Ruth and Hoshi anchored their chairs, but I could tell they were praying.

I was the only one who saw Stu come into the room. I scanned her face. Bad news? Good news? "Stu! What's happened?"

The prayers abruptly stopped. Stu took a deep breath. "He's okay—shot in the back, but not fatal—"

"*Thank* ya, *Je*-sus!" Florida shouted. Chanda gripped her head and started jumping up and down. Several burst into tears and dropped to their knees. "Hallelujah!" . . . "You are a *mighty* God!" . . . "Ha! Satan, you're a liar!" filled the room for several moments.

I wanted to say, "Hush! Hush! Let's hear what happened." But obviously some of the other women had heard what they needed to hear. Delores Enriquez still had her son! José was not dead! The "enemy" had been thwarted!

GRADUALLY THE STORY CAME OUT—what Stu knew of it, anyway. She and Edesa had not been allowed to see José, only family. They'd paced and prayed in the waiting room for a couple of hours while José had surgery to insert a tube in his chest cavity—she wasn't sure why. At one point several police came in, asking to speak to José Enriquez. Stu and Edesa could only wait helplessly. Finally Delores came out, worry mixed with relief.

Evidently José had taken his siblings to the park near their house in the Little Village neighborhood. José's sister Emerald said a bunch of gangbangers—Spanish Cobras—were hanging in the park, "doin' business." José had told them to move somewhere else *(Unbelievable! Pretty brave for a fourteen-year-old,* I thought) so the kids could play. The Cobras started yelling, so José had corralled the little ones and was hustling them out of the park, when . . . here Emerald said she didn't know *what* happened. But she heard car tires screeching, then some gunshots—and suddenly her brother was down on the ground, groveling in pain.

Stu said Delores had broken down weeping at that point in the story. "It could have been Emerald—the twelve-year-old—or any of her 'babies.'" The police weren't making any statements at this point, Stu added, but witnesses in the park said José got hit by a bullet when a bunch of Latin Kings showed up and started a shouting match over Cobras doing business on King turf.

"King turf?" I blurted.

Yo-Yo spoke up. "Cobras makin' a *big* mistake if they mess

with the Latin Kings. Kings are *everywhere,* and they don't take kindly to anybody messin' with their turf."

I stared at her. How did she *know* that? Prison education? But I'd heard enough. Kids getting hit by stray bullets just going to play in the park? I brushed aside the nagging thought that I'd been quick to assume José himself was in a gang, just because he got shot. I latched on to the most important thing: Delores still had her son; they'd get through this.

The big-faced clock in the room said nearly eight o'clock. Most of us still needed to get showered and dressed for the day—in a hustle if we didn't want to miss breakfast. Several others must have had the same idea, because we started drifting toward the door. Crisis was over.

But I heard Yo-Yo's voice again. "What are you guys going to do?"

I turned back, prepared to offer my short list: shower, clothes, breakfast.

"How do you mean, do?" Ruth asked in that funny, backward way of hers.

"About Delores. What are you going to do about Delores?"

There was an awkward silence, which Yo-Yo took as an invitation. "You guys been talkin' all night to the Big Guy upstairs about Delores's boy. Looks like He gave a pretty good answer . . . for starters. But everybody just goin' to go home? Like this prayer group never happened? Delores might still need you, you know."

9

*L*ater, sitting with Avis and Florida in the Sunday morning worship service in the ballroom, I thought about what Yo-Yo had said. For somebody who wasn't into the "Jesus thing," Yo-Yo had sure seemed to nail the "Jesus thing" that time.

Avis had said it was a good question. "Let's meet one more time after the morning worship and talk about what we want to do."

Sunday worship was the fourth main session of the weekend—not counting the banquet—and to tell the truth, the pounding gospel music had begun to burrow its way into my soul . . . "The devil is defeated! We are blessed!"

That was true enough this morning. Last night I, for one, had thought Delores might be attending her son's funeral. Not Avis, though. She obviously wasn't about to accept defeat—hers or anyone else's—as long as she had breath to claim victory. That took faith—a lot more faith than I seemed to have. Funny. I'd always presumed I had a strong faith. *Let those Commies come and send me to Siberia unless I recant! Ha! Do your worst!* But on an everyday level, my mind tended to weigh in all the "realities." *Most people don't get healed from cancer . . . Denny got bumped from the high school coaching job he wanted . . . A lot of poor people pray, but they still go to bed hungry . . .*

The music was going over the top. "I'm coming back to the heart of worship . . . it's all about You, Jesus . . ."

I closed my eyes, for once oblivious to what Florida and Avis were doing. *I want to learn how to worship You, Jesus. I want a bigger faith. I want to learn how to pray. And, yes, I want to know what You created me for . . .*

When the morning speaker—Evangelist Olivia Mitchell again—asked, "Who wants God to show you who He created you to be? Who wants to step into your spiritual destiny? Come on down here to the front. We're going to pray for you," I planted my feet firmly. No way was I going up. I didn't want to cry or have hands put on me or get laid out. I could pray right here in my row, thank you.

But when both Florida and Avis went up—and I saw Nony and a couple of others from our prayer group up front—I reached down for some courage. *Jodi Baxter, didn't you just tell God you wanted to learn more about worship . . . about faith . . . about prayer . . . about yourself? Well, go get prayed for, girl!*

Fortunately for my shaking knees, there were so many women who came to the front for prayer that the speaker just touched each woman on the forehead with oil and kept praying as she passed down the line. But even that brought tears to my eyes, to feel that touch, to be included in the prayer. I had the strange sense I was being sent on an adventure into the unknown . . . without a map.

WHEN THE SERVICE WAS OVER, the ten of us in Prayer Group Twenty-Six—Edesa had stayed at the hospital with the Enriquez family—gathered once more in Meeting Room 7. One of the other prayer groups was also meeting in the room, so we pulled our chairs closer together in order to hear.

"Well," Avis said, "Yo-Yo asked what we're going to do about Delores. What are you thinking, Yo-Yo?"

Yo-Yo slouched in her chair like a denim-clad log, shoulders and fanny barely touching the chair, her legs stretched out their full length, her hands jammed in the pockets of her bib overalls. "Yeah. The way I see it, something got started here, and you guys stood up with Delores in a big way with that chain prayer thing. But it ain't over yet."

We all glanced at each other, then a few suggestions trickled out.

"If we had her phone number, we could call her, let her know we're still praying for her."

"Or maybe some of us could visit José in the hospital—Cook County, wasn't it, Stu?"

I took a leap. "I've been thinking about what Yo-Yo said. There's no reason we couldn't continue this prayer group."

"Oh, really!" Adele snorted. "My guess is the folks in this room live all over the city. Lawndale . . . Little Village . . . Austin . . . and half a dozen other neighborhoods. Not an easy commute to get together at 7:00 A.M. for a prayer meeting."

I could feel my ears turning red. But I pressed on. "I realize that. But if we had each other's telephone numbers and e-mail addresses—"

"What? Like a phone chain?" Florida asked.

Stu groaned. "That could take forever to get around—or get stuck in somebody's voice mail."

"But how about e-mail?" I pressed. "If we had each other's e-mail addresses and each created a 'group list' in our address book, then if someone has a prayer request, they could send it to the whole group with one e-mail."

The idea sat out there for a moment or two, then Florida piped up. "I like that. That works for me."

Stu tucked a long blonde lock behind her ear. "But maybe not everyone has e-mail. Let's see hands of those who don't."

Yo-Yo and Chanda were the only ones who waggled their hands.

"Not to worry, Yo-Yo. My e-mail is your e-mail." Ruth patted Yo-Yo's knee. "I'll bring it to the café when I get my rugelach." We had no idea what rugelach was, but the rest of us couldn't help but laugh.

"But what about Delores and Edesa?" Stu pressed. "What if they don't have e-mail?"

"I'll call them and find out." I lobbed the ball right back into her corner. "Did you get Delores's phone number last night?" I dug around in my tote bag and pulled out my notebook. "Look, I'll send this around and everyone can put down their e-mail addy *and* their phone number. Snail-mail address, too. Then we can make a list—can't tell when it might come in handy."

"You are the queen of list-makers, girl!" Florida crowed.

"Um," said Hoshi. We all looked at her. The Japanese student had said so little in the group that even "um" got our attention. "I have e-mail, fine. But if we create a group list in our address book, we need a name. Not just 'Number Twenty-Six.'"

Chuckles rippled around the circle again.

"Just call it Prayer Group," said Stu. She sounded annoyed.

"Prayer Group, yada yada, whatever," said Yo-Yo.

Ruth twisted her motherly self to the side and looked at Yo-Yo like she'd just said something brilliant. "I like that. The Yada Yada Prayer Group. It means something, I think."

"Yeah. 'Whatever,'" echoed Adele. She shook her head as though she couldn't believe we were having this conversation.

I snatched back the initiative. "Yada Yada it is—whatever it means." I wrote it at the top of the page of my notebook, scratched my address, phone, and e-mail on it, and started it around the circle. "I kinda like it, too." *It kinda fits this motley crew,* I didn't say. *And we'll never agree on a name, so "whatever" is fine.*

Avis smiled. "Well, I don't know about Yada Yada as a name, but keeping in touch and sharing prayer requests by e-mail is a good idea. Jodi, will you send that list to all of us by e-mail? But we still have Yo-Yo's question to answer. What are we going to do about Delores? I think it would mean a lot if a few of us—wouldn't have to be everybody—could visit José in the hospital. And the rest of us could call Delores and share a promise from the Word or pray with her on the phone."

"Now you're talking," said Yo-Yo. "Sign me up to visit José."

I TENTATIVELY SIGNED UP to visit José Enriquez with Avis on Monday night if he was still in the hospital—pending Denny's schedule, since he sometimes had to coach late afternoon sports at West Rogers High School. As we packed our luggage and said our good-byes to Flo, I felt really weird. We'd been thrown together for three days and two nights, right down to our toothbrushes and sleep shirts . . . and now I wasn't sure when—or if—I would see Florida again. Our lives were about as different as two people's could be, but I liked her. Really liked her. I could only imagine everything she'd been through, but she was so . . . so upbeat. So close to God. Where did that come from?

"Sorry about the snoring," I told her sheepishly as we folded up the sleeper sofa and returned the cushions to their rightful place. "*Next* time you take the bed, and I'll take the floor."

"Next time?" Flo wiggled her eyebrows. "Well, girl, you come visit me, and for sure I'll take the bed and give you the floor." She laughed. "Only got one bed, anyway. The kids are already sleeping on the floor."

I tried not to look flabbergasted. Kids sleeping on the floor? Oh, well. Not my business. But I did have something I was curious about. "Flo, when we were sharing stuff for prayer, you asked us to pray about getting your family back together again. What did you mean?"

Avis, coming out of the bathroom with her cosmetic bag and toilet kit, heard my question and gave me a look. Like maybe I was getting too personal.

"That's okay. You don't have to say," I added hastily.

Florida shrugged, her brow knit into a frown. "No, it's all right. Just hard to talk about. Truth is, I can't find my baby. DCFS took all three of 'em when I was strung out on drugs and put 'em in foster homes. Carl—their dad—wasn't in any shape to take care of 'em, either. Since I've been straight, I've got the boys back— Cedric, he's eleven, the one who's ADD, and Chris, he's thirteen. But my girl—she'd be eight now—the foster family who had her just . . . disappeared. Even DCFS can't find 'em." Florida's eyes puddled. "Scares me sometimes that maybe I won't find her."

"Oh, Florida!" I put my arms around her in a tight hug. I couldn't think of anything else to do.

"Not find her? Oh, no, we're not going to go there," Avis said firmly. "That's Satan telling you one of his rotten lies. Father"— and she started right in praying—"we rebuke Satan and all his lies. We reject discouragement. We claim victory right now for finding Florida's little girl . . ." The three of us stood in a little huddle for several minutes while Avis prayed. When she was done praying, I didn't want to let go of their hands, didn't want the moment to end. But we parted, finished packing quietly, and headed for the lobby to check out.

"You got a ride?" Avis asked Florida as we said our good-byes beside the hotel's revolving door.

"Yeah, Adele said she'd drop me off. We don't live too far."

"Are you in Rogers Park, too?" I asked, surprised. I hadn't had time to look at the list of addresses that had gone around.

Florida nodded. "Yeah. Almost to Edgewater. Only a couple of miles from you guys, though."

As Avis and I pulled out of the hotel parking lot, I saw Florida outside the revolving doors with her bag, a cigarette in one hand. At that moment, I didn't blame her. If I couldn't find my little girl, I'd probably be dragging on a cigarette, too.

10

Avis dropped me off in front of the house. I couldn't believe it was already 3:30—but then our prayer group had gone past noon, so by the time we tried to get a "quick lunch" in the hotel café, the line had been pretty long. We'd made the deadline to check out by two o'clock—barely— but the traffic on I-90 going into the city crept along in typical freeway gridlock. We made better time once we got off on Touhy Avenue heading east toward Lake Michigan, even with stoplights.

"See you tomorrow," Avis said as I got out in front of our two-flat on Lunt Avenue in Rogers Park. "Back to real life. No more maid service."

I grinned weakly. I was glad to be home . . . but part of me hated for the weekend to end. I wasn't sure why—getting to know the women in the prayer group was part of it. But I wanted time to think about everything that had happened since Friday night, to sort it out. I couldn't wait to tell Denny—he'd be real interested to hear about it.

Picking up my suitcase, I walked up the steps to the porch and stood there. Should I ring the bell? Or use my key? I used my key, let myself into the foyer where carpeted stairs led up to the second-floor apartment, then unlocked our first-floor door on the right. Slipping off my shoes and hanging up my jacket in the hall closet, I could hear the television in the living room—a baseball game, no doubt. Then I heard male laughter—several adult voices.

Rats. Denny had company.

I could almost taste the resentment that surged upward from my gut. Didn't Denny know I'd be home about now? That we hadn't seen each other for two whole days and nights? That I'd want some time together to catch up with each other?

I swallowed, telling myself I was being childish. I didn't even know what the situation was yet. Pasting a smile on my face, I walked in my stocking feet toward the living room archway and stopped.

Three guys—four, counting Denny—lounged on the couch, the floor, and two overstuffed chairs, eyes glued to a Cubs game on the TV as they booed a call by an umpire. Willie Wonka, our almost-deaf chocolate Labrador, lay sprawled happily on Denny's feet. Nearly empty bowls of chips, popcorn, and salsa competed with a cardboard pizza box and cans of pop on the coffee table and lamp tables. And brown bottles. Bottles? The bottles didn't compute for a moment. And just then Denny looked up and saw me in the archway.

His face lit up. "Hey, babe! You're back!" He leaped up, bottle in hand, and gave me a big smooch.

Beer on his breath. The bottles were beer bottles.

He turned back to the other guys. "Larry . . . Greg . . . Bill . . . you remember my wife, Jodi."

I recognized the men now—coaches and assistants who worked with Denny at the high school. Larry could be Michael Jordan's brother, complete with shaved head. A chorus of "Hi, Jodi!" wafted my way, cut short by a whoop as the Cubs batter connected.

"Denny?" I said, giving the bottle in his hand a dark look.

He looked amused. "Don't worry about it, babe. One of the guys brought a six-pack. *One* six-pack. Not a big deal."

"But what if my parents walked in right now? . . ."

"Your parents, I assure you, are safely ensconced in Des Moines, Iowa, where they belong." I could tell he was teasing me, his gray eyes twinkling under dark eyebrows and the thick strand of dark hair falling over his forehead. "Say, did you have a good time at the conference?"

"Yeah, I—"

Loud groans from the living room. Denny stepped back where he could view the TV. "I want to hear all about it, hon. Only one more inning in the game." He still stood only three feet from me, but he was gone.

Turning on my stocking feet, I stalked down the hallway, past Amanda's bedroom on one side and the dining room on the other, past the one and only bathroom . . . I came back to the bathroom. The door was closed. I knocked tentatively.

"Busy!" came a female voice on the other side of the door.

"Amanda? It's Mom. I'm home."

"Oh, hi, Mom! Glad you're back," said the disembodied voice of my fourteen-year-old.

"Come see me when you're out—I'll be in my bedroom."

"Okay."

I continued on down the hall and peeked into Josh's room. No sign of life, except for the mold and unsightly creatures probably breeding in the piles of dirty clothes, CDs, schoolbooks, magazines, and snack dishes littering every inch of the floor. My mouth tightened. Didn't Denny tell the kids to clean their rooms on Saturday?

Probably not. Nagging was *my* job. Everybody was on vacation when Mom went away for the weekend.

I headed for our bedroom at the back of the house, tempted to slam the door with gale force, but I thought better of it with "company" in the house, so I left it open a crack. Throwing myself onto the bed, hot tears welled up and wet the comforter. I grabbed a tissue from the bedside stand and dabbed my eyes, then blew my nose.

Some homecoming.

"Mom?" My fourteen-year-old stood silhouetted in the doorway. "Ohmigosh. You've got big black smudges under your—" Amanda, her butterscotch hair twisted in a clump on the back of her head and gripped with a big white plastic claw, sat down on the edge of the bed and squinted at me. "You okay?"

I rolled my eyes and allowed a self-deprecating grin. "Yeah. Never learned the art of bawling without ruining my mascara. I'm fine. Just, you know"—I jerked my head in the direction of the living room—"disappointed."

She looked confused. "Why? Dad's just watching the game with some guys."

"I know. I just . . . never mind. How was your weekend?"

"Great! Dad took me out for brunch Saturday—we went to the Original Pancake House up in Wilmette. So cool, Mom! I had one of those Dutch babies—couldn't even finish it."

I smiled, trying to ignore the pang in my chest. It'd been a long time since we'd been to the Original Pancake House, a virtual North Shore museum of stained glass as well as to-die-for breakfast creations. "I'm glad, honey. That's neat."

"Oh. What time is it? Gotta go. The youth group is having a meeting at four-thirty about our service project trip to Mexico. Josh is already over there." She bounced off the bed then leaned over and pecked me on the cheek. "'Bye." And she was out the door.

Thirty seconds later she was back. "The game isn't over. Can you give me a ride to the church?"

I sighed. Welcome back to the real world.

WHEN I GOT BACK FROM TAKING AMANDA over to Uptown Community—it was only about a mile, but Denny and I didn't like her walking alone, even in the afternoon—the game was over, the guys were gone, and Denny was dutifully cleaning up the living room. "Hey," he said as I walked in. "Thanks for taking Amanda.

Hope you didn't mind. It was a great game—Cubs won by seven runs!" He had that hopelessly silly look of the sports addicted.

I shrugged. "Didn't mind. Got to steal a quick hug from Josh—who knows when I'll get to see him otherwise."

Denny balanced several bowls in each hand as he headed for the kitchen beyond the dining room. "Yeah. He's taking this 'youth leader' role for the Mexico trip pretty seriously. Hey! You sit down," he called back over his shoulder. "I'll finish this up, then I want to hear about your weekend! You want some coffee? Tea?"

"Tea." That would be nice. I settled in one of our secondhand overstuffed chairs in the living room—decorated in a charming hodgepodge that Denny called "early attic." I felt my spirit relax. I'd gotten myself worked up over nothing. The kids were gone . . . Denny and I could have some time to ourselves now . . . everything was okay.

Five minutes later Denny came back with the teapot, two mugs, the honey bear, and a couple of spoons on a tray. "Okay," he said, handing me one of the steaming mugs. "Tell me about your conference."

Now that I had his attention, I hardly knew how to tell him what had happened this weekend. So I just started at the beginning—our unexpected roommate . . . getting assigned to a prayer group for the weekend . . . wearing our jeans to the banquet ("You're pulling my leg!" he said, his eyes getting big; then he burst out laughing) . . . the news about José getting shot and the all-night prayer chain . . . and finally, our decision to keep the prayer group alive to pray for each other.

Denny set aside his mug and pulled me over to sit beside him on the couch. I nestled down into the crook of his arm, feeling warm and safe. "Sounds like an amazing weekend. How did it go rooming with Ms. Johnson?"

Ms. Johnson? I pulled back to look at him. He had a smirk on his face. Of course. That's what I always called Avis at school. She was the principal, my boss, after all. "Good. Good. We got along great." But suddenly I felt a bit schizophrenic. All weekend she had been "Avis"—a friend, a "sister." And yet, now that I thought about it, I didn't know a whole lot more about her than I did before the conference. Except that she could lose herself in worship—totally unlike her calm, reserved, everything's-under-control presence at school. I knew she had grandkids—their pictures were all over her office at school—but she'd never said anything about a husband. Was she married? Divorced? Never married?

How had we managed to get through the entire weekend—and all that sharing in the prayer group—and I still had no idea if there was a Mr. Avis?

I just sat in the crook of Denny's arm, thinking . . . when I spied a stray brown bottle on one of the lamp tables. "Denny?" I turned to look at him again. "What's with the beer? I mean, I thought we agreed, no beer in this house."

"Oh, is that what we did? I thought it was you saying *you* didn't want any beer in the house. Though you don't seem to mind the occasional bottle of good wine."

"Yeah, but . . . that's different." Denny knew my background; why was he being so cavalier about it all of a sudden? I was too little to remember much about my father's drinking—just the feeling of panic when the yelling started, my big brothers holding me in one of the back bedrooms, covering my ears to drown out the sounds of my father shouting at my mother and the crash of things getting thrown around. But then my father got saved at a little Bible church—saved and "delivered from the demon of alcohol," my mother often said. After that, drinking of any kind —along with smoking, gambling, and cussing—was right up there with the seven deadly sins. To my mother's delight, we became the church-goingest family in Des Moines, and everyone had marveled that Sid Jennings was a changed man.

Denny, on the other hand, came from a mainstream church background, where drinking wine and even beer was an accepted part of the social culture. By Denny's own admission, he'd been more of a church attender than a Christ follower till college, even got a little wild with the weekend parties. But then he'd had a real renewal of his faith with a Christian college group on the university campus—somewhat to the bewilderment of his parents, who were a little worried he might turn "fundy."

Denny's parents had graciously offered to buy the wine for our wedding reception, nearly giving my parents apoplexy. We managed to convince the senior Baxters that *not* serving wine at the reception dinner would be more "sensitive" to my family, who didn't drink—and besides, would save tons of money.

They gave us two nights in a luxury hotel instead.

"How different?" Denny's tone was not confrontive, but also not concerned.

"Just . . . different." I felt on the defensive. "People don't go out and get drunk on *wine*. But you hear about all these stupid beer parties at the universities, and . . . and, who do the cops pull over for DUIs? Beer drinkers!" Now I was finding my groove.

"Hey, hey, hey! Wait a minute." Denny's tone went up. "When did we jump from drinking a beer while watching a Cubs game to getting pulled over for drunk driving?"

"Well . . . it starts somewhere."

"Jodi Marie Baxter. You're being unfair. I'm totally on the same page with you about drunkenness! It's wrong. It's stupid. The Bible warns against it. But drinking a glass of wine with our meals—as you do from time to time—or drinking a beer with the guys in my own living room is not a sin. I didn't even buy it. Larry brought it, and I made the decision that to make a big deal about it would be to push him away, a 'holier than thou' thing. Especially when we drink wine from time to time. What kind of hypocrisy is that?" He paused. "Besides, remember that Bible study we did on Jewish festivals? Wine is a symbol of harvest, of God's blessings. You know that."

"Wine, not beer," I said stubbornly.

Denny stood up abruptly. "Oh, good grief, Jodi. Let's not fight about this. It's really *not* a big deal. Look, you just got home . . . I'm glad you had a good time . . . the kids and I managed fine . . . this is the first time the other coaching staff have been to my house, and they had a great time . . . Let's leave it at that." He picked up the tray and headed for the kitchen.

I sat motionless on the couch, wishing I still had his arm around me, wishing I hadn't said anything. Tears threatened again, but I blinked them back stubbornly. Maybe Denny was right. Maybe I was inconsistent. Still . . . I didn't like him drinking beer in our house, not with the kids around, for sure, and I wished he wouldn't. For me, if nothing else.

The clock on the mantel of the gas fireplace struck six. I shook myself. I needed to go over my lesson plans for tomorrow—we were working on one-digit multipliers in math, and I'd wanted to de-velop some games to make it fun—and do the prayer group e-mail list.

A surge of energy got me up off the couch. The prayer group. If we were going to hang together as the Yada Yada Prayer Group, I needed to get on the computer and send out that list.

11

I settled down at the computer in the dining room—
might as well do the list first, I reasoned, before the
kids got home, suddenly remembering that they still had
homework—and got out my notebook with the page the prayer
group had filled out. As I started to type in names, addresses,
and e-mails, I couldn't help but guffaw. I could practically guess
whose e-mail address belonged to whom, even without looking
at who wrote it down.

AprinciPal@MMBE.org . . . Avis, of course.

Flowithflo@wahoo.com . . . guess who.

Yid-dish@online.net . . . oh, that *was* funny. Ruth, the Yiddish
Dish. Ha!

ShineBaby@wahoo.com . . . had to be Adele's shop.

Nony's was easy: BlessedRU@online.net.

Stu's was blatant advertising: GetRealStu@GetRealEstate.com.

I felt a little silly typing our family e-mail address on the list:

BaxterBears@wahoo.com. Denny's idea, of course, when the Chicago Bears were hot. But now it sounded like a children's picture book. Oh well.

Hoshi had a Northwestern University address, and I didn't have anything for Delores or Edesa yet. Chanda and Yo-Yo did not have e-mail—hopefully Adele and Ruth would help us stay in touch with them somehow.

"Whatcha doin'?"

I turned to see Denny leaning in the doorway between the dining room and kitchen. His gray eyes were gentle, a little sad—that puppy dog look he got when he wanted everything to be okay.

"Making a list, checking it twice . . . to see who's been naughty or nice."

That got a laugh. So I told him about our conference prayer group wanting to stay in touch, even choosing a name for ourselves.

"The *Yada Yada* Prayer Group?" Now his eyes were crinkled up in silent laughter, the corners of his mouth twitching.

"Don't laugh," I ordered, but I was grinning myself. "If you met all these women, you'd see it fits this group perfectly."

"And it means . . .?"

"Don't have a clue. 'Whatever.'"

Denny moved behind me and massaged my neck. "Hungry? You want to go out for a bite somewhere? Kids aren't back yet . . ."

The last bit of tension between us seemed to evaporate. It was tempting . . . but. "Sounds great . . . but I want to get this done before Josh and Amanda get back and tell me they've got a ten-page paper due tomorrow morning, and will I *please* get off the computer?" I looked up hopefully. "But a toasted cheese sandwich sounds good. With horseradish. And a pickle. If you're offering."

"Coming up."

Denny went back into the kitchen, and I stared once more at the blinking cursor on the screen. Okay, I had the list done and ready to send, but I needed to make an address subgroup so I could send it with one click. And maybe I should summarize what different women had asked prayer for during the weekend and send that, so we could keep praying for those situations.

The foster family who has my little girl seems to have disappeared.

Flo's words popped into my head so strongly, I actually looked around, thinking she was standing right there telling me again. Ohmigosh. If we were going to be a real prayer group, we certainly should be praying for *that*. But . . . Flo had only told me because I'd blundered into her business. Would she mind if we prayed about it as a group? Why would she?

At least I could ask.

Working quickly, I created a subgroup in my address book called "Yada Yada," then copied the list into an e-mail message and hit "Send." Then I called up a new message:

To: Florida Hickman
From: Jodi Baxter
Subject: Prayer for your daughter

Flo! Hope you got home okay. How are the boys?

I'm wondering . . . could Yada Yada pray about finding

your daughter? Ever since you told me that the foster family has disappeared, I've been thinking THIS is the very reason we need to continue the prayer group. Please consider letting the group know how we can pray. In the meantime, I will pray . . . hard.

I stared at the message on the screen, realizing how little I knew this woman. Then a troubling thought crossed my mind: if Flo had e-mail, that meant she had a computer. A computer . . . but no beds for the kids?

Odd.

BEEP . . . BEEP . . . BEEP. I automatically flung out my arm and hit the snooze button on the alarm. For a moment, I was confused. Had the prayer group decided to pray before breakfast again? Had my snoring chased Florida out of the bed again?

Then I felt movement in the bed, and Denny's arm pulled me close under the comforter. I smiled sleepily as I pressed my back against his warm, bare chest. This was definitely better than sleeping by myself in the corner of a king-size hotel bed, even without maid service.

Five minutes later, the alarm went off again, and I flung off the comforter. Monday morning at the Baxter household had begun.

One hour and thirty minutes, four rounds of banging on the bathroom door, two slices of burnt toast, one shoe hunt, pooling pocket change for city bus fares, and three wails of "Where's my whatzit?" later, I headed out the front door for the fifteen-minute walk to Bethune Elementary. I felt like a bag lady in walking shoes, a bulging backpack (extra sweater and flat shoes to change into) slung over one shoulder, a huge canvas tote bag full of rectangle shapes (baking pan, old Christmas card boxes, box of cereal, and the like) for my students to measure the perimeter of rectangles in math, and my smaller canvas lunch-bag-with-water-bottle in the other.

"C'mon, hon! I'll give you a ride," Denny called, letting the engine of the minivan run while he cleaned bird poop off the windshield. My mistake. I'd left the car parked on the street last night after picking up the kids from church. Usually there weren't any parking places on the street—at least we had a garage off the alley— but yesterday, there it was, a parking place *right in front of the house.* An urban miracle! It would've seemed a shame to leave it empty.

But I forgot about the bird poop.

"No thanks! Need the exercise." I lifted the tote bag in a half-attempt at a wave and set off down the sidewalk at a good pace. Walking was my fifteen minutes of mental space between household chaos and school chaos every day.

I hummed as school kids passed me on the run, their book bags bumping on their backs like loose turtle shells. "Hi, Miz Baxter!" a few of them called. But for the most part, they seemed to function on the principle that school hadn't started yet and therefore they weren't obligated to acknowledge adults. That was all right with me. All too soon we'd all be on the conveyor belt that pulled us through the school day. Bells ringing . . . announcements on the loudspeaker . . . passing out worksheets . . . moving desks into modules for science projects . . . the constant hum of thirty eight-year-olds, like a classroom of crickets . . .

I'm coming back to the heart of worship . . .

It's all about You, Jesus . . .

I realized I'd been humming some of the worship songs from the conference. The words carried me along like inner breezes.

The playground was full of kids running—always running—backpacks and jackets dumped along the tall chain-link fence or against the deep red brick of the old school building. The May sunshine tempered a chill wind coming off Lake Michigan and prowling through any available open space.

I pulled open the double doors and stepped into the relative quiet of the before-school hallway. Glancing into the school office, I saw Avis talking with one of the secretaries. She caught my eye, and I gave her a smile, but I thought, *Good morning, Ms. Johnson. Back to the real world.*

But to my surprise, she held up her index finger in a wait-a-minute signal.

I lowered my tote bag to the floor. In less than a minute, she came out, dressed in a cranberry suit and chunky gold earrings. Were school principals supposed to look that smashing?

"Hi, Jodi." She smiled, but I wasn't sure if it was a "friendly principal" smile, or a warm now-we-know-each-other-a-little-better smile. "Recover from the weekend yet?"

"Not sure I want to. It was . . . great."

"Yes, it was. And you did the group list already! I was so surprised to get it this morning when I came into the office. That's great."

"Good." I nodded. "I'm glad."

"But I wanted to ask you . . . do you want to go see José Enriquez tonight? And hopefully Delores, if she's there."

José! I had totally forgotten I'd signed the list to go with Avis tonight. I hadn't told Denny or checked to see if he needed the car or anything.

"Oh! Yes . . . I want to. Can I let you know for sure a little later?" I probably should offer to drive, since Avis had ferried me to the conference and back. But did I really want to drive around the Near West Side at night? Not really.

Avis agreed with a wave and turned toward her inner office while I picked up the tote bag once more and headed for my third grade classroom. It was pretty much as I had left it on Friday, except the floor had been swept, the trash emptied, and the desktops had been scrubbed free of dried paste and eraser marks. Bless the janitor. Through the bank of windows along one side of the classroom, I could see the blur of feet dancing in and out of a set of twirling jump ropes to the tune of a timeless childhood chant:

> Strawberry shortcake
> Huckleberry Finn
> When I call your birthday
> Jump right in . . .
> January, February, March, April . . .

Still a few minutes to get ready for the day. I unloaded my bags, changed my shoes, and stowed my lunch in the desk drawer . . .

noticing the paperback New Testament I kept there. Kept there, and it usually stayed there, too. This was a public school, for goodness' sake. But this morning I pulled it out. In my head I could hear Nony "praying Scripture," one verse after the other. I felt an inner longing to be that full of God's Word, so that it came pouring out like that.

Well, why not?

I opened the book and turned to the Psalms, included at the back. The pages fell open to Psalm 95. My eyes skimmed a few verses silently . . . *Come, let us sing for joy to the Lord; let us shout aloud to the Rock of salvation.*

I was struck by the irony. Reading "sing for joy" and "shout aloud" silently—that was me, all right. But if Florida or Nony were standing in my shoes right now, they'd take "Sing!" and "Shout!" pretty literally.

Well, why not?

"Come, let us *sing for joy* to the Lord!" I said in a loud voice, picking up a piece of chalk and proceeding to write down the day's new math problems on the board. "Let us *shout aloud* to the Rock of salvation!" I did a little dance step and moved down the board. "Hallelujah!"

Gosh, that felt good. So good it made me laugh, just as the bell rang.

I put down the chalk and stowed the New Testament back in the drawer. Time to hustle out to the playground, stand in front of the ragtag line known as "Ms. Baxter's third grade," and escort them back to the nest of learning. Another typical Monday . . .

Or was it?

12

That afternoon at the last bell, it took only ninety seconds for twenty-seven third graders—three were absent—to disappear from Room 3C, leaving behind the usual glut of forgotten items: two hooded sweatshirts, an overdue library book, several hair bands and barrettes, a red sock (a *sock?*), somebody's copy of the math homework page, even a blue-and-red backpack. I peeked inside the backpack. Johnny Butler's, of course. His backpack resided more hours in the classroom than it did at home. Unfortunately, his parents never seemed to notice.

Piling the left-behind items into my Darn-Lucky Box covered with gold foil—I charged the kids a quarter to redeem items, and they were "darn lucky" to get 'em back—I glanced at the clock: 3:05. I'd had no time to contact Denny at the high school during the day, and now he'd be busy with after-school baseball practice. I wracked my brain, trying to remember if anything was happening tonight in the Baxter family that would curtail my going to the hospital, but my mind was blank.

That was either a good sign or a bad sign.

Taking a chance, I made a quick trip to the office and told Avis (though I remembered to ask the school secretary, "Is Ms. Johnson available?") that I was pretty sure I could go tonight and would pick her up at six-thirty. *That* was a leap. *Okay, God, I'm counting on You to grab Denny by the scruff of the neck and haul him back home by six—and please don't let him bring half the team home for supper.* Well, it hadn't happened yet, but I wouldn't put it past him.

Back in my classroom, I consulted my lesson-plan book to see what I could do now to get a jump on the next day. Following my finger down the language arts column, I found "contractions." "Ha!" I announced to the empty room. These kids were pretty good at contractions already—*ain't . . . cain't . . . gonna . . . whassup*—though I doubted I'd find those in the third grade syllabus. I finally decided to make a puzzle out of strips of heavy paper so the kids could play with words like *do not* and *is not* that could be joined together, with "wild apostrophe" cards to cover the dropped letter. As for math, the kids had enjoyed measuring "real" rectangles, so I toyed with the idea of having a contest to see who could bring in the most interesting "rectangle" the next day—the class could vote and the winner would get a prize. Could be risky, though. No telling what the kids might come up with—and I didn't want to incur the wrath of a parent whose jewelry box went "missing."

For science, we were supposed to compare "consumable versus recyclable" household items. Jotted down another list of stuff to bring from home. Toothpaste . . . bath soap . . . shampoo . . . would do for consumables. The recyclables were easy too: newspaper . . . metal can . . . plastic grocery bag . . . glass bottle . . .

Glass bottle. Yesterday's upset with Denny dusted itself off and tightened my face. Sure hoped I could find an empty bottle besides the brown *beer* bottles I'd stashed under the newspapers in the recycling bin on the back porch.

I smacked the side of my head with the flat of my palm. *Nope. Don't go there, Jodi. Denny said it isn't a big deal, so don't make it a big deal.*

By four o'clock I was ready to change back into my walking shoes, gather up my bags, and head out of the school. The afternoon sun had warmed up to a comfy sixty-five degrees, and the walk home was pleasant—though if I had three wishes, I'd use two of them to be walking along a country road (one) and to be ten years old again (two).

On second thought, I didn't really want to be ten years old and have to go through puberty and pimples again.

"Hellooo," I called out as I let myself in the front door, mentally rehearsing what I could make for supper and keep hot if I had to leave. "Anybody home?"

Willie Wonka's nails scrabbled down the hall and slid to a stop around my dropped bags, snuffling and sniffing in each one.

"Hi, Mom." Amanda's voice floated from the dining room. "Just me. Josh and Dad are still at school . . . Hey, who's 'FlowithFlo'? We got a strange e-mail message from somebody, but *I've* never heard of her. Should I delete it?"

THAT'S IT, I DECIDED, as I slowed the minivan in front of Avis's apartment building. I've got to get my own e-mail address. Nearly gave Willie Wonka a heart attack by pounding down the hall screeching *"No!"* with—I hoped—the accuracy of a heat-seeking missile. Amanda had looked startled then rolled her eyes when I ordered her away from the computer. But, I'd reminded her, she wasn't even supposed to be *on* the computer unless Denny or I were home.

But it all worked out. The e-mail from Florida had simply said, "Okay to put my girl on the list. Her name is Carla." No signature; no context. (No wonder Amanda felt suspicious.) But I felt nonplussed; sounded like Florida was leaving it to *me* to write up the prayer request and send it to Yada Yada. But I didn't know diddly-squat about the situation! Why didn't she write it up and send it herself? She had the list now.

But as I stared at her daughter's name—*Carla*—on the screen, my attitude softened. What did it matter, really? I didn't have to say much. We just needed to pray that Florida could find her little girl, her Carla.

"Mom? Are you crying?" Amanda's voice behind me had sounded alarmed.

"No . . . no," I'd sniffed. "Well, maybe a little. Tell you later."

But I hadn't had time to tell her. I didn't want to write up the prayer request in a rush, so I told Amanda she could use the computer now and went into the kitchen to scare up supper. By the time Denny and Josh got home—by six o'clock, thank You,

God—I had the makings for tacos on the counter assembly-line style, apologized for not giving Denny advance warning about going to the hospital this evening to see Delores's son, but did he mind if I took the minivan?

"No problem," he'd said. "But it's going to be dark by the time you get home. Want me to go with you?" I could tell he was a little worried about me driving in an unfamiliar neighborhood— with good reason. Even though we'd lived in the Chicago area for twenty years, even though we'd lived on Chicago's north side for nine months, I had never once been to Cook County Hospital.

But armed with a map Denny printed off from the computer, I kissed everybody good-bye—even Willie Wonka—and set out for Avis's address. But—as usual—I couldn't find a parking place, except a nice empty spot in front of a fire hydrant. Taking a gamble, I pulled in, left my hazards blinking, and dashed into the foyer. *D. Wilson . . . T. Coleman . . . A. Johnson . . .* that was it. I punched the white button beside her name.

The intercom crackled. "If that's you, Jodi, I'll be right down."

I grinned and ran back to the minivan so I could move it if a police car snuck up on me.

"Hi!" said Avis a few minutes later, opening the passenger-side door and climbing in. "Glad you found me okay." I noticed she was carrying her Bible, a big thick thing. It hadn't even occurred to me to bring mine—though if it had, I probably would have brought my pocket-size one. Avis clicked the seat belt. "Which way are we going?"

"Down Lakeshore Drive into the Loop"—the name of

Chicago's downtown, circled by a loop of elevated trains—"then out the Eisenhower Expressway." I didn't know if that was the fastest way, but it kept me on major arteries. I glanced at Avis. "You been to Cook County Hospital before?"

She nodded. "Long time ago, though, in the old building. Haven't been there since they built the new one. I think it's called Stroger Hospital now—after the county commissioner."

That was news to me. I don't think I could have told anybody who the county commissioner was, and now they'd named a hospital after him.

The traffic was still pretty heavy as we headed into the heart of Chicago proper, but the lake was beautiful once we got on Lakeshore Drive heading south. Bikers and skaters filled the bike path that snaked for miles along the shore. On the other side of the drive was the Gold Coast, where classy old apartment buildings rubbed elbows with businesslike steel-and-glass condos. I reminded myself that I was driving and to keep my eyes on the road because I was tempted to gawk at the penthouses on top of the older buildings.

"I have this fantasy," I confessed to Avis, "of marching into one of those buildings someday and asking whoever lives in the penthouse if I could please just come up and look around. Ever want to do that?"

She bent her head and looked up as the buildings flashed by. "No. Never thought about it."

Okay. That one didn't fly. I didn't really want to talk about school—somehow I wanted Avis to be Avis tonight, not Ms. Johnson. So I told her about Florida's e-mail. That got her interest, and we talked about what to say to the group. Before I knew it, Avis was praying out loud for little Carla—her eyes open, talking just like Jesus was sitting in the backseat. "Jesus, we know *You* know where Carla is, and we pray for a hedge of protection around her right now. You know the foster family, too, and why they've gone missing. Thank You, Holy Spirit, for the work You're going to do in reuniting Florida's family. *Thank You!*"

I think we prayed right through the city, out the other side on the Eisenhower Expressway heading west, right off the exit ramp at Damen Avenue—just like Denny's computer map said—until we saw the huge hulk of the hospital loom just two blocks south of the expressway. The sign said, "John H. Stroger Hospital of Cook County."

THE ELEVATOR DOOR PINGED OPEN, and Avis and I got out on the sixth floor in the middle tower. It had taken a good while to find a parking spot in the parking structure, then we took an elevator to the ground floor and walked and walked—the length of a football field at *least*—past the outpatient pharmacy, past out-patient clinics for ophthalmology . . . oral surgery . . . pain control . . . clinic after clinic, each with its own waiting room with rows of connected black-and-tan steel benches, divided into "chairs" by steel armrests and individual vinyl pads on seats and backs. Finally, we came to the main reception area, stark and functional, and got our visitor passes. I'd seen signs for the ER pointing to the other end. Did the hospital extend a similar length in that direction? It felt like a skyscraper lying on its side.

"This might be a new hospital," I murmured to Avis in the elevator, "but they sure didn't waste any money on carpets or wallpaper or green plants to soften all this glass and steel."

The young woman at the sixth-floor reception desk—still not a plant in sight—efficiently told us how to find our way to the patient rooms. After a few rights and lefts, we stopped at a nurses station and asked for José Enriquez. A nurse in a blue-print tunic looked at the sign-in sheet. "He already has several visitors . . ." She let her voice trail off, as if hoping we'd offer to leave or wait. But we just let it hang there. "Guess it's all right if you don't stay long," she finished.

The door to José's room was slightly ajar. We heard a multitude of voices inside. I hung back and followed Avis into the room. In the first bed, a man in his late twenties or early thirties—dark-haired, nutmeg complexion—spoke rapid Spanish with two older women, one of whom kept fussing with his sheets and shaking her head. Probably his mother.

Beyond the curtain that hung between the two beds, I saw a man—short and solid—sitting mute and poker-faced in a chair in the corner, like a bullfrog on a log. But I picked out a familiar voice on the other side of the curtain: Delores. We pushed farther into the room, nodding apologetically to the man in the first bed.

"Avis! Jodi!" Delores Enriquez, standing on the far side of the hospital bed, lit up with delight like we'd arrived with birthday cake. Beside her a girl about twelve with large dark eyes, her hair pulled back with a yellow headband, smiled shyly. "I'm so glad to see you!" Delores babbled. "Oh, my . . . and that girl, Yo-Yo, came last night. She really surprised me—oh!" Our friend put a hand to her mouth then gestured toward the bed. "Listen to me. And I haven't even introduced you to my son. José? This is . . . is . . ." Delores turned toward us in consternation and whispered, "I don't remember your last names."

Avis smiled at the teenage boy in the bed, who was looking at us through a mask of wariness and pain. "I'm Avis Johnson, José. And this is Jodi Baxter. We got to know your mother at the women's conference this weekend—before this happened. We've been praying for you."

The boy's eyes relaxed slightly. *"Señora* Johnson . . . *Señora* Baxter." He shifted slightly in the bed, wincing in discomfort. Suddenly I was aware of the tangle of tubes attached to various parts of his body, some clear and dripping various fluids, others gray and snaking to various machines behind the bed. One larger tube was strapped to his chest.

Delores turned toward the man filling the chair in the corner as though to introduce us—I'd already guessed he was José's father— when three knocks sounded on the door. "José Enriquez?"

Avis and I stepped aside as a large black man in the uniform of a Chicago police officer entered the room and loomed at the end of the bed.

13

The police officer was followed by another, a woman with a short blonde ponytail, carrying a huge book like a photo album. "Mr. and Mrs. Enriquez?" The first officer shook hands with Delores and extended a hand to the man in the chair but got only a short nod. "My name is Officer Clay, and this is Officer McCloud of the Victim Advocacy Unit. I was here Saturday night after your boy got out of surgery. We have a few more questions we need to ask José."

Avis and I had only just got there, but I suddenly felt like extra baggage above the limit at an airline security gate. "We can—" I jerked a thumb toward the door. "We'll find a waiting room."

"Gracias," Delores nodded. "But please don't leave. *Esmerelda"*— she pushed the young girl forward—"show the *señoras* where to go."

Again the dark-eyed girl smiled shyly and—to my surprise— took my hand and led us toward the door.

"One moment," said Officer Gray. "Emerald, you were with your brother in the park when he was shot, is that right?"

The girl's smile faded. She nodded.

"If you don't mind, Mrs. Enriquez, we would like to talk to the girl, too. We have some pictures—maybe she can identify someone."

The frog on the log stirred. "Leave the girl alone," Mr. Enriquez muttered. "What can she know? She was scared. All our babies were scared."

But Delores mutely nodded at Officer Clay and shooed us out with her hand.

Outside the hospital room, I was sorry I'd suggested going to the waiting room. The policeman's presence had shut up the chatter around the other bed. They probably wanted to eavesdrop . . . just like me. If we hung around right outside the door, we might be able to hear the policeman's questions.

But Emerald, still holding my hand, led us around a corner to a room with large glass windows looking out into the hall. A sign said, "Waiting Room." Beneath it was the word, *"Espera."*

We waited. Emerald hummed a little tune, sitting on her hands. Avis had her eyes closed. Praying, no doubt.

"What grade are you in school, Emerald?" I asked.

"Seeex."

"What's your favorite subject in sixth grade?" That's what I said. But I wanted to say, *What did those gangbangers say when José asked them to leave the park? Were you afraid? What did you do when José got shot? Who called the police? Did anyone help you? What—?*

Emerald shrugged. "I don't know. Art maybe."

Art maybe? "I'm a teacher—did you know that? But I teach kids younger than you—third grade." I leaned over and lowered my voice to a stage whisper. "*Señora* Johnson is the boss of our school. *She's* the principal."

Avis arched an eyebrow and opened one eye. Emerald giggled. She clearly didn't believe me. "My sister Luisa is grade three. Rosa's the baby—she's in kindergarten."

I added up the names. "Aren't there five of you?"

The dark hair bounced up and down. "My other brother, R. J. He's ten."

"Were you all in the park—"

The door to the waiting room opened, and Delores and the two police officers came in. "Ladies, if you don't mind, we'd like to ask this young lady a few questions," said Officer Clay. We were clearly being dismissed.

"Go talk to José," Delores urged apologetically. "We'll come back in a few minutes."

Avis and I obediently found our way back to the hospital room. "Not sure I want to be alone with Mr. Stoneface without Delores," I murmured to Avis just before we went in.

The chatter had resumed around Bed One. We hustled past, nodded to Mr. Enriquez, and came around to the other side of José's bed. My heart seemed to squeeze. Anchored by tubes to the hospital bed, José seemed younger than his fourteen years. A *child* with a bullet wound? It was crazy.

"It could have been the girl—or one of the others."

I jumped at Mr. Enriquez's voice. It was as if Delores's husband had read my mind. Suddenly, I felt ashamed of my flippant attitude toward the man. He was obviously hurting, hurting badly, in his own way.

"We are terribly sorry this happened to your son, Mr. Enriquez," Avis said gently. She turned to José. "But we are so grateful God spared your life, José. That's something to thank God for, isn't it?"

José nodded politely and winced.

Avis opened her Bible. I knew she was warming up now. "Your youth is a great gift, José—did you know that?" The pages of the huge Bible flipped. "Let me read you something." She turned a page or two more. "Here it is, First Timothy, chapter four . . . 'Don't let anyone look down on you because you are young—'"

"That's right," José muttered, his voice suddenly dark with anger. "Those Cobras just flipped me off 'cause they bigger. Makin' that park so nobody can use it but them. But they better watch out. One day they gonna be sorry they messed with me."

I caught Avis's eye. I didn't think this was where she'd been going with that verse.

"Let me finish the verse, José." Avis's tone held a bit of her "principal" authority. "'Don't let anyone look down on you because you are young, but *set an example* for the believers in speech, in life, in love, in faith, and in purity." She closed the Bible and laid a hand gently on José's hand, avoiding the IV line. "That was *you*, José—what you did in that park. Even though you are young, you were an *example* to your younger brother and sisters of doing the right thing—even an example to those Cobras, or whoever they were. That took a lot of courage. But you had that courage. Courage to do the right thing."

José frowned, as if considering what Avis was saying. Or ignoring it. It was hard to tell.

"Do you mind if we pray for you, José?" Avis said "we," but she didn't really wait for an *okay* from either the boy or me. She just began praising God for sparing José's life. A nurse came in to check José's tubes and machines; Avis just kept praying. When the nurse left, I began to pray, too, whispering, "Yes, God . . . Heal José's wounds, Jesus . . . Thank You for his courage, God"—an undercurrent to Avis's prayer, which was growing stronger and bolder.

"We're claiming *victory* for José's life, Father God! Right now, in the name of Jesus! Satan, you can't have him!—or his brother, or his sisters, or anyone in his family. Hands off, Satan! This is God's child!"

I couldn't help sneaking a peek through my eyelashes at the visitors for Bed One as Avis back-talked "the enemy." The two older ladies stared open-mouthed in our direction. I didn't look at Mr. Enriquez to see how he was reacting to Avis's prayer. But I closed my eyes again, realizing it didn't really matter. Avis wasn't trying to offend anyone—but she believed in the importance of prayer so much that she just did it, even if it did.

Oh God, how many people have I not prayed for or with because I was too afraid of offending somebody?

"*Gracias, Dios.* Thank You, Jesus!"

I opened my eyes. Delores and Emerald had come back. I gave my new friend's plump body a squeeze as we clustered around the bed and pulled Emerald into the crook of my arm. But I felt a little hypocritical. I wasn't sure I could be so . . . so enthusiastic in *my* praise if that was *my* son lying in the hospital bed with a gunshot wound in his back.

IT WAS DARK by the time we got out of the hospital, and once we got on Lakeshore Drive heading north, the city was spectacular, dressing all the buildings in gossamer gowns of twinkling lights. To our right, the city lights lit up the foam atop the gentle waves of Lake Michigan, like so much liquid cotton rolling against the shore.

"Who's going to the hospital tomorrow?" Avis asked, as I pulled up in front of her apartment building.

"Nony, I think." I dug around in my tote bag, pulled out my notepad, and turned on the interior light of the minivan. "Right. Nony tomorrow, and Ruth on Wednesday. Stu is Thursday, and Adele on Friday if he's still in the hospital." The doctor had told Delores it would be anywhere from four to seven days until the hole in José's lung healed and they could take out the tube that was draining air and fluid from his chest cavity.

Avis was quiet a moment, thinking. "Maybe you should send those folks a reminder by e-mail. It'd be easy to forget."

"A *reminder?*" I rolled my eyes. My kids already accused me of nagging them to death. Would these grown women feel the same way? But I probably *would* remind the people on this list, because I couldn't help it.

Avis laid a hand on my shoulder. "Don't worry about it, Jodi. It's going to be hard to keep this group informed and praying together. Go for it. You're good at that."

I flushed gratefully. "Okay. I'll, um, send out Delores's and Edesa's e-mail addresses"—thank God I'd remembered to get them from Delores before we left the hospital—"and just add the visitation list so everyone has the same info."

She opened the car door. "Great. And don't forget the prayer request about Florida's daughter."

I laughed. "Now who's nagging!"

But as Avis got out of the car I felt a strange disconnect. I'd spent gobs of time with Avis the last few days and still knew nothing about *her* family, *her* background. On impulse I beeped the horn. She turned back and peered into the open passenger window, eyebrows raised as a question mark.

"Uh . . . would you like to have dinner with us sometime this week?"

"Dinner?" She glanced away, breaking eye contact. "I'm usually pretty beat after a day at school. But thanks for the invitation. Maybe another time."

With a wave she was gone. I'd been dismissed.

Five minutes later I pulled into our alley, clicked the garage door opener several times till our garage door finally rolled up, and parked the car inside. I hated the walk from the dark garage to our back porch at night, even though it was only twenty feet. I didn't feel truly safe till I got in the back door and locked it behind me. *A cell phone would be nice,* I thought, stabbing my key into the door lock. *Then I could call Denny when I drove in and he could come out to the garage and escort me in.*

"Woo woo woo," barked Willie Wonka, scrambling up from the mat just inside the back door where he always waited if anybody in the family was "out."

"That you, Jodi?" Denny's voice sailed from the front room, where I could hear the TV.

"Yeah, it's me! Be there in a minute!"

Noting gratefully that the kitchen had been cleaned up, I dumped my purse in the dining room and stopped by the kids' bedrooms before heading for the front room. Amanda had the cordless and gave me a wave, pointing to the phone. Josh was sprawled on his bed, working on homework in his lap, his boom box playing noisily at his elbow. I went in and stood by his bed, just looking at my son. Almost as tall as Denny now. Losing his adolescent gawkiness. Sandy-haired. Too short, though; almost a buzz cut. Not like Denny and me at that age, imitating the hairy hippies of the '70s. Ho ho! How Josh and Amanda laughed at our high school pictures, with those gaudy bell-bottoms and all that hair. That was ancient history now—the last century, Josh liked to remind us. Gosh, he was good-looking—especially when he laughed, which was often. Next year he'd be a senior, and then . . . off to college.

"What?" He looked at me funny. "You okay, Mom?"

"Yeah." I bent over and kissed him on the forehead. "Just glad you're alive."

TO HIS CREDIT, Denny turned off the TV when I brought in two mugs of tea and curled up on the couch beside him. He listened thoughtfully as I told him all about the visit to Cook County Hospital. "It's called Stroger Hospital now," I told him, feeling informed.

"Uh-huh." Denny was obviously not going to work too hard to change the name in his mind. I grinned. Me, either.

"Both José and Emerald picked out a mug shot of the guy José talked to in the park. José said he's a Spanish Cobra. That doesn't mean he's the shooter, though. Other witnesses say some Latin Kings drove up and started shooting. The police said they'd talk to the guy, though. It's a start." Suddenly I shivered, in spite of the hot tea. "Oh, Denny, I never worried about gangs before, because . . . I mean, it sounds terrible, but at least the gangs tend to leave the white kids alone and . . . what?"

Denny was giving me a funny look. "Jodi, there are white gangs, too."

"What do you mean?"

"Honey, at West Rogers High we've got Skinheads and Stoner groups . . . the Insane Popes here on the North Side are Greek, basically a white gang. And girls—don't forget girls. A lot of the gangs have female counterparts."

I just looked at him.

"Besides," Denny added, "that's not the point here. From what you say, Delores's son wasn't in a gang, just an innocent bystander. We've seen it in the newspaper before—some kid killed accidentally in a drive-by."

True, but it had always seemed . . . far away. Not up close and personal.

Denny reached out a finger and tipped up my chin. "Hey, don't get all morose. I wish I could meet these new friends of yours. I'm feeling left out. Sounds like an interesting bunch. An ex-con named Yo-Yo . . . an ex–drug addict . . . a Japanese university student . . ."

"You will . . . I hope." Suddenly I wanted to see the women in the prayer group—the Yada Yada Prayer Group—again. It had been great to see Delores tonight and meet part of her family and pray in person for José. How could we make that happen for the rest of the women?

"That reminds me," I said, pushing myself off the couch. "I've got to send out an e-mail. Won't take long."

"Promise?" Denny waggled his eyebrows suggestively then picked up the remote. "Okay. I'll catch the news for a few minutes, then come to bed."

Willie Wonka followed me into the dining room and plopped himself under the computer desk, leaving no room for my feet. The screensaver contorted on the computer screen, like a Slinky toy on amphetamines. I called up e-mail. Two or thee spam junk ads . . . a reminder from Uptown Community about the Mother's Day potluck after worship next Sunday, please bring a friend . . . and something to "Yada Yada Prayer Group" from "Yid-dish@online.net." Ruth.

Chuckling already, I clicked it open.

To: Yada Yada Prayer Group
From: <u>Yid-dish@online.net</u>
Subject: "Yada Yada"

So who's the brilliant person who came up with the name, Yada Yada? I knew it meant something. I looked it up in my Hebrew dictionary. "**Yada:** to perceive, understand, acquire knowledge, know, discern." And a whole lot more. Here's one I like: "To be known, make oneself known, to be familiar." And another: "To distinguish (yada) between right and wrong."

If we add an "h" it gets even better. "**Yadah:** to speak out, to confess; to praise; to sing; to give thanks." Later it says Yadah "essentially means to acknowledge . . . the nature and work of God."

How about those jewels, Yada Yada sisters?

Ruth

I sat staring at the computer screen, not quite understanding the tears that wet my cheeks.

14

When I got home from school the next day, Willie Wonka nearly bowled me over in his urgency to go outside. Normally we just let him pee and poop in the backyard in the morning and Josh walks him when he gets home from ball practice. But today I played on Amanda's sympathies and sent her around the block with Willie Wonka while I logged on to the computer.

There were several e-mails to Yada Yada, mostly in response to Florida's missing daughter. A couple of the responses said things like, "Oh, Florida, my heart aches for you. Of course I'll pray!" and "That's so awesome about what *Yada Yada* means."

Avis, of course, cut to the chase: "Cling to Romans 8, sister! 'If God is for us, who can be against us? He who did not spare his own Son, but gave him up for us all—how will he not also . . . graciously give us all things?' (v. 31–32)."

Nony's e-mail took it to the next level: "Satan, beware! You can't have this child, either! Florida, I'm praying Isaiah 10:1–2 for you and your precious Carla." Hmm. Would have to look that one up.

And then there was Stu's e-mail.

To: Yada Yada
From: GetRealStu@GetRealEstate.com
Subject: Missing foster family

Florida, I'd like to hear more about the situation. I worked at DCFS for several years after college and still have some contacts there. Maybe we can pull some strings and cut through some red tape to get your daughter back. E-mail me privately if you don't want to put out the details to the whole group.

Stu

I glared at the screen. Why did Stu's e-mail rub my fur the wrong way? She was only trying to help, right? Right. That was just it. Stu acted like she had all the answers. For half a second I hoped she wouldn't be able to find those "strings" she wanted to pull—and almost slapped myself. *Jodi Baxter, get a grip. Bottom line, you want Florida's daughter to be found, right? Who cares if God uses a real-estate-agent-wannabe-social-worker?* Okay, okay, I told myself. Still, it bugged me that she invited Florida to "e-mail me privately."

I clicked "next." A response from Adele: "Sure. Get the white folks to pull strings, and all will be well. Whatever. I'm praying, Florida."

Ouch. I didn't know whether to wince or giggle. Adele's sharp tongue sure could snap you like a rubber band. I kinda liked it when she set Stu straight. But what *exactly* did she mean by "get the white folks to pull strings, and all will be well"?

"Mom? Can I—?"

I jumped. "Amanda! Don't sneak up on me like that!"

"Sneak?! Willie Wonka and I got back five minutes ago! But I gotta use the computer—got a paper due tomorrow."

I sighed. Did *anybody* with teenagers have a life? Seemed like all I did was juggle around *their* schedules. They needed the computer . . . they needed a ride . . . they needed the car . . . could they eat early? or late? They had a practice, a game, a youth meeting . . .

I clicked the "close" box and headed for the kitchen. Oh, well. It was time to start supper anyway, and my plants could use a good soak. And lesson plans for tomorrow. Always lesson plans.

"Oh . . . Mom? You're supposed to sign this."

I turned in the dining room doorway. "Sign what?"

"This." Amanda held out a sheet of paper with all the enthusiasm of going to the dentist, making me walk back to take it. A Spanish test . . . with a big fat red F at the top.

"Amanda! What is this?" The school year was almost over! How could I not know she was doing so badly? "This isn't . . . this isn't . . ."

"No, it's not the final." She pulled a pout, a talent bestowed on fourteen-year-olds the day adolescence was invented. "Just a quiz . . . but my teacher said you had to sign it or I'll get an F for the semester. How fair is *that?*"

I grabbed a pen and scrawled "Jodi Baxter" across the bottom of the paper. "Fair? Fair? You're on rocky ground, young lady, talking about *fair.*" I threw the pen back onto the desk. "What's going to keep you from getting an F for the semester all by your own sweet self with grades like *that?*"

"But Spanish is *hard,* Mom." Amanda dragged out the word "hard" like she was pressing it into existence. "And the teacher doesn't teach good."

"*Well.*"

"What?"

"'The teacher doesn't teach *well.*' Forget it. But you can't blame the teacher, Amanda."

"I can't help it if I don't understand what he's saying." The pout deepened to personal injury. "Why'd you and Dad move us from Downers Grove anyway? *That* high school is rated one of the best in the state."

I winced. "Don't change the subject," I snapped. "What about homework? Have you turned everything in?"

"I guess. Yeah. Mostly."

I stood there, hands on my hips, feeling frustrated. Frustrated with Amanda for waiting this long—it was May, for goodness' sake!—to say she was struggling with Spanish. And only then because the teacher made her get a parent signature on a failing quiz. Frustrated with myself for not noticing. For not asking. What did her teacher say at the last parent-teacher conference? For the life of me, I couldn't remember. I'd never taken Spanish in high school; might as well be Greek to me. That was my excuse, anyway, for why I never asked to see her homework or how Spanish class was going.

Pretty lame excuse.

And then there was the sore point about Chicago schools. Amanda had been looking forward to entering high school with all her friends and had thrown a royal fit when we—mostly Denny— decided to move. Denny had been concerned too. Chicago schools in general seemed tougher, less endowed. We finally decided to send the kids to Lane Tech College Prep, one of the better high schools, even though it was farther away than West Rogers High where Denny got a coaching job. But . . . moving had been tough on both kids. A sacrifice.

I took my hands off my hips and rested them lightly on Amanda's shoulders. She did not pull away but slumped under my touch. "Honey, I'm sorry. Sorry I didn't know you were having a hard time. Maybe it's not too late to get some help. Can you stay after school? Ask your teacher—?"

"I don't want to ask him! He's . . . I don't know. I'd rather get help from somebody else. But I don't know who."

I opened my mouth to protest, then closed it again. Okay, so Amanda didn't click with this teacher. Maybe her own stubbornness; or maybe he "didn't teach good." We just needed to get her through this class, help her to pass, maybe get some help in summer school to prepare her for Spanish II. But who? That was a good question.

"Look. I'll talk with Daddy, see if he has any ideas. Just work on your paper." I hadn't even asked what paper she was writing. "What are you working on?"

"Oh, it's kinda cool. We had to read *To Kill a Mockingbird*, and now we're supposed to draw parallels—what's the same and what's different—between the social issues in that book and the social issues in our own neighborhood today. It has to be at least two pages long, double spaced."

I liked the way Amanda's eyes lit up talking about the paper. At least the funk she was in about Spanish hadn't spilled over to her English class. I was glad I'd asked.

DENNY WAS UPSET about Amanda's Spanish quiz, as I knew he would be. I didn't say anything till we were doing dishes after supper when I could speak to him privately. "I feel like it's partly my fault because—"

"Jodi! This is *not* your fault. Amanda has to take responsibility for her own grades. If she needs help, she should ask for it."

I glanced into the dining room to make sure Amanda wasn't parked in front of the computer. Empty. Competing CDs blared from both kids' bedrooms. "I know. It's just . . . I haven't checked on her homework or asked how the class is going for weeks." *Maybe months,* I thought.

"She could also *ask.* Haven't we drilled that into the kids? 'If you don't know, *ask!*' 'There are no dumb questions!' 'Learn how to learn!'"

He looked so comical, punctuating each axiom with a dirty plate before putting it into the dishwasher that I started to laugh.

"What?" He grinned. "Okay, you're right; we both should've

asked. Maybe I could help. I took three years of high school Spanish . . ." His voice trailed off, and he stared at me, another dirty plate in hand. His admission must have punched a rewind button in his mind, because he said, "Good grief, Jodi. That was over twenty-five years ago! Are we really that old?"

"Uh-huh. Twentieth anniversary coming up. Not that you'd forget or anything."

"Sheesh." Denny poured dishwasher soap into the little soap cups in the door and closed it with a *whump.* "Twentieth anniversary, huh?" He kissed the back of my neck as he headed out of the kitchen. "August . . . August, right? I didn't forget the month—just the year."

I watched his back as Denny went through the dining room and disappeared down the hall toward Amanda's bedroom. Nice bod. Stockier than when we got married twenty years ago, but still in good shape. Firm muscles, only a slight pot. I smiled, remembering those first couple of years before Josh was born. We'd moved to the Chicago area—but out in the 'burbs—because I wanted to teach and he wanted to coach. We thought there'd be a lot more opportunities in a large urban area. There were—but the head coaching job he'd wanted at a choice high school out in Downers Grove had never materialized. Too much competition. And the city schools—too many politics. Disappointing. But Denny wasn't the kind of guy to wallow in disappointment. He started volunteering at Uptown Community Church in their outreach program . . . and the rest, as they say, is history.

Almost twenty years married, though . . . that was some kind of milestone, all right. Some couples would take a cruise, or fly to Cancun for a weekend in the sun. Not likely for the Baxters. But we *would* celebrate, I vowed, drying the counter with the dishtowel and tossing it toward the towel rack. (Oops, missed.) Maybe a party, invite our friends . . . then sneak away to Starved Rock or some other resort out in what passed for "country" in Illinois. I wondered what I could get for cheap on Priceline.com?

The dining room was still empty—I could hear the muffled voices of my spouse and child, calm enough, from Amanda's bedroom—so I pulled one of the table chairs up to the computer and moved the mouse. The screensaver dance froze then disappeared into its little black hole or wherever screensavers hide when they're not needed.

I called up our e-mail server. Only one new message—from Nony.

To: Yada Yada
From: BlessedRU@online.net
Subject: José Enriquez

Dear Sisters,

Picked up my two boys after school and took them to visit José today. I was so touched to see the answer to our prayers on the mend and in his right mind. Hallelujah! God is good . . . all the time!

Edesa was there when we arrived . . . then Delores came after her shift ended. At first I thought it was just a nurse coming in to check José's tubes—took me a second to recognize Delores in her pink flowered pediatrics tunic and stethoscope. She looked so official. Got a laugh out of that.

Edesa left to pick up the other Enriquez children at their after-school program. What a sweet sister she is to Delores.

José tried to be polite but seemed exhausted, so we went out to the waiting room to talk and pray. Delores says to tell EVERYBODY in Yada Yada that she appreciates our prayers and visits so much. Her other children are quite upset. We need to keep the whole family in our prayers.

My boys (Marcus, 11, and Michael, 9) were tongue-tied during our visit—but once we got in the car they had a zillion questions. A good teaching moment.

Love to all,
Nonyameko

P.S. I LOVE the meanings of Yada Yada/Yadah Yadah! Can we keep both meanings even though we spell it just one way?

Nonyameko. I'd forgotten that was her full name. How beautiful. And it was interesting to hear Nony talk . . . normal, like any other mom. Maybe it was the conference. Maybe it was those gorgeous African prints she wore. Maybe it was the way she "prayed Scripture" like it was her mother tongue. But I hadn't quite imagined her doing ordinary things like picking up her kids at school or laughing over Delores's nurse's uniform.

I called up "write message," typed in "Yada Yada," put "Prayer Request" in the subject line . . . then stopped. Any prayer request I had seemed so paltry and insignificant compared to Florida's missing daughter and José's recovery from a gunshot wound.

On the other hand, what was the point of a prayer group if we couldn't pray about everything? I went on.

To: Yada Yada
From: BaxterBears@wahoo.com
Subject: Prayer Request

Hi Sisters! Jodi again. This may not seem very important, but I just discovered my daughter Amanda is failing Spanish! I never took Spanish—for some reason I took French as my foreign language, which would make sense if we lived in Quebec or Europe. But Chicago? My husband took high school Spanish, but that was in the Dark Ages. (No comments needed.) Please pray that we find a tutor or someone who can help Amanda in the next few weeks to pass this class, and maybe get some help during the summer so she'll be ready for Spanish II next fall.

Thanks, Nony, for your report from José's hospital room. Anyone else who visits, please give our love to

Delores and send us more praise or prayer reports. Delores is probably too overwhelmed right now to give us news and requests.

Everybody sleep tight! I'm so glad God put you—

The computer *pinged!* meaning I had a new message. I diminished the e-mail I was writing and called up the new message.

Another one from Stu.

To: Yada Yada
From: GetRealStu@GetRealEstate.com
Subject: Church on Sunday?

Hi, people—but specifically Avis and Jodi. What time does your church start on Sunday morning? I haven't really found a church home here in Oak Park. Thought maybe I'd visit some of the churches you all come from. Uptown sounds interesting. Could you tell me the address? I figure it'll take about 45 minutes from here to get to Rogers Park in Sunday morning traffic.

Or do they do a big sappy Mother's Day thing? Not sure I'm up for that.

Thanks! Stu

P.S. Florida, my offer still holds. Let's get your girl home!

I groaned. Oh, great. Just what I needed. Leslie Stuart the Great coming to my church. Like we needed more white folks from the suburbs!

Resisting the urge to delete it, I closed her message and brought mine back onto the screen. I wished I'd sent my e-mail *before* Stu sent hers, so I could pretend I hadn't gotten it till some other day. Could I send mine now without answering her question about church?

Blowing out my frustration, I finished the last sentence: "I'm so glad God put you all in my life" . . . went back and deleted "all" . . . and hit "send."

15

Somewhere between breaking up a fight in the hall between two fifth graders and scraping fish sticks off the bottom of my shoe in the lunchroom the next day, I realized I missed Florida. She had plopped into my life—into my hotel room, to be exact—unexpected, unapologetic, and certainly a bit unusual. But she had accepted me at face value, talked openly about the challenges in her life, and seemed to have the determination of a locomotive on full throttle.

I wanted to be more like her.

Not the drugs. Oh God in heaven, thank You for sparing me from the dragons she's had to slay just to lead the semblance of a normal life!

But coming through the fire . . . whole, her faith intact, her will to overcome fueled by *knowing* what rock bottom is like. And thankful. I missed hearing her voice cry, *"Thank* ya, Jesus!" during worship. I missed the way she wrinkled her nose and said, "Girl, you are so funny" (which translated probably meant, "Jodi, I can't figure you out, but *whatever"*). I missed her energy, popping in and out of rooms, looking out for other people. I even missed the matter-of-fact way she had to "step out for a cig," even though I hate the smelly things.

But that was Florida, the whole package. Take it or leave it.

We were together at the women's conference for less than forty-eight hours, yet I felt . . . changed, somehow, by knowing her. But unfinished, too, like taking a bite of chocolate and knowing I had set it down somewhere, because the expectation for the whole thing is still unsatisfied in my mouth.

I would call her tonight, I told myself as I herded my class back to our room after lunch. Within minutes I had to comfort a weeping LaKeisha, the child's small, bony shoulders shaking because Mean Old Kevin had poked a pencil through the watercolor picture she'd worked so hard on for Parents Day. Kevin, sitting in the corner as penance for his misdeed, rocked the chair legs back and forth and sent imaginary darts in my direction. Once LaKeisha had calmed down, we would practice "conflict resolution," which usually required some form of restitution from the perp—though for the life of me, I couldn't think what could restore LaKeisha's masterpiece to its original third-grade perfection. The pencil hole went right through the forehead of her portrait of our school namesake, Mary McLeod Bethune.

"It's still a beautiful painting," I pointed out, though that brought on even louder wails. LaKeisha was certain in her heart that wasn't so. "But," I went on, "Mrs. Bethune suffered a good many problems establishing a school for black girls a century ago. She might say that hole in your portrait is a good reminder of all the difficulties she faced."

Sniff, sniff. The wailing stopped, and I gave LaKeisha a tissue to blow her nose. "That—*hic*—really be so, Miz Baxter?"

"Yes, I think that's what she'd say."

Mollified, LaKeisha took her picture and pinned it proudly to the bulletin board. The crown of little beaded braids all around her head bounced—just like Florida's had at the conference.

Just like Florida's . . .

I walked over to the bulletin board. "LaKeisha, how old are you?"

She beamed up at me, tears forgotten. "Eight. But I'll be nine in June when I graduate to fourth grade." And she skipped away.

I don't know why I asked. I had a whole classroom of eight-year-olds, though at this time of year they were turning nine like popcorn. Eight years old. Just like Florida's Carla. If Carla went to this school, she could very likely be in my classroom.

The dismissal bell rang. The quiet work suddenly erupted into orderly chaos—but the faces of the children who filed past me froze in my mind, frame after frame, like pictures snapped with a digital camera. What if Carla *was* in my classroom, but her foster parents had given her a new name? No, no . . . that couldn't be so. That would be too weird. Too coincidental. There were scores of Chicago neighborhoods where Carla's foster parents might live —maybe they'd even skipped town altogether without telling DCFS.

But I was so rattled with the possibility that I forgot to ask

Avis on my way out of school what to do about Stu's e-mail about visiting Uptown Community this Sunday.

AS IT TURNED OUT, I didn't call Florida that night or even the next. Josh had a soccer game against the Senn Bulldogs, Lane Tech College Prep's archrivals, so Denny, Amanda, and I sat on the sidelines yelling our heads off for the Indians—then had to cope with a disappointed Josh because Lane Tech lost by one point, which affected their standing in the playoffs. The following night—Thursday—was Bible study at Uptown, a rather mind-numbing affair with Pastor Clark trying to unpack the Book of Revelation and the meaning of endtimes prophecies. How can anybody really know what the leopard-like beast with ten horns and seven heads means, or who the "twenty-four elders" are? *Really* know, I mean.

Avis likes this study though. Denny, too. They like digging into prophecy verse by verse. Which is a good thing for me. If there's anything critical I need to know—like Jesus is coming back next week—I'm counting on them to tell me.

I caught Avis after Bible study. "Did you get Stu's e-mail, wanting to come to church here at Uptown on Sunday?" I paused, leaving her to fill in my meaning.

The outer corners of Avis's plum lipstick flickered upward a fraction. "Yes. Yes, I did. I answered it this morning—no, yesterday—when I came in to the office." She shrugged. "Gave her the address and told her it was a great Sunday to visit since we're having a potluck after worship, and no, Uptown didn't overdo the Mother's Day thing. 'Course I told her she didn't have to bring anything as a guest."

"Oh." *Knowing Stu, she would anyway. Probably flaming cherries jubilee or something equally exotic.* "I—uh—didn't know how you'd feel about that after she made such a fuss about *not* having a leader for the prayer group."

Avis wagged her head. "Jodi, if I got offended every time somebody said something insulting or silly or ignorant, I'd spend most of my life in a funk. Don't have time to be offended. Takes too much energy. I'd rather spend that energy on praising or praying."

I nodded like I understood. I didn't. How could she not be offended by that little episode? *I* was offended, and it wasn't even me Stu had dissed.

"Well . . . good. Just wanted to be sure one of us answered." *Lies, lies, all lies, Jodi.* "See you tomorrow." I did smile then. "Last week this time we were looking forward to the women's conference."

Avis chuckled. "Right. All we have to look forward to *this* Friday is staff meeting after school."

Oh joy. I had totally forgotten. "Right. See you then."

When Denny and I got home from Bible study, Josh was on the Internet—doing research for his American history paper, he said. "Huh," said Denny, peering over his shoulder at the long list of web sites about the Vietnam War. "Vietnam was 'current events' when I was in high school." He slouched into the kitchen, shaking his head.

"Midlife crisis," I murmured to Josh—then made him take a break to scoop Willie Wonka's poops in the backyard.

"But it's dark, Mom."

"I noticed," I said, handing him a flashlight.

I saved his research as the back door banged and called up e-mail for BaxterBears. Several new messages addressed to Yada Yada *pinged* onto the screen. Good. At least husband and off-spring had been quickly trained to not delete anything till I'd had a chance to read it, though Josh thought the name was a hoot. ("You starting a Star Wars fan club, Mom?" he'd teased.)

I opened the first message.

To:	Yada Yada
From:	Edesa55@CCC.edu
Subject:	Spanish

Hola! I'm on the school computer and others are wanting to use it, so can't be long. God bless you all for the visits to José. It means so much to Delores and the whole fam-ily—even Ricardo, though he won't tell you so.

Jodi, about your daughter. I want to teach Spanish and could use the practice. Would you like me to tutor Amanda? Delores is taking two weeks off to stay with José when he comes home so won't need me for babysitting for a while. I could come to your house, if that works best for you.

Edesa

"Denny!" I screeched. "Amanda! Look at this!"

As they read the message over my shoulder, I told them what I knew about Edesa—that she was from Honduras and Spanish was her native language, that she was a student at Chicago Community College (I was guessing—but what else could <u>CCC.edu</u> mean?), and she babysat for Delores Enriquez. "They met at Church of the Holy Spirit or something-or-other in Spanish."

"Cool," Amanda said.

"What does she charge?" Practical Denny.

"What's the party?" asked Josh, bungling in the back door with Willie Wonka and the pooper-scooper. When we told him he said, "Sweet. Can I have the computer back now, Mom?"

"Give me a few more minutes," I growled, shooing them all out of the dining room except for Willie Wonka, who leaned happily against my leg. I sent a quick reply back to Edesa, thanking her profusely for her offer and asking how much she charged, then opened the next message.

To: Yada Yada
From: <u>Yid-dish@online.net</u>
Subject: [blank]

To pray the foster family be located is good. To know the child is safe, smothered in love, and cared for like their own daughter—of course you want to know. But if all is well, is it the best interest of a child to be taken away and returned to a parent she may not even remember after so many years?

Ruth

I had to read Ruth Garfield's message three times before it sank in. Was she saying Florida's little girl *shouldn't* be returned to her? Then, horrified, I realized her message had gone out to the whole group. Including Florida.

I clicked "next," got something about Internet virus protection, clicked "next" . . .

A message from Florida. I was almost afraid to read it.

To: Yada Yada
From: FlowithFlo@wahoo.com
Subject: Re: [blank]

Do I need advice? God is God all by Himself and knows what is best for me and my family. Do I need prayers? NOT IF YOU'RE PRAYING AGAINST ME!

16

I was so shaken by the exchange between Ruth and Florida that I tossed and turned all night. Why in the world would Ruth raise a question about whether Florida's daughter should be returned to her? And Florida . . . I was the one who'd urged her to share about Carla with the whole group. But I hadn't expected this!

All day long their e-mails haunted me. That, plus a rotten night's sleep, made me as snarly as the troll under the bridge in Three Billy Goats Gruff. I suspect the children had an extra reason to be glad when the dismissal bell rang *besides* the fact that it was Friday.

As I sat in the staff meeting after school trying to look alert—major agenda: Parents Day coming up the end of May, and Illinois testing—I wondered what Avis thought about the latest exchange between Ruth and Florida. But she was all business, and afterward several other teachers got to her first.

I thought about checking e-mail when I got home, but Amanda informed me that she'd been invited to a birthday party—tonight—which meant doing the usual parental inquisition: Why was I only hearing about this now? How well did she know the girls being invited? Would any boys be at this party? Any R-rated videos? Who was going to supervise? Which elicited the usual, "Mo-om. I don't know! Shelly just gave me the invitation today, and I'd like to go. It's just a birthday party, for cryin' out loud."

Why shouldn't she go to a birthday party? Jiminy Cricket from Disney World whistled cheerfully in one ear. *They'll gossip about all the boys at school, decide to color some poor girl's hair with a box of L'Oreal Ruby Fusion, squeal over birthday CDs, glitter eye shadow, and ankle bracelets, and gorge themselves on pizza and white bakery cake with "Happy Birthday Shelly" on top in gel frosting . . .*

Why should *she? Because her parents are probably out of town!* screamed Jiminy Cricket from the 'hood into my other ear. *Because you've never met this girl, because boys will crash the party with six-packs of beer—or worse, and next thing you know, you'll be getting a call from the police station!*

I tried to remain calm. "Let me call Shelly's mom and find out what's what." Which I did. Shelly's mom wasn't home yet, but I was informed by Shelly herself that her mom would be around all evening. Did I want her to call? "Yes," I said and left our number. But, I warned Amanda, if we didn't connect, she couldn't go.

As it turned out, Ms. Mom did call me back, sounding surprised I had any questions. But she assured me the party would be supervised, and no boys, beer, or bad movies would be allowed.

"Is PG-13 all right?" she asked sweetly. "We're going to the video store soon." *Depends on which movie!* I wanted to shout. But wasn't sure how far I should keep pushing. I let Amanda go to the party—at which point she asked if she could borrow ten dollars and could I drive her to Target on Howard Street to buy a birthday gift?

So much for my Friday evening.

Denny and Josh, who both had after-school games, only saw us in a blur as they came in the door and we absconded with the minivan. At Shelly's home—a condo half a block from Lake Michigan—I insisted on going up the elevator and delivering Amanda to the door, even though it meant leaving my car double-parked and risking a thirty-dollar fine. Amanda, of course, was *totally* embarrassed, but I said, "Just wanted to meet your mom!" to Shelly when she opened the door, giving her my sweetest smile. Amanda and Shelly disappeared somewhere into the labyrinth of hallways and rooms, but I stayed in the doorway till a woman dressed in a business suit with an extremely short skirt—never could figure out the rationale of that combination—came to the door. We exchanged a few pleasantries, then I excused myself with a cheery, "Well, gotta go. I'm double-parked, and if I get a ticket, Amanda's taxi bill is going to be thirty bucks!" I was just joking, but the lady gave me a very strange look.

No ticket. Just an irate car owner I'd been blocking, so I refrained from shouting, "Thank You, Jesus!" and beat a hasty retreat. By the time I nearly tripped over Willie Wonka inside the back door, I was ready to crash—but not before I shanghaied Denny to pick up Amanda from the party at ten-thirty. Not just because I wanted to go to bed early and fall asleep over a good book—I'd already decided *not* to check e-mail; whatever Yada Yada was up to could wait till I got a decent night's sleep—but mostly to let Shelly and her mom know that Amanda's dad was a Big Guy.

I WOKE TO A LUXURIOUS STILLNESS. The red numerals of the bedside digital said 5:47. Still early. I could go back to sleep, but—figuring I'd fallen asleep before ten last night—I'd already had almost eight hours. The prospect of some early morning quiet time all to myself lured me out of bed.

All bedrooms were quiet. Josh had been out playing pool at a friend's house; Denny must have retrieved Amanda with no problem. Good. Let 'em all sleep.

Willie Wonka followed me into the kitchen and whined at the back door. By the time he was ready to come back in, I had a big mug of fresh coffee and was looking for my Bible. With chagrin, I found it in the hallway, tucked inside the tote bag along with the journal I'd taken to the women's conference last weekend. Had the whole week really gone by and I hadn't once cracked it open?

Well, I wasn't going to beat myself up about it. Weekday mornings were hard, getting everybody off the school. But this morning I'd make up for it—just me, God, and Willie Wonka, I grinned, tucking myself into the La-Z-Boy near the bay windows facing the street.

For a while, I let the Bible just lie on my lap as I sipped my coffee, staring out the window at the waking world. A couple of dog-walkers, a car every now and then, a gradual brightening as the sun came up over the other side of the lake . . . but tucked in here among all the buildings, it would be quite a while before actual sunshine filtered in. I couldn't remember where I'd been reading the last time, so I just started to pray silently, thanking God for my family, our jobs, our health, our church—my usual litany of thanksgivings.

Whoa. I had a whole new list of people and things to pray for—all the requests people had mentioned in the prayer group last weekend, plus additions from the Yada Yada e-loop. My silent prayer became more specific as I remembered Edesa asking prayer for her family in Honduras . . . Yo-Yo taking care of her siblings . . . José Enriquez coming home from the hospital, maybe today? . . . Hoshi's Shinto parents coming to the States from Japan this summer . . . finding Florida's daughter . . .

As I prayed, I closed my eyes and imagined the group of virtual strangers praying together at the women's conference. And all at once something felt wrong with my prayer. Something was missing . . .

Praise.

I must have said it aloud—loudly—because Willie Wonka's silky brown ears, hiding his growing deafness, perked up, and he looked at me with a doggy question in his eyes. "Praise," I repeated, rolling the word around in my mouth. "Willie, why do I always launch right into thanking God for this or that blessing in my life when I pray, and then whip out my list of things I want

God to do?" Willie Wonka must have decided this didn't really concern him, because he put his head back down and sighed.

I got out of the chair, dumping my Bible on the floor, and started pacing around the room. Why had it been so easy for the other women to praise God—just for who God is—at the women's conference? Not just in the main sessions, but in the prayer group, too. All our prayer times had started that way, with worship, just praising God, worshiping Him, being glad to know Him—no strings attached.

I never started my personal prayer times with worship, not really. Not like Avis and Nony did. Suddenly a great bubble of thankfulness welled up inside me for giving me a glimpse last weekend into a new spirituality—new for me, anyway—a spirituality my sisters of color seemed to possess in greater depth than I'd been exposed to.

I grabbed my Bible off the floor; I needed a prop. I flipped it open to Psalms and landed at Psalm 150. Okay, I was going to paraphrase like Nony did, and make it between God and me.

"God, I praise You in Your sanctuary! I praise You in Your mighty heavens! I praise You for Your acts of power, for Your surpassing greatness. I'd praise You with a trumpet if I had one—or a harp or tambourine! I praise You with dancing—"

Hey, I could do dancing. I twirled around the room, startling Willie Wonka and sending him scrambling for a safer spot. "Let everything that has breath praise You, Lord! Hey, hey, hey! Praise the Lord!" I tumbled onto the couch out of breath.

"Jodi?"

Denny's voice startled me right off the couch. How long had he been standing in the archway from the hall?

"Ohmigosh, Denny. I'm sorry. Did I wake you up?"

"Yeah. But it's okay." He scratched the back of his head. "What's going on?"

I started to laugh. "Just trying out what it would be like to 'get down' before the Lord—you know, like King David. Sorry if I woke you up . . . hey." I retrieved my coffee mug and pushed him onto the couch. "Don't go away. I'll get you some coffee, then I want to talk to you about something."

Returning with my refill and a fresh mug for Denny, I let the coffee do its job till my frumpy husband looked halfway awake behind his eyes. Then I told him about the two e-mails from Ruth and Florida.

"I know." He scratched his head again, as if waking up his brain cells. "I saw them last night after you went to bed."

"I don't know what to do! I'm the one who asked Florida if I could tell Yada Yada to pray about finding her daughter. Never dreamed it would turn controversial. Now maybe she's mad at me. Didn't Ruth know how her 'suggestion' would sound to Florida?"

Denny nodded thoughtfully. "That's one of the problems with e-mail. Too easy to shoot off a message without really thinking it through. And you don't have to look the other person in the eye when you say something."

The windup wall clock—a wedding present from my grandparents—ticked loudly as we both sank into our thoughts. A tiny fear tickled the back of my mind. What if Yada Yada fell apart

146

before it even got started? *Oh God, don't let that happen! I need this group. I need these sisters . . .*

"Denny!" I knew exactly what I needed to do. "I'd like to go see Florida today. Any reason that wouldn't work? What's happening today?" My mental calendar came up blank.

"The men's group at church is doing some repairs and painting at Uptown—told Josh he needed to put in a few hours with me. Guess you could have the car . . ."

"Don't need the car. I hate trying to find parking. I'll get her address and take the el or something."

Denny frowned. "What if you have to walk in an unfamiliar neighborhood?"

I smiled. I liked it when Denny worried about me. And I certainly wasn't above letting Mr. Big Guy part the waters or scare off the bad guys on my behalf. But I felt strong and confident today. "It's daytime. I won't take a purse. I'll keep to busy streets. Don't worry, I'll be fine—oh. What about Amanda? If you're gone and I'm gone . . ."

"Take her with you. I'd feel better if there were two of you anyway. She's a good screamer too."

"Whaddya mean, 'too'?" I threw a couch pillow at him—but it wasn't a bad idea. Amanda was a friendly kid; she'd probably hit it off with Florida's boys. I scrambled off the couch, eager to begin the day, but Denny grabbed my sleep shirt and pulled me back onto his lap. "On one condition—that we go out tonight. Both kids were out last night. They can just stay home tonight, and *we'll* go out. Promise?"

17

*D*enny decided to jog to the lake and back, but I opted to start the laundry that was crawling out of the bathroom hamper and inching its way across the floor. Ran down to the basement to throw in a load, then got in the shower, wondering how early I could call Florida. She had kids—she couldn't sleep in that late, could she?

Had my hair all soaped up when the water suddenly slowed to a trickle. Shoot! The washing machine was refilling. Wrapping myself in a towel, I ran down to the basement hoping I wouldn't bump into our upstairs neighbors, shut off the machine, and dashed back to the safety of the bathroom. Stupid water system.

Finally, squeaky clean and balancing two pieces of wheat toast on top of a glass of OJ, I turned on the computer and called up the address list I'd made for Yada Yada. There. Florida lived in the 5600 block of Magnolia . . . where was *that?* Digging out a Chicago map, I figured she lived pretty close to Broadway and

Bryn Mawr—not too far, maybe three miles. There was an el stop at Bryn Mawr too. Good.

Denny got back from his jog and jumped into the shower, bellowing "Buffalo Gals Gonna Come Out Tonight" slightly off-key—until the rinse cycle on the second load of laundry started in the basement, at which point he yelled bloody murder. I ran down to the basement and hit the stop button, making a mental note to turn it on again when he was out of the shower. Only eight-thirty . . . probably too early to call. Taking a deep breath, I checked our e-mail and skimmed through the forwards and ads and stuff addressed to Denny and the kids. Nothing from Ruth, nothing from Florida. Hmm. Was that good or bad after almost two days? There *was* a long e-mail from Stu citing case studies of foster children successfully being returned to their parents and giving web links to look up . . .

Oh, brother, I thought. I didn't even bother to read it.

And a new one, dated seven o'clock this morning, from Adele.

To: Yada Yada
From: ShineBaby@wahoo.com
Subject: Prayer for our kids

Florida, don't let "friendly fire" shoot you down. Keep the faith, baby.

Saw José last night. Doctors are sending him home today. I think it's too soon—he's still in pain and has trouble breathing. "They" say he just needs time to heal. Delores says thanks for all the visits and prayers. Keep 'em up.

I winced. "Friendly fire"? That kind of language felt like throwing gasoline on live coals. I'd been worried about how Florida felt. But now I was worried about Ruth.

Was about to shut down when I realized I'd skipped over an e-mail from Edesa because it wasn't addressed to Yada Yada, but to BaxterBears: "You don't have to pay me—I need the experience! But when do you want me to come? I'm free this Saturday late afternoon." That was today!

I considered waking Amanda to ask if she had anything going on this afternoon and decided it didn't matter. She was failing Spanish, and this was her lifeline. She probably wouldn't appreciate me planning her *whole* day—but I could call going to see Florida a special mom-daughter time, like she had with Denny last weekend.

I picked up the phone and dialed Edesa's number.

BY THE TIME I TOLD EDESA HOW TO FIND US, called Florida and asked if I could "drop by" this morning, rousted Amanda and sweet-talked her into coming with me to visit one of my new friends ("instead of cleaning your room," was the way I put it), it was almost eleven when Amanda and I hiked the three blocks to the Morse el station. I bought a pass from the machine good for four rides, stuffed the card into the electronic turnstile, then handed it back to Amanda so she could put it through again.

We heard a train pull into the elevated platform above our heads and did a mad dash up the stairs, but it was northbound, heading for Howard Street—Chicago's northern city limit—where any remaining commuters would transfer to the Purple Line serving the North Shore communities.

"Did you tell your friend I was coming?" Amanda asked, stuffing her hands into her jeans and suspiciously eyeing two teenagers with low-slung jeans and zigzag designs shaved into their clipped heads. I suddenly saw Amanda as the male species must see her: butterscotch blonde hair pulled back into a ponytail at the nape of her neck, leaving wisps of stray hair curling around her face; a budding figure; rosy skin marred only by a few concealed zits on her forehead. *Humph!* I told myself. *I should have left her home.*

"Um, sure I did. And her name is Florida—Mrs. Hickman to you. She said she'd *love* to meet you."

I smiled, remembering Florida's barely disguised surprise when I called. *"Uh-huh. You and your daughter 'just happen' to be in my neighborhood and want to drop in?"*

"No, Florida," I'd said, realizing how easy it would've been to give that as a reason—but obviously, Florida was no fool. *"I've been missing you this week. So I said, 'Heck with the housework. I'm gonna go have coffee with Flo.' Or whatever you drink at your house."*

Flo had laughed out loud. *"Girl, you takin' your life in your hands with that one. Sure, come on. House won't look like Martha Stewart, but I'm cool. And I'd love to meet Amanda. I'll go kick my menfolk out of bed—time they was movin' they butts anyhow."*

The southbound Red Line pulled into the Morse Street Station with a metallic squeal, and the doors slid open. Only one person got out—Morse was the second stop after Howard Street and most people who got on at Howard were heading downtown. The boys who looked like they might trip over their pants held back and let Amanda and me get on first. Nice, I thought. I hadn't expected that. The car was about half-full, but Amanda and I got two aisle seats across from each other.

Denny and I always told out-of-town guests they had to ride the el if they wanted a genuine Chicago experience—though I suspect the riders who were privy to it for everyday transportation were unimpressed by people who rode the train "just for fun." As the train picked up speed, it snaked perilously close to apartment buildings whose second-floor windows looked out eye to eye with commuters on the elevated train. How could the people who lived in those apartments stand it? No wonder most of the windows had their blinds pulled. But how depressing was that?

"Look, Mom!" Amanda pointed out the window on her side of the train at a back porch loaded with hanging baskets and flower boxes, a profusion of bright colors spilling over the sides. "Cool," said Amanda. "Like 'bloom where you are planted.'"

Out of the mouth of babes . . . I shook my head. Could *I* bloom if God planted me with the back of my house butted up against the elevated train tracks with a deafening din clattering past every fifteen minutes? *Why not?* a voice argued from somewhere inside my head as another flower-bedecked rear porch flew by. *What does scenery have to do with it?*

"Morse" . . . "Loyola" . . . "Granville" . . . the el pulled up along each platform stop, exchanged passengers, then rolled out again. Shutting out the *clickety-clack, clickety-clack,* I listened harder to the voice in my head, remembering the speaker at the women's conference—Olivia Mitchell. Even when she got up to speak, the praise went on for several more minutes. *I don't need your permission to praise!* she'd told us. *You don't know where God has brought me from!*

"Mom? Mom! Isn't this where you wanted to get off?"

The train doors had slid open, revealing the word BRYN MAWR in block letters on the platform sign. "Yes!" I jumped up, grabbing Amanda's hand. "Let's go!"

We walked a few blocks on Bryn Mawr, crossed Broadway, and hit Magnolia just one street over. Florida's apartment building was just half a block south—a six-flat. In the foyer I punched the button that said "Hickman, 3rd Fl. N."

A tinny voice said, "Who is it?"

"Jodi and Amanda."

A loud buzzer echoed in the small foyer, and I jerked open the door.

"Mom," Amanda whispered as we climbed the worn, carpeted stairs, "I feel funny. I don't even know these people."

"I know, honey." I felt funny, too, and I *did* know these people—Florida, anyway. "But thanks for coming with me. Means a lot."

Two doors stood on either side of the landing at the top of the stairs. Before we could read the little paper names inserted in the door nameplates, the door on the right opened. Florida stood there in T-shirt and jeans, cigarette in hand, a big smile wrinkling her nose.

"Jodi! Give me a hug, girl."

I gave her a big hug, feeling like my own smile was wrapping itself around the back of my head. Gosh, I really had missed her.

"This your baby?" Florida stepped back and gave Amanda a head-to-toe once-over. I suddenly felt appalled. How stupid of me!—flaunting my daughter, when Florida's daughter was missing. But Florida seemed oblivious to my self-chastisement. "Why didn't you tell me she was such a beauty! Mmm-mm. You better get yourself a shotgun and keep it loaded." She held out her arms, the cigarette ash growing longer by the second. "C'mere, darlin'. Let Aunt Florida give you a hug."

This seemed to please Amanda tremendously, and she returned Florida's hug with a grin. Florida opened the door wider. "C'mon in. Don't mean to leave you out in the hall. Chris! Cedric!" she yelled somewhere over her shoulder. "Turn that thang down and come meet some friends of mine."

The living room to our left was dim, lit only by a video game bouncing on a TV screen. Two young boys reluctantly put down their controllers and came to the doorway to shake our hands. Chris, Florida told us, was thirteen; Cedric was eleven. Even though Amanda was only one year older, I noticed she towered over Chris by a good three inches. Both boys had Florida's warm hazelnut skin; embarrassed grins escaped as she bragged on how well they were doing in middle school.

"What game are ya playin'?" Amanda asked, moving into the living room. "I've never seen it before. Can you teach me how?"

"I guess," Chris shrugged.

"Sure!" beamed Cedric. "It's really fun."

I stared at Amanda's ponytail as the three kids settled down on the floor in front of the TV. Would wonders never cease? Two minutes ago Amanda didn't even want to be walking up the stairs.

"Come on back to the kitchen," Florida said, leading the way down a long narrow hall. "I've got coffee on."

I sneaked a peek into the two bedrooms to my left as we headed toward the kitchen—a double bed, unmade, in one; a double mattress on the floor in the other. The second room was so small the mattress practically touched both walls.

A man with tired eyes in an otherwise pleasant face sat at a round table in a room just off the kitchen that seemed to serve as all-purpose room. A computer monitor and keyboard sat atop a small desk in one corner, surrounded by schoolbooks and stacks of mail; a sewing machine sat on a recycled end table. The chairs around the table didn't match. The man must be—

"Carl, this is Jodi Baxter, one of the women I met at the conference last week."

Florida's husband reached out a hand and murmured a greeting, but he seemed puzzled as I shook his hand. "Not the same one who was here last night?"

Florida snickered and headed for the coffeepot. "You got eyes, Carl! Stu was taller, had long blonde hair."

I was startled. Stu was *here* last night? But Carl seemed embarrassed. "Sorry. Just took me a minute. You know, you both . . . you both . . ."

"White," Florida finished, returning from the small kitchen

with a big grin and handing me a cup of black coffee. "These white people all look alike, don't they?"

I couldn't help but laugh. "I'm really glad to meet you, Carl—your handsome boys, too," I said, trying to smooth the awkwardness. But what was there to say next? I couldn't ask about his job; Florida had said he was unemployed. I turned to Florida. "Stu was here last night?"

"Yeah." Florida sat down at the table and motioned me into a seat. Carl seemed to take the cue and excused himself. "She wanted to talk about Carla, get whatever information she could about the DCFS case. I . . . gave her the folder we had with letters, forms. She said she'd be sure to return it." Florida looked at me. "What? You think maybe that wasn't a good idea?"

She must have seen the strained look on my face. I certainly felt my mouth tighten, my forehead frown. But what *was* I thinking? That Stu had gotten here first. I had wanted to visit Florida in person, show her I really cared about her and her family . . . and Stu had beaten me to the draw.

I shook my head, trying to shake my petty thoughts loose. Florida seemed to be waiting for my answer. I made a stab at one. "Uh . . . I don't know. Maybe. Do you have copies of all those papers?"

"No. But Stu said she'd photocopy them and return my originals." Florida stubbed out her cigarette in an ashtray and muttered, "One of these days God and me gonna have a talk about *this* habit . . ." Her thoughts seemed to drift, then she sighed. "Guess I shoulda made copies first, but she seemed eager to get the process started. Though for the life of me, I don't know what she can do. She doesn't even work at DCFS. Not now, anyway."

I pushed past my own conflicted feelings to reassure her. "I'm sure Stu just wants to help if she can. But it would be good to get those originals back as soon as possible." I looked around the room. There was one framed poster on the wall—the poem "Footprints" done in fancy calligraphy. Christian pop art. But no framed photographs. "Do you have a picture of Carla? I'd love to see it."

"Those were hard times, Jodi. Didn't take many pictures." But Florida got up and rummaged in one of the desk drawers, then handed me a snapshot of a little girl about two years old, holding a ball. The quality was poor, but the grin on the little girl's face was bright, the eyes laughing—just like Florida's.

"She's adorable," I breathed.

Florida's shoulders slumped. "That's the last picture I have of her—two years old. She'd be eight now. I try, I really try, to imagine what she looks like, but I can't. And sometimes I'm afraid . . . afraid I won't find her again, or if we do, afraid she won't know me anymore, won't want to come back." Tears slid down her cheeks.

Tears were filling my own eyes. I clasped Florida's hands in both my own. "No, no. We're not goin' there." *Good grief,* I thought. *I sound like Avis.* "Look what God has done for you already! You're 'five years saved and five years sober'—isn't that what you said?"

"Yeah." Her smile was tentative, like a small break in the rain clouds. "Five years this June. After they took the kids from me."

"You've come so far, Florida! God has been putting your family back together again—look at your two beautiful boys! And your husband, too." I lowered my voice to a conspiratorial whisper. "Good-lookin' guy, you know, even if he doesn't have a job. Yet."

"Yep. You're right. God's been good . . . all the time. Hasn't brought me this far to leave me." The old fire rekindled in her eyes. "And I can't be around negative people who think otherwise."

"Ah. Ruth's comment." It couldn't be avoided. It had to get out on the table.

"You got that right!" she shot back. "What does she know about me, or . . . or Carla . . . or our situation, or . . . anything!"

AMANDA AND I STOPPED AT A LITTLE CAFÉ on Broadway for Chicago hot dogs and milkshakes before catching the Red Line back to Rogers Park. "That was fun, Mom," Amanda said, trying to keep the trimmings from falling off the bun as she took a big bite of her hot dog. "Chris and Cedric are nice. Thanks for bringing me along." These last words were muffled by the wad of food in her mouth.

I nodded. Aside from talking with her mouth full, I was proud of her. Amanda had really risen to the occasion. I wasn't so proud of myself. The visit to Florida had clearly shown me two things:

We had to patch up the rift caused by Ruth's comment before Yada Yada ripped apart at the seams.

And I really was jealous of Stu.

18

*M*load of laundry was sitting on top of the dryer, sopping wet. Rats! I'd forgotten to turn the washing machine back on after Denny's shower. It looked like our upstairs neighbors—a working couple who never seemed to be home—had moved my unfinished load so they could do some laundry while we weren't home. With only two households using the washer and dryer, it usually wasn't a problem. But now I couldn't remember whether my load had been in the wash or rinse cycle.

I gave up and ran it through all over again.

When I came into the kitchen from the basement, I could hear Amanda and Edesa exchanging Spanish phrases in the dining room. *"Cómo te llamas?"* . . . *"Me llamo Amanda."* . . . *"Cuánta gente en tu familia?"* . . . *"Hay cuatro personas en mi familia."* Caught that one. Something about "my family."

Edesa had arrived right at four o'clock. Amanda seemed to

take to her right away, probably because she was young and pretty and shook Amanda's hand with a delighted smile—unlike Mr. Ortez, Amanda's teacher, fiftyish, who seemed to have a perpetual frown engraved between his flabby jowls. Now that I thought about it, that frown would not make me want to ask for extra help, either. But Edesa hadn't wasted any time getting down to business. She'd asked for Amanda's last few quizzes to get an idea of what her weak areas were and they'd set right to work.

Denny and Josh came home from the men's workday at Uptown Community right in the middle of the Spanish lesson, and of course had to tromp into the kitchen for something to eat. I followed them, trying to get them to muffle the sounds of two hungry males pulling out chips and salsa and popping cans of Coke. "What's for supper, Mom?" Josh said in a failed attempt to keep it to a whisper.

"Your mom and I are going *out,*" Denny said. "Supper is whatever you and Amanda can find to eat."

Amanda's voice floated in from the dining room. "Can Edesa stay for supper?"

"No, no. That's all right. Thank you anyway," Edesa protested. I looked at Denny. *Now* what?

As it turned out, Denny admitted later it was a delightful time getting to know Edesa over a quick supper of quesadillas—tortillas topped with melted cheese and piled high with shredded lettuce, chopped tomatoes, chopped green onions, and salsa—with a side of packaged red beans and rice. It was one of our "easy meals"— ready in thirty minutes—and I didn't think much about it until

Edesa held up one of the store-bought flour tortillas and said with a teasing grin, "My mama makes these from scratch . . ." *Pat-pat-pat-pat*—she flipped the tortilla from side to side between her palms. ". . . and bakes them in a brick oven. Mmmm. Now *that's* a tortilla."

I was horrified. Edesa must've thought we were trying to give her an "authentic" Honduran meal or something. But before I could get out a protest, she pointed at my face—I'm sure my mouth and eyes were round as Cheerios—and burst out laughing. Amanda, Josh, and Denny joined right in, though why they felt the joke was on *me,* I don't know.

But that sparked a lot of questions from Josh and Amanda about the town in Honduras where Edesa grew up. Most of the population, she said, was *mestizo*—mixed Amerindian and European—with blacks, whites, and indigenous Indians making up about 10 percent. Her people were descended from African slaves who rebelled in the Caribbean and were exiled to Honduras by the British. "Unfortunately, racism exists in Honduras, too," she said, her eyes liquid and dark, like looking into a deep well. "We are still considered 'outsiders.' When Hurricane Mitch hit the coast in 1998, no one sent us any aid, especially those of us who belong to Pentecostal churches—a small minority in a largely Catholic country."

By the time we finished talking, it was getting dark, and Denny was concerned about Edesa riding the el alone. So, for our "date" we gave her a ride home to the Near West Side—not too far from where Delores lived, she said. The night was clear, and the brightest stars could be seen in the darkening sky as we drove down Lake Shore Drive, in spite of the brilliant lights from Chicago's skyline. The Loop was alive with horse-drawn carriages, partygoers heading for restaurants or the theater, and families silhouetted against the colorful sprays of Buckingham Fountain enjoying the May evening. But when we had spit out of the other side of the Loop like a watermelon seed zipping west on the Eisenhower Expressway and finally turned off on the narrow one-way streets of the Near West Side neighborhood, the darkness seemed to close in around us.

"Sweet girl," Denny said, coming back to the car after walking Edesa into the dim pocket of her apartment building foyer and making sure she got inside okay. "Now what? Too late for a movie—unless you want to go for the late show."

"Uh-uh. Not with church tomorrow," I groaned. But I did have an ace up my sleeve. "Wanna try out the Bagel Bakery? I hear they got awesome Jewish pastries." I waggled my eyebrows knowingly and fished out a scrap of paper where I'd written the address from the yellow pages that afternoon. "On Devon somewhere."

Denny looked at me suspiciously. "Do I detect another Yada Yada conspiracy afoot? Jodi . . ."

"Only if you want to," I amended hastily.

"Hey," he said, turning the key in the ignition. "I'm only along for the ride." But his hangdog look was so exaggerated I punched him on the shoulder. "Okay, okay," he agreed. "Why not? I didn't have anything else to suggest anyway."

IT WAS ALMOST EIGHT-THIRTY by the time we pulled into the parking lot of the tiny strip mall on Devon, and the Bagel Bakery was hopping. Denny held the door for me. "Popular place."

Inside, a warm, homey smell pulled us into the waiting arms of the bakery. Loaves of bakery bread and freshly made bagels and bialies—rye, pumpernickel, onion, egg, wheat, cinnamon—and various sugary pastries filled the glass cases. An overhead menu—fast-food style—offered soup, bagel and bialy sandwiches, cheese blintzes, kugel, potato latkes, and kreplach, whatever that was.

Denny eyed the food as plates were handed to waiting customers, trying to figure out what was which, but my attention was drawn by a young woman with short, spikey hair behind the bakery counter. "Half a pound of ruggeleh?" she was saying to a customer. "Do you want the raisin-filled or raspberry . . . both? You got it." A moment later the customer walked toward the cashier with her white paper bag.

"Yo-Yo?" I ventured.

The young woman behind the counter stared at me for a moment, then broke into a huge smile. "Jodi? Hey, Jodi! Speak of the devil . . . and is that your man?"

I grinned. "Yeah. That's Denny." I pulled "my man" away from the food counter. "Denny, this is Yo-Yo, one of the women in my prayer group at the conference."

"Right. 'Yada Yada,'" he teased, as if giving the secret password. "I'm delighted to meet you, Yo-Yo, and everything looks so good I may stuff myself."

"Go right ahead! Get something to eat. I'll take a break in a few minutes and come join you." She turned to another customer. "What you want tonight, Mr. Berkenstein?"

Armed with a pumpernickel bagel piled with lox and cream cheese for Denny, and a spinach and cheese blintz for me, we looked around for a table. The place was full of men, women, and children—a gray-haired grandfather over there, tickling a dark-haired cutie who tried to protect her "tickle zones" amid peals of laughter . . . a mother scolding, "Eat! Eat! I paid good money for that kugel!" . . . teenagers huddling in a corner . . . and a table of four women, dyed heads all bent together like a cootie convention. I noticed that almost all the males—young and old—were wearing small, black, embroidered caps, anchored to their heads with clips or bobby pins.

"You need a yarmulke," I teased Denny, edging toward a booth that was being cleared by a young man in a white apron.

A few minutes later Yo-Yo came out from behind the counter, wiping her hands on her apron, revealing her signature denim overalls underneath. "Hey, Jodi," she said again, sliding in beside me on the yellow vinyl seat across from Denny. "What brings you here?"

"To see you," Denny offered. "We're supposed to be on a date, but . . ." He tried on his hangdog expression again.

"Don't pay any attention to him. He's fine. And he'll be fat, too, if he hangs out here much longer." I tipped my head toward the general hubbub around us. "This place always this busy?"

Yo-Yo shook her head. "Nah. But Saturday night after Shabbat ends, they flock in like bees around honey. Sunday morning, too."

"Shabbat?"

"You know . . . like Sunday for you, only Saturday. We close at sundown on Friday, open at sundown on Saturday." She shrugged. "Get Friday night and Saturday off, anyway."

"You Jewish, Yo-Yo?" Denny asked between bites of his bagel.

"Me?" She guffawed. "I ain't nothin'. But it's a good place to work. Ruth got me the job, you know. Speaking of Ruth . . ." Yo-Yo craned her neck, scanning the lively tables and the people who kept coming in. "Ruth and Ben usually come in Saturday night. Haven't seen 'em yet, though—oh. But you can meet Jerry." With hardly a break she raised her voice and yelled, "Jerry! *Jerry!* C'mere!"

A young boy about twelve or thirteen untangled himself from the knot of teenagers clustered around the corner table and came over to our booth. He wasn't wearing a yarmulke, though I thought he could've used one of those clips to keep the shock of lank, brown hair out of his eyes.

"Jerry, this is . . ." She looked blank for a moment. "Jodi!" she hissed. "What's your last name?"

"Baxter."

"Mr. and Mrs. Baxter, friends o' mine. And *this*"—she swatted the boy playfully on his rear—"is my kid brother. Say hi, Jerry."

"Hi Jerry." The boy snickered at his own joke, then gave a little wave. "Nice ta meetcha." He grinned and backed away toward the corner table.

"Kids," Yo-Yo snorted. "Ain't got the manners down yet. I'm still working on keeping 'em fed and a roof over their heads. Pete

—that's the older one, he's sixteen—he's out with some friends tonight. Scares me to death to let him out of my sight."

The enormity of Yo-Yo's situation—working a full-time job, trying to raise two teenage brothers—left me speechless for several moments. Denny, too. I could tell he was watching the boy as he melded back into the group of young people.

"Yo-Yo," I said, "have you gotten any of the e-mails from Yada Yada this week? I know you don't have e-mail yourself, but Ruth said—"

"Yeah, yeah. Ruth has printed out stuff and brought it to me every couple of days." She lifted an eyebrow. "Hope it works . . . keeping that prayer thingy goin', I mean. People got some stuff, don't they?"

That was the truth. I desperately wanted to ask if Ruth had talked to her about that whole foster-care business, but Yo-Yo jumped in again. "Hey. Maybe Yada Yada needs to get together, rather than just computer talk, ya know? Got plenty of reasons. Why don'tcha throw Florida a party—a five-year sobriety party? Man, if *I'd* been on them drugs and stayed clean for five years? *I'd* want to party—not party party, but you know, with folks like you and the rest of them women I met at the conference. 'Cause that's major stuff—Hey! There's Ruth and Ben. Hey, Ruth! Ben!" she yelled across the crowd. "Look who's here!"

19

I saw Ruth Garfield's eyebrows lift as they came in the door, and she headed our way, her husband trailing behind. Yo-Yo hopped off the vinyl seat. "Look who's here—Jodi and . . ."

"Denny. Denny Baxter." Denny slid out of his seat, stood, and shook hands with both Ruth and Ben. Ben looked about sixty, with wavy silver hair and crinkly friendly eyes. "I'm really happy to meet you, Ruth." Denny clasped her hand in both of his. "This Yada Yada group seems to have taken over our house ever since Jodi got back from that conference." He motioned to the padded bench he'd just vacated and slid in beside me. "Sit down, please!"

Yo-Yo grinned at the Garfields. "The usual? I'll get it. You guys talk. I gotta get back to work anyway."

"Got any beer, Yo-Yo?" Ben gestured at Denny. "Want a beer, Denny?"

"Sure. Thanks."

"Make that two, Yo-Yo!"

I felt my face go hot. Denny was going to drink a *beer,* right here in public, in front of my new friends? One of which was a "Messianic Jew," or whatever a Christian Jewish person was called, and Yo-Yo wasn't a Christian at all! *What's wrong with this picture, Denny?* I wanted to yell.

I felt like the "picture" had flash-frozen, but it was probably only for a millisecond, because Ruth reached across the table and grabbed my hand. "Oh, Jodi, I *am* so glad to see you. You don't know . . ."

"Uh . . . me, too, Ruth. I know it's only been a week, but it seems like a year!"

"I know." She tossed a look at the two men, who were already jabbering away. "Looks like Ben and Denny hit it off."

I shifted nervously. What did she mean by that? Drinking buddies already?

"Tell me, how is everybody?" Ruth asked eagerly. "I mean, in Yada Yada. Have you seen anybody else since last weekend?"

My knotted muscles relaxed slightly. I'd been worried that Ruth had been blown out of the water by Florida's strong reaction to her "suggestion" about kids in foster care. But she seemed to genuinely want to know about the others.

"As a matter of fact, today especially! I saw Florida this morning"—I purposely dropped this in, but moved right on—"and Edesa, bless her heart, offered to tutor my daughter, Amanda, in Spanish, so she was at our house today. And let's see . . . oh, yes, Avis and I went to see José Enriquez last Monday night, so we both got to see Delores—"

"Yes! I did too! On Wednesday. That poor boy—broke my heart, it did. But Delores . . . that's a strong woman! If my child had gotten shot . . ."

I leaned forward slightly. Denny and Ben were talking about the latest Cubs and White Sox scores. "Do you have children, Ruth?"

Ruth looked down at the Formica tabletop. But only for a second. She came up smiling. "No, no, never did." Lowering her voice to a stage whisper, she jerked her head slightly in Ben's direction. *"He's* number three. You'd think one of those times . . ." She brushed a lock of hair off her forehead, as though brushing off the subject. "Eat, you two! Don't wait on us. Ours is coming."

As though playing the prophet, Yo-Yo appeared with a large bialy—sliced and filled with something that looked like sautéed vegetables, pizza sauce, and melted mozzarella cheese—that she set down in front of Ben, and a bowl of matzo ball soup and an onion bagel that she set down in front of Ruth. "And these are for you," she said, whipping out two bottles of cold beer from the pockets of her tunic and setting them down in front of Ben and Denny. Last out of her pocket was a bottle opener. "Enjoy, folks. Gotta get back to work."

My mad came back. I couldn't believe it. Denny really was going to drink that beer, right here and now.

"How did you guys meet Yo-Yo and her brothers?" Denny asked, polishing off the last bite of his lox-and-cream-cheese bagel and washing it down with a swig from the bottle.

I wanted to snatch it out of his hand . . . but Ben said, "Ho ho, now that's a story." That got my attention; I'd been wondering the same thing all week.

"Story, schmory. Not such a big deal," Ruth protested, but I could tell she was warming up. "I work as a secretary, right? I type, I take dictation, I answer the phone, I smile, I make the coffee, I cheer everybody up. Always making the boss guys look good—but for what? So they can make money. *Pffffft.*" Ruth thumbed her nose and rolled her eyes. I didn't dare look at Denny for fear we'd both burst out laughing. "So I tell God, I says, 'God? If I'm gonna smile myself to death, I want a better return on my efforts.' I'm thinking money, see? But I forgot to factor in God's sense of humor. God's got a cosmic sense of humor, you know. Remember Queen Esther? And Haman? Ho, ho, I nearly fall down laughing every time we celebrate Purim. To think—"

"Oh, no," Ben groaned. "Noodle, don't get started on Esther. Back to Yo-Yo."

Noodle? He called her Noodle! Oh, that's a stitch!

"What's the hurry? The place on fire?" Ruth gave an exaggerated sigh. "Okay, okay. You want a *short* story, you get a short story. A woman in my office—nice black lady—visits women down at the county jail. So I'm thinking, *That's nice.* Then I think, *If I have to make nice, I'd rather make nice on someone who can use it more than the fat cats I work for.* So I go with this lady to the jail one night. Turns out she does a Bible study—you know, a Christian thing—with whoever wants to come. But it didn't matter who—Christian, Muslim, Jew, whatever. These gals wanted to talk; I like to talk—"

"Got that right," muttered Ben, giving Denny the eye.

Ruth swatted him with her paper napkin. "You *said* tell the story!"

"Nah. I said, 'Now *that's* a story.'"

"Oh, please don't stop now," I interrupted. "I really do want to hear how you met Yo-Yo."

"See?" Ruth said, flicking her fingers at Ben like an annoying fly. "All right, where was I? . . ."

Ben hoisted his beer bottle with an indulgent smile of resignation.

IT WAS ALMOST MIDNIGHT by the time we got home. "Ben and Ruth . . . they're something else." Denny was grinning when we got back in the car.

I laughed. That was the truth. All the way home I thought about Ruth's story, how Yo-Yo had drifted into the Bible study at the county jail, always sitting in the back. When the "nice black lady" found out Ruth was Jewish, she asked her to tell some Old Testament stories to the women. That knocked my socks off! . . . Finding a common denominator even though Ruth wasn't a Christian. Apparently Ruth was a great storyteller. Yo-Yo kept asking, *"Why did God do this?" "How come God did that?"* Ruth said she didn't have a clue, but the Bible study lady started to explain how the Old Testament fit together with the New Testament.

"It got me thinking—" Ruth had said.

"Thinking, not talking, eh?" Ben winked at me.

Ruth had swatted him with the napkin again. *"So one day I went to this Jews for Jesus–type church—"*

"Yeah. Can you beat that? An oxymoron, if you ask me."

Ruth ignored him. *"So now on Saturday I go to synagogue with Ben—when he goes, that is—and on Sunday I go to church. With other Messianic Jews."*

"What's a guy to do?" Ben had shrugged. *"She's got a foot in both pots."*

In spite of all the banter, I suspected he adored her. "For that matter," I told Denny on the way home, "Ben seems more attached to Saturday night at the Bagel Bakery than Saturday morning at the synagogue. He wasn't wearing a yarmulke, for one thing."

Denny grunted. "Huh. You could be right."

Ruth had liked Yo-Yo from the start. *"A plain talker—when she talked,"* she had said with an eye on Yo-Yo, busy behind the bakery counter. Then one week Yo-Yo wasn't there. Or the next. Ruth found out she'd been given two years at Lincoln Correctional Center downstate. Eighteen months with good behavior. Ruth wrote a couple letters to Yo-Yo and got one back.

"That did it," Ben had butted in. *"She dragged me down to Lincoln to visit the girl. Not my idea of how to spend my day off—at a women's prison."* But a hint of a smile had softened his words.

That's when they discovered that Yo-Yo had two younger stepbrothers she worried about plenty. Their mother had a "drug problem," and the boys were dropping through the cracks. *"Whatever she did to get arrested, I think she did it for those boys,"* Ruth had said.

"That's really something," I murmured as Denny turned the minivan into our alley and clicked the garage opener. "How Ruth and Ben hunted up Jerry and Pete and took 'em places and did things with them while Yo-Yo was in prison." Ben had said they'd only met the mother once, and she'd been so strung out when they came to the door that she hadn't asked any questions about who they were or where they were taking the boys. Just, *"Fine, go."*

All the lights were on, and both of our kids were still up when we got home—cat's away, the mice will play—but we chased them into their bedrooms and settled down on the living room couch with some chamomile tea, my stocking feet in Denny's lap. Willie Wonka flopped on the floor with a huge sigh.

"Whatsa matter, Willie?" Denny said, scratching the dog's silky ears. "Mad at us?" He put on a growly voice. "'Bout time you two got home. Don'tcha know I can't go to sleep till everybody's in?'"

I was only half-listening, still thinking about our evening at the Bagel Bakery. I had hoped to talk about Ruth's e-mail about "what's best for the child." In Ruth's shoes, I would probably be scared off from saying anything more to Yada Yada after Florida's hot reaction and Adele's sarcastic comment about "friendly fire." At one point, I thought I'd found the perfect opening to bring it up . . .

"It was Ruth's idea, really," Ben had acknowledged, *"to take those boys under our wing . . . kinda like foster parents, even though they didn't live with us. And she helped Yo-Yo get custody when she got out. She's got a knack for that."*

"Oh!" I'd said, little lights going on in my head. *"Have you worked with the foster care system, Ruth?"*

"Now that's another story," Ben had said. *"I'll need another beer if we go there. You, Denny?"*

I mentally glared at Denny, but to my relief he shook his head. Ruth, however, dodged the ball. *"Talk, talk, talk—that's all I've been doing. What am I, a monopoly? Jodi, how did you meet Denny? A good catch he is, I'd say! He could give my Ben a few pointers."*

And so we'd chatted and got acquainted right up till Yo-Yo kicked us out at closing time. My "good catch" had been thoroughly charmed by Ben and Ruth, and Yo-Yo, too—which was fine, but I was left still wondering if Yada Yada was going to hang together or not. At least Ruth had seemed eager to hear about the other women in the prayer group, even though we'd verbally danced around the "elephant" in the middle of the room as though it wasn't there. Maybe she was okay . . .

"Denny," I mused, nursing the last of the tea in my mug, "what do you think about throwing a five-year sobriety party for Florida, like Yo-Yo suggested? . . . Denny?"

Romeo was snoring softly at the other end of the couch. Well, let him. He was still going to get it for drinking that beer tonight.

20

I didn't feel like praising the Lord when I woke up. I overslept, the laundry was only half-done, I'd totally forgotten to plan something for the Mother's Day potluck—who came up with that dumb idea, anyway?—Denny seemed oblivious that I was mad about the beer, and Stu was coming to Uptown Community that morning.

Hallelujah.

For the next hour and a half we did the "Baxter Hurry Scurry," and at two minutes to ten we hustled up the stairs of the double storefront Uptown occupied to the large upstairs room that served as the sanctuary. Well, at least Josh and Amanda and I did. Denny was still driving around trying to find a parking space. I snuck into the kitchen with my Easy Chicken-and-Rice Casserole and hoped I'd remember to stick it in the oven at eleven o'clock.

I sniffed. Fresh paint. The work crew yesterday must have painted something.

The Reilly twins were passing out carnations to everybody as they came in—red if your mother was still alive, white if she had "passed on." In one corner of the large room the music group—two guitars and a keyboard—was warming up. Josh settled in at the soundboard—his new passion. Avis was talking with Pastor Clark at the front; she must be leading worship this morning.

And Stu had already arrived. She was wearing a smart lavender suit—overdressed for this crowd—her ash blonde hair coiled into a professional bun at the nape of her neck. She waved at us with the red carnation she was holding and pointed at the empty folding chairs next to her.

"Oh, Lord," I muttered, "she saved seats for us."

Stu was sitting in the third row near the front beside a young couple in jeans and T-shirts. Two street people dressed straight from the Salvation Army sat just behind her, a situation that was sometimes challenging to the nose. We often had more street people on potluck Sundays, I'd noticed. Otherwise our congregation was pretty much a casual mix of "wuppies"—white urban professionals—both married and single, who wanted something a bit different than traditional church, with a hopeful sprinkling of color here and there and a whole mess of kids. Kids . . . somewhere along the way I'd lost mine but spied Amanda sitting with some of the other young teens.

Get a grip, Jodi. I smiled back at Stu and headed—slowly—for the third row. *Just because Stu is a go-getter doesn't make her your rival or anything. Go on; she looks glad to see you.*

"Hey, Stu." I plopped down into a chair beside her. "You

made it." The smell factor from the row behind us didn't seem too bad today.

"Yes! Found it with no problem." She grinned at me. "Guess you have to live a long way away to arrive early."

I opened my mouth and shut it again. Great. She just couldn't help commenting about me squeaking in at the last minute, could she?

Stu waggled her carnation. "This is nice. Everybody gets to celebrate Mother's Day."

Avis's voice filled the room from the microphone. "Praise the Lord, church! If you have your Bibles, please turn with me to Isaiah Fifty-Two." Hiding the flush that had crept into my face, I dug into my tote bag and got out my Bible. Avis's voice rang free and joyous, so different from her contained demeanor at school, like she'd just kicked off shoes that pinched after a long day at the office. "How beautiful on the mountains are the feet of those who bring good news, who proclaim peace, who bring good tidings, who proclaim salvation, who say to Zion, 'Your God reigns!'" she read. "Listen! Your watchmen lift up their voices; together they shout for joy. . . ."

Denny's familiar bulk sat down in the chair beside me. Parking place at last. Out of the corner of my eye I saw Stu turn slightly our way, waiting. "Oh," I whispered, trying not to interrupt Avis's Scripture reading. "Denny, this is Stu . . . Stu, my husband, Denny."

Denny reached a hand across my lap and shook Stu's warmly. "Yada Yada, right?" he whispered.

"Right," she murmured, giving him a bright smile. Too bright, if you asked me.

". . . The ends of the earth will see the salvation of our God," Avis finished, closing her Bible. "Let's stand and worship God this morning as men and women who have received good news! *Salvation* is ours because of Jesus Christ. *Peace* is ours because of Jesus. Like the watchmen on the walls, we can shout and sing a joyful song!"

The guitarists strummed an introduction as the words to a song based on Isaiah 52 appeared on the portable screen behind them. I found it hard to concentrate with Stu standing beside me but dutifully sang the words: " . . . How lovely on the mountains are the feet of him . . . who brings good news . . . good news . . ." We came to the end of the song, and immediately the music group launched into another. Uptown prided itself on providing "contemporary worship," but the quick way we hustled from song to song was certainly different from the worship at the women's conference last week, when one song seemed to last anywhere from ten to fifteen minutes. We had lingered over the words, singing them again and again till they worked themselves deep into the soul.

I watched Avis. As worship leader, she was mostly in charge of setting a theme, reading Scripture, maintaining the flow. As the music group galloped from song to song, she gradually seemed to tune them out, lost in her own worship of the Savior. Her eyes were closed—were those tears?—her hands raised, and I could see her lips moving—not to the song, but just saying, "Glory! Praise You, Jesus! I love You, Lord!"

How did she do that? It wasn't like anything profound had

happened today to kindle such deep worship. Last week, with five hundred other women worshiping over the top, sure, I could let go, too. Well, at least what passed for "letting go" for Jodi Baxter. But here at Uptown? Would I dare be the only one to shout out, "Thank You, Jesus!"

Probably not.

But with Avis . . . it didn't seem to matter. She worshiped the same here at Uptown as she did at the Chicago Women's Conference, regardless. How did she do that?

Because she is thankful. She loves the Lord with all her heart.

The words were so clear, it was like someone spoke inside my head. I squeezed my eyes shut. *Lord, I know I said I want to learn more about worship. But it's so hard. I get distracted . . . by people around me . . . by things I have to do . . . by my runaway thoughts.*

During the next song, I kept my eyes closed, shutting out everything around me. When the familiar words ran out, I just did what Avis did, filling in with "Glory!" and "Thank You, Jesus!" and "I love You, Lord!" More like a murmur than a shout, but my heart began to fill. God had been pretty good to me. I needed to be more thankful—and tell Him so.

THE SERVICE WAS OVER, and I was introducing Stu to the people around us when I saw several folks head for the kitchen. I stopped in midsentence: the potluck! And my casserole was still sitting on top of the stove, stone cold.

"Jodi? Are you okay?" Stu looked at me quizzically.

"No . . . yes! Yes, I'm fine. Denny?" I plucked on my husband's sleeve. "Could you introduce Stu to some folks? I've . . . I'll be back in a minute."

I didn't head for the kitchen. I headed for the women's bathroom, a two-stall affair with plastic flowers in a vase on the counter between the two sinks in an attempt to dress up the drab little room. Except it wasn't drab today. The small room had a fresh coat of sunny yellow paint. Well, good for the work crew.

The bathroom was usually pretty busy right after the morning service, and today was no exception. When a stall became free, I locked the door and sank down on the toilet seat. I wasn't sure whether to laugh or cry. Why did I forget today of all days? With Miss-Do-Everything-Right visiting. Why did I always end up feeling a day late and a dollar short when Stu was around?

On the other hand, Jodi, you forgot because your focus was on worshiping today. For a change.

I blinked back the tears that had started to pool. Okaaay. The bad news was that I'd blown it as far as the potluck went. How bad was that? There would probably still be plenty of food—or at least "enough." The good news was that I'd given God more of my attention than I usually did on a Sunday morning. I could live with that, couldn't I?

When I came back into the large room, Stu was talking to Pastor Clark, who had given a pretty good sermon that morning (I'd even taken notes). While she was busy, I slipped into the kitchen where half a dozen helpful people were putting out all the dishes on the counter that opened into the big room. Even my uncooked casserole sat among the others, still in its aluminum foil cover. Hoo boy, folks would get a surprise biting into that raw rice. With an apologetic smile, I whisked it away and stuck it in the refrigerator.

Denny and I sat with Avis and Stu at one of the many long tables that had been set up around the big room. To quell my guilty conscience, I didn't fill my plate very full, though I did make a point to take some of Stu's pasta salad. Okay, so I was wrong about the flaming cherries jubilee. "Where's your chicken-and-rice?" Denny asked, his mouth full of Avis's super cornbread. "I wanted some but didn't see it."

"Um, sorry. It met with a little accident. The pasta salad is good, Stu." Actually it was only so-so, but who was I to find fault? At least it was edible.

Denny stopped midbite and looked at me. "Accident? Ha. You forgot to put it in the oven, didn't you!" He thought that was very funny. "Oh, you should have seen us this morning, throwing that thing together. And then she forgets to put it in the oven! Ha ha ha ha ha!"

Thanks, Denny. Thanks a lot.

Stu grinned. "Well, at least we know what you're going to get for supper, Denny."

I decided to take it on the chin. "Yep. And Monday night, and Tuesday night . . ."

Everybody laughed.

"I enjoyed the service today." Stu pushed back her empty paper plate. "The teen mission trip sounds great. And the carnations were a nice touch—a nice way to include everybody on Mother's Day. I'd like to come back."

Oh, great, I thought. "Sure," I said.

"Watch out," Denny teased. "That commute from the 'burbs is why we ended up moving to Rogers Park."

"Actually," Stu continued, "I've been thinking about visiting all the different churches Yada Yada folks attend. If we really want to keep this prayer group going, I'd like to see each woman in her own context."

Hmm. Kinda liked that idea. Wished I'd thought of it.

"Even better—what if *all* the women in Yada Yada visited each other's churches? But we all came on the same Sunday?—say the last Sunday of the month till we've visited everybody. Shouldn't be too hard to organize through the e-loop . . ."

I figured *"I'll be glad to set it up"* would be her next words.

"I'll be glad to set it up," Stu finished.

Avis frowned thoughtfully. "But that could be five or six churches—a lot of Sundays to miss being at one's own church."

"Well, spread it out—maybe every two months."

Okay. So what if it was Stu's idea. I actually liked it, though spreading out those church visits over a year might be most realistic. But as long as we were talking about getting Yada Yada together, I decided this was a good time to float the idea about a five-year sobriety party for Florida.

"It's actually Yo-Yo's idea," I said modestly. "Last night Denny and I went to the Bagel Bakery where she works, got to see Ruth Garfield and meet her husband, Ben, too." *Sorry, God, couldn't help dropping that in.* "It would primarily be a celebration for Florida, but we could also make time to share and pray for each other—like we did at the conference."

I would have checked with Denny, but he had disappeared across the room to talk to some of the street people. "We could host it at my house," I added.

Avis nodded thoughtfully. "Sounds good."

Stu nodded. "What about Memorial Day weekend? That'd give us two weeks to plan it."

"Can't be a Saturday," I said. "Yo-Yo works Saturday night—big night at the Bagel Bakery. And it was her idea."

"If we did it Sunday afternoon, we could invite the sisters to come to Uptown in the morning—the first 'church visit'—and then go over to your place." Avis seemed to be warming up to the idea. "Do you want me to send out invitations, Jodi?"

"But speaking of Ruth . . ." said Avis, suddenly backing up.

Ah. The elephant in the middle of the room.

"Yes!" Stu immediately turned from invitations to indignant. "Why in the world did she send that e-mail? Implying that Florida wanting her daughter back might not be 'in the best interest of the child'! Sheesh."

"It was more generic than that," I defended. "Sometimes returning foster kids to the natural parent *isn't* in the best interest of a child."

"Yes, but why bring it up in Florida's case?" Stu shook her head. "What does she know?"

Good point. I'd wondered, too. "I wanted to ask Ruth about

it when I saw her last night. But our husbands were with us and, you know . . ."

Avis's lips twitched in a small smile. "Right. Husbands. Women talk better when they're not around."

My ears pricked up. She said *husbands*. Was she talking about her own? Was she still married? Divorced? Avis was an extremely attractive woman, even in her mid-fifties—but as far as I knew she'd never mentioned a husband before. Why—

But the conversation had turned back to Ruth.

"Can't blame Florida for reacting the way she did," Stu was saying. "With friends like that, who needs enemies?"

Avis leveled a gaze at Stu that would stop most students at Bethune Elementary in their tracks. "I certainly hope you didn't say that to Florida. At worst, the comment was thoughtless. At best, Ruth may . . ." She didn't finish her sentence.

"May what?" I prompted.

Avis shook her head. "Never mind. We're all speculating anyway. We don't know. But . . . after the reactions she got, do you think Ruth will come to Florida's sobriety party?"

Good question. But at least we were finally talking about the elephant.

21

We had the *cooked* chicken-and-rice for supper, at which Denny and the kids had surprised me with a raspberry pie from Baker's Square and three flats of alyssum, petunias, and impatiens to plant in the backyard as my Mother's Day gift. I felt overwhelmed by the flowers, afraid they'd die in their little plastic pots before I had time to get them in the ground.

"So whaddya think?" I asked Denny, flopping down on the couch after finagling a promise from Josh and Amanda that they'd help me dig up the flowerbeds. "Should we make this party for Florida a surprise or tell her about it?"

"Huh?" Denny half-turned toward me, his eyes still glued to a documentary on public television about avalanches.

"Never mind." I got up.

"No, no, that's okay." He hit the mute on the remote. "What's up?"

I reminded Denny what Yo-Yo had said last night about a

five-year sobriety party for Florida and said both Avis and Stu liked the idea. "Should we make it a surprise or tell her about it?"

"Tell her. You want to make sure she'll come." He hit the sound back on.

"Uh, can we have it here?"

"What? Sure." On screen, the film crew was skiing for their lives, trying to outrace the avalanche. If I wanted a fur coat or a trip to Ireland, now would be the time to ask.

I called Florida. "Really?" she said. "Yo-Yo said that? That girl's all right."

She said Sunday on Memorial Day weekend would work for her. "Can I bring my kids? They're a huge part of what I got to celebrate."

Kids? I hadn't counted on *kids* when I offered to have it at my house. What would we do with kids? "Uh, sure. We'll think of something to keep them entertained." Something like Josh and Amanda. My name was going to be mud.

"You gonna invite the whole Yada Yada group?"

"Uh, sure. That's the idea. To celebrate with you."

A silence thick as wall putty seemed to clog up the line. Then, "Well okay. Can't nobody rob me of my joy, right?"

"Right," I said softly.

Everybody would be invited, but would "everybody" come?

I stood by the kitchen phone after we hung up. This whole thing didn't make sense. I liked Florida—really liked her. And I liked Ruth, too. What a stitch she was! I was sure they could be friends, if anybody could be in Yada Yada. What had happened?

"Hey, Josh," I said, stopping by the desk in the dining room, where he was pecking away at his history paper. "Let me know when you take a break. I gotta send out an invitation tonight."

BY THE TIME MEMORIAL DAY WEEKEND LOOMED on the calendar, I had gotten responses back from almost everybody saying, Great, let's do it, don't know about church but I'll see, what can we bring? Yo-Yo didn't have e-mail so I called her. Turned out she worked on Sunday, too, but was going to try to get off. Chanda didn't have e-mail, either, so I'd tried her number and left a message, but she hadn't called back. So that was everybody so far . . .

Everybody except Adele and Ruth.

Ruth . . . guess I wasn't surprised. She might need a little coaxing. Needed to call her, too. But what was Adele's excuse? It had been almost two weeks! How long did a simple yes or no take to send by e-mail?

Prayer requests from Yada Yada had been piling up, too. The most urgent was from Delores. On top of José's medical bills and slow recovery, her husband, Ricardo, had lost his job! "Without Ricardo's paycheck, I need to go back to work," she wrote. "Probably a good thing. Having both José and Ricardo underfoot all day is driving me *loca!*"

Hoshi had gotten a letter from her parents about their visit to Chicago this summer, but she still hadn't had the courage to tell them she'd become a Christian. "Pray for me I won't be afraid."

Nony wrote a long epistle detailing the growing famine in

Zimbabwe, Mozambique, Botswana, and other countries surrounding South Africa, and once again asked prayer about returning to Africa to work for the good of her people. "P.S. Mark and I would like to send Marcus and Michael to a Christian summer camp. Any suggestions?"

Hmm, I thought. *I could pass on the camp brochures we get every summer, since Josh and Amanda are going on the mission trip instead.*

And of course there was the ongoing prayer that Florida's little girl would be found. No word on whether Stu's efforts were turning up anything new.

I meant to pray every day for all these things; I really did. But school had been a zoo the last couple of weeks. End-of-year fever made nearly all the kids infected with can't-sit-still-itis until I was about ready to declare an epidemic and stay home. And Parents Day was coming up the week after Memorial Day, meaning that I'd probably spend most of the Monday holiday decorating my classroom. Bummer.

Chicago's lakefront officially opened on Memorial Day, and Chicagoans flocked to the parks and beaches like Ulysses clones drawn by the Sirens' song. Even a crowd-hater like me. For one thing, the mosquitoes and bees had not yet begun to recruit troops and draw up battle plans for Labor Day, pretty much leaving the parks bug-free. For another, people-watching was at its greatest as bikers, joggers, dog-walkers, and baby strollers were practically bumper to bumper, and everybody and his Uncle Jimmy hauled their Weber grills to the lakefront for a family reunion. It was as if Chicago itself shook off the winter doldrums to celebrate the beginning of summer.

Which made going back to school the next day—for three more weeks!—grounds for mutiny in the hearts of students and teachers alike.

But now that Saturday was here, I might as well suck it up and make the most of the three-day weekend. Like groceries. I hadn't done a serious shop since before the women's conference, just darting into the store to pick up milk or bread or hamburger on our way somewhere else. But, as Denny subtly pointed out, the vittles situation was starting to get serious when the only cans on the pantry shelf were dog food.

Besides, I had to shop for Florida's party. Which meant chicken. *Lots* of chicken. I hoped "Baxter grilled" instead of Kentucky Fried would be okay.

After reminding Amanda that Edesa was coming at four o'clock for tutoring and laying down the law to both kids that their rooms had to be clean—not just kicking stuff under the bed—before they could do anything with friends, I set out armed with my list of errands. I'd dropped off the dry cleaning and stood in line at the post office—both near each other on Devon—and was heading back up Clark Street toward the fruit market and new Dominick's grocery store when I saw the red-and-blue sign:

ADELE'S HAIR AND NAILS

I was so startled, I hit the brakes, meriting serious horn honking from the car behind me and getting a single digit salute as the driver swerved around me into the oncoming lane. I circled the block and drove slowly north on Clark once more, on the lookout for a place to stop and gawk. Adele's Hair and Nails—that was it, all right. I'd totally forgotten that Adele had said her shop was on Clark Street, a two-lane artery through Rogers Park boasting so many ethnic businesses that the shop signs looked like someone shook up the alphabet and scattered the letters like so many dice.

A car pulled out of a parking space, and I pulled in. Why not? I was here; Adele was in there, doing her thing. Why not just go in and ask if she could come to Florida's party? We were both Yada Yada. Why not?

Because you're a big chicken, Jodi. Adele hadn't exactly warmed up to me at the women's conference, and at least there I had the relative safety of the whole prayer group. But now . . .

I looked at the shop about two car lengths away. It looked innocent enough. Posters of women—mostly black women of different hues—with perfect skin and various hair styles ranging from waves to weaves stood behind an array of hair products in the window. Twinkle lights outlined the window—left over from Christmas?

Didn't look like a lion's den. But that's what it felt like as I locked the car, fed the meter, took a deep breath, and pulled open the door.

22

A bell tinkled over the door as I walked in, and I was greeted with a strong, not unpleasant smell reminding me of the Tonette home perms my mom used to give my grandmother. And music—a male vocalist singing gospel something. Three beauty-shop chairs were parked in front of the long mirror covering the wall to my left, but only one was occupied. On the right side, behind the counter, I could see a couple of hair dryers—those standard beehive contraptions that looked like hairdos on a *Simpsons* cartoon.

A young woman wearing a smock and tight-fitting latex gloves was sectioning the hair of a woman in the first chair and daubing on a white substance at the dark roots with a small, square paintbrush. She looked up. "Be with you in a minute."

I looked around the waiting area. Don't know what I'd expected, but not a comfy sofa and matching love seat making an L around a large coffee table. Another woman with light honey skin sat on the love seat paging through a copy of *Essence* and carrying on a conversation with the woman getting her hair done. "Her baby is just the sweetest thing," she was saying. "Sings like an angel."

"What? How old is he now?"

"Nine, maybe ten. He's good enough for the Chicago Children's Choir, I swear."

I edited my vision of an actual baby "baby" that could sing like an angel and sat down on the couch, giving the three woman what I hoped was a friendly smile. I picked up a copy of *O*—Oprah's magazine—from among the available reading materials: *Ebony, Jet,* and *Essence,* plus several issues of neighborhood newspapers. And a Bible.

"Whose CD is that she's got on? Kirk Franklin's new one?"

"Sounds like Fred Hammond to me."

I'm not sure which surprised me more: the Bible on the coffee table, the gospel music flooding the salon, or the coffeepot, half-full, plugged in on a little table beside the love seat. A cake server snuggled among the Styrofoam cups, powdered creamer, and packets of sugar revealed some kind of cake or pastry under its glass lid. Everything looked so . . . inviting. Sit down. Stay awhile.

Somehow, "inviting" and "Adele" were concepts that seemed like the north and south ends of a magnet.

"Can I help you?" the beautician asked, moving from the chair to the counter as she toweled white goo off her latex gloves.

I came to the counter, my mind scrambling. Should I just ask for Adele, or . . . maybe I should get something done. Nails! Why not get my nails done for Florida's party tomorrow? I was tempted to grin, remembering all the painted nails around the circle at the women's conference. Mine excluded. How much could it be? Might be fun.

"Um . . . do you take walk-ins for a manicure?"

Lifted eyebrow. "You don't have an appointment?"

"No, uh, you see . . . I was just driving by when I saw Adele's shop—Adele Skuggs, right?" I glanced past the young woman toward the back of the shop. "Is Adele here by any chance?"

The young woman arched both absolutely perfect eyebrows as if to say, *"You* know *Adele?"* but obediently called over her shoulder. "Adele? Lady here wants to see you."

"Give me a minute! I'm doing a comb-out!" That was Adele's voice all right. I smiled at the young woman, who returned to her client, and perused the shelves of beauty products that lined the wall just inside the door. Dudley's Oil-Sheen Spray & Moisturizer . . . Mizan Holding Spritz . . . KeraCare Detangling Shampoo . . . and several other brands of conditioners, moisturizers, and fixers, as well as small plastic packages labeled "Wave Caps."

"Well, look who's here. Jodi Baxter of the Baxter Bears."

I whirled. Adele had appeared behind the counter, big as life. Same short reddish 'fro. Same big gold earrings. Same little space between her front teeth. Same ability to tie up my tongue in a triple knot. The lion in the lion's den was looking at me with an amused smile.

"Hi, Adele. I . . . was just driving by and saw your shop! Decided to drop in and say hi . . . uh, *and* get my nails done, if you take walk-ins." I held out my fingers. "They're in pretty bad shape."

Adele did not look down at my hands.

"Or," I added hastily, "I could make an appointment for another time if you're too busy. Last-minute idea anyway. Just thought I'd get gussied up for Florida's party. Tomorrow, you know." I was starting to stumble over my own words, and I knew it.

Adele's eyebrows lifted a fraction. "Florida's party. Tomorrow."

"Right! I sent out an e-mail to Yada Yada about it, but maybe you didn't see it. A five-year sobriety party for Florida. It was Yo-Yo's—"

I stopped in midsentence. A little old lady with dark freckled skin and graying hair appeared in my line of vision, pushing a walker between hair dryers and beauty chairs and muttering loudly. "Cain't get nothin' ta eat in this rest'runt . . . lousiest service in th' South . . . jest gon' find mahself 'nother place ta eat . . . bunch o' pig-headed—"

"MaDear!" Adele grabbed but missed as the old woman shuffled past in her pink slippers—at a pretty fast clip, in my opinion—making a beeline for the front door. Adele caught her before she got to the handle and turned her around. "You want somethin' to eat, MaDear? Come on. I'll fix something for ya."

I stood transfixed, watching Adele usher the little woman in front of her, keeping a firm grip on "MaDear's" bony shoulders, which were encased in a faded blue housedress. Just as they were about to turn a corner beyond the hair dryers, Adele called out, "Come on back, Jodi. Think I can squeeze you in."

Startled, I glanced questioningly at the woman on the love seat. "Are you . . .?"

"Me? Nah. I'm waitin' on Takesha, here, to do my hair."

The young woman in the white smock—Takesha, presumably—nodded. "Go on. If Adele say she can squeeze you in, she can squeeze you in."

The woman in the chair, her hair standing stiffly at all angles, laughed. "Yeah. She the boss."

I walked toward the back and turned the corner into another leg of the shop. Two comfy-looking black vinyl chairs were poised on white porcelain pedestals that looked like mini-bathtubs. For soaking feet obviously, I told myself. Two more chairs were lined up in front of little white tables with all sorts of small gadgets and bottles of nail polish. Manicures.

Adele had parked her mother in a rocking chair and was tying her in with a padded Velcro belt. "Here you go." She handed her a sandwich that she took out of a small refrigerator.

The old lady patted Adele's hand. "Yo' sweet." She looked up quizzically. "What yo' say yo' name is?"

"Adele, MaDear." Adele blew out a breath, as though easing the level of pent-up frustration. "Since the day I was born."

She seemed to notice me then, standing in the middle of the narrow aisle. "Go on, have a seat. I've got a comb-out to finish. Be with you in five."

I sat down at one of the manicure tables, dizzy with the events of the past two minutes. Adele's mother was more "demented" than my grandmother ever was. Maybe it was Alzheimer's. Out of the corner of my eye I watched the old lady take her sandwich apart, laying each piece separately on her skinny lap: slice of bread, square of rubbery American cheese, slice of balogna, another slice of bread. Then she proceeded to lick the mayonnaise off each one.

"'Bye, Adele! See ya in a couple of weeks. 'Bye, MaDear." The comb-out waved in the general direction of Adele's mother and disappeared toward the front.

"Takesha!" Adele yelled after her. "Cash out Sister Lily, will ya?"

Then she was back. She eyed her mother. "Hmm. Oughta keep her busy for a while. Okay . . . you wanted a manicure?"

"Yes . . . I mean, if you're sure . . . I didn't have an appointment . . . how much do your charge?"

"Relax, Jodi." Adele was washing her hands in the hair-washing sink. "It's all right. I was kinda surprised to see you, I guess." She looked me up and down as she toweled her hands. "Sure you don't want a pedicure, too? Ten for the manicure, twenty for the pedicure . . . but I'll give you both for twenty-five. For coming in. Call it a first-time promotion."

I was tantalized. Why not? I'd cut it off the grocery bill—somewhere.

Sitting with my bare feet in the Jacuzzi footbath, I watched Adele lay out her clippers and scrubbers, oils and lotions. "Pick a color," she ordered, motioning toward the rows of nail polish. Oh, gosh. I didn't think I could go blood red. "That one," I said, pointing at a soft coral color.

"Ah. Living dangerously, eh?" Her shoulders shook in a silent chuckle.

But when Adele, big and black, pulled up a low footstool and took my left foot out of the bath, a sense of . . . of impropriety welled up inside me. I couldn't do this! Adele was practically kneeling at my feet, rubbing some kind of cuticle oil on each toe . . . it felt wrong! Like the old days, before Civil Rights, when white women like me sat up high and mighty on their thrones and black women scrubbed the floors.

"Jodi! Stop jerking your foot. I'm gonna gouge you good with this cuticle cutter if you don't hold still."

"Adele . . ." My voice came out in a squeak. "I feel . . . awkward having you work on my feet. I mean, you own this shop . . . don't you have a girl or somebody who does feet?"

Adele sat back and looked at me. Just looked at me. And for some reason, I started to cry. Big ol' tears just slid right down my face.

Finally she spoke. "Well, ain't you somethin' else. Know who you sound like, Jodi Baxter? Big ol' full-of-himself Peter. 'Oh, Master! You shall never wash my feet!' Just couldn't swallow it. And what did Jesus say?"

I just stared at her.

"He said, 'If I don't wash your feet, Big Boy, you ain't one of mine.' Well, something like that." She chuckled at herself. "Then ol' Peter says, Well if that's the case, give me the whole bath!"

Adele, still sitting on the footstool, put one hand on her ample hip and shook a finger at me. "Well, Jodi Baxter, I ain't gonna give you a whole bath, but feet are my business, and this *ain't* a big deal. And if we gonna do this . . . this Yada Yada thing, better get used to it. You wash feet sometimes; you get your feet washed sometimes. Ain't that the way it s'posed to be? Now hold still."

I PULLED INTO THE GARAGE an hour later than I thought I'd be, the back of the minivan full of groceries. Hitting the grocery store after getting all twenty digits oiled and lotioned and painted like a queen was a bit of a letdown. Here I was, still in my gym shoes covering up my now-gorgeous toes, when I *felt* like dancing barefoot in the grass wearing a gauzy gown, like those women who float through TV commercials for some kind of pain reliever.

But the temperature was creeping upward in the garage; it was going to be a warm Memorial Day weekend. Better get the cold stuff into the fridge right away—especially those packages of chicken for Florida's party tomorrow.

Sorry I'm late, I rehearsed telling Denny in my mind, *and I just spent twenty-five dollars we probably don't have—but it was worth it. Adele Skuggs is coming to Florida's party tomorrow, and she promised to bring Chanda—"minus Chanda's three kids if God has any mercy at all,"* was the way Adele put it.

Trying to be careful of my newly polished nails, I scuttled toward the back door, a gallon of milk in one hand and a bag of chicken in the other. "Sure hope Josh or Denny is around to help me haul in all these groceries," I mumbled. "And Josh and Amanda better have their rooms clean, too."

Willie Wonka was on hand to greet me, poking his nose into

the bag of chicken before I even got inside the door. I swatted his nose. "Anybody home?" I yelled. "I need help with the groceries!"

No answer. But I heard the shower running. Peeking into the dining room, I saw a couple of notes on the table, one in Amanda's pretty cursive, the other in Denny's scrawl.

"Finished my room. Dad said I could go to the mall with Trisha's family. They promised they'd get me back by 4:00."

"Jodi—Gone for a run. Josh playing ball at the park. Love you. D."

Humph. Denny must be back from his run and in the shower. So much for help lugging in groceries. But they got points for at least leaving a note.

I picked up the bag of chicken and opened the refrigerator door . . . and felt my own temperature rise. It had been almost empty when I'd left this morning. Plenty of room to store all that chicken until tomorrow. But now the lower shelf was full—with two six-packs of beer. Minus one bottle.

23

I hauled in the rest of the groceries like a queen bee with her stinger in backward. Now Denny was not only "having a beer with the guys" while watching a game, but stocking up the refrigerator! (*Stomp, stomp, stomp* across the back porch.) What was he stocking up *for?* Florida's party? Over my dead body. (*Slam* the car door.) How did he buy them anyway? I had the car. (*Slam* the back door.) And what's with the missing bottle? Drinking by himself? In the middle of the day? (*Slam* the refrigerator door)—

"Jodi? What in the world . . . ?"

I whirled around. Denny was standing in the kitchen doorway in his jeans, barefoot and shirtless, leaning on one arm against the doorpost. He looked pretty yummy—but I was *not* going to be distracted from my anger.

I flung open the refrigerator door and pointed. "That."

He didn't move from the doorway but folded his arms across

his chest. "That. Uh-huh. All this slamming of doors is because I bought some beer."

"*Some* beer? Looks to me like you laid in quite a supply . . . for what? Not Florida's party. She's a recovering *addict,* for goodness' sake, Denny." He wanted stubborn? He was going to get stubborn. I folded my arms across *my* chest.

A little grin tipped one corner of his mouth. "Hey. You got your nails painted." The grin widened. "Jodi Marie Baxter, Miss Simplicity herself, has gotten herself—"

"Don't change the subject." I tucked my nails under my folded arms . . . but I could feel tears gathering behind my eyes, like an anxious teenager who didn't get asked to the prom. I'd wanted Denny to notice my nails, to like it that I got dolled up—but not in the middle of an argument. I tilted my chin up. "When did you buy this stuff? *I* had the van. Why so much? You got a party planned I don't know about? And looks like the party's already started—"

"Good grief! Give me a break, Jodi!" The grin disappeared, and he half-turned to go—Denny's usual defense when I rode in with six-shooters blazing. But he pointed a finger at me. "You're right. You had the van and took your own sweet time getting home, too. Did you ever think I might have errands to do? But no problem, I decided to go for a run down at the lake. Beautiful day for a run— or hadn't you noticed?" Sarcasm dripped off his words as though sweating from the heat in his voice. "Worked up a real thirst on my run. Stopped in at the Osco on Morse on my way home to get something to drink. And you know what, Jodi? They had a special on cold beer. Buy one six-pack, get one free. And you know what else, Jodi? That cold beer looked mighty good and I drank one. One measly beer . . . and my wife wants to take it all the way to the Supreme Court. Sheesh." He threw up both arms in disgust and this time completed his exit.

I watched him disappear into the hallway beyond the dining room, trailed by Willie Wonka, who'd been standing between us, watching us with worried wrinkles above his doggie brows. My tears came out of hiding, pursued by silent sobs as I tackled the plastic grocery bags all around my feet.

Okay, so I probably didn't handle that the best way. I stuffed frozen orange juice, frozen vegetables, and hamburger into the freezer.

Should've waited till we could talk about it instead of jumping all over him. Canned goods, pasta, and cold cereal went into the cupboards.

Should've known that would backfire; always does. I dumped the bags of onions and potatoes into their little plastic bins under the sink.

Didn't say anything last weekend when he had a beer at the Bagel Bakery . . . huh! Look where that got me. Gave him an inch, and he took a yard. Paper towels, toilet paper, and napkins got squeezed into the tall cupboard by the back door.

What does this say to the kids? It's okay to have a beer? And he better not give me that "but even you drink wine sometimes" bit. Last time I read the papers, it was "beer parties" that got busted, not dinner parties. I pulled out the crisper and dumped in carrots, celery, and lettuce.

I paused with the refrigerator door open again, staring at the offending six-packs. It bugged me to have my refrigerator full of beer. I wanted them *out* before the kids got home. Not only that, but I didn't want them there with Yada Yada coming to my house tomorrow. People like Avis and Nony probably thought *any* alcohol was wrong. And it might be a stumbling block to someone like Hoshi, who was new in her faith . . . or Chanda, who seemed rather borderline when it came to Christian behavior.

I hauled out the six-packs and took them to the garage, setting them in a corner under an old bushel basket. I'd tell Denny before he "discovered" they were gone and . . . well, we'd deal with it later.

EDESA DECLINED OUR INVITATION to stay for supper after her tutoring session with Amanda at four o'clock—said she was going to babysit for Delores and Ricardo that night so they could get out of the house.

"Isn't José too big for a babysitter?" I teased.

"Absolutely!" she laughed. "But . . . he cannot take care of his younger brothers and sisters yet. Besides, he is bored. He likes me to play cards."

"What about tomorrow—can you and Delores come to Florida's party?"

She smiled. *"Sí!* Wouldn't miss it. Can we bring Emerald?"

More kids. "Uh . . . sure." Emerald was sweet. She wouldn't be any trouble.

Josh, bless his heart, walked Edesa to the Morse Street el stop. While he was gone, I asked Denny if we could talk privately a minute. Amanda was on the phone talking to a girlfriend, so we went out on the back porch and sat down on the steps.

"Denny, I . . . I'm sorry I jumped all over you about the beer."

He pursed his lips and nodded, but didn't say anything.

"But I really don't want it in the house for Florida's party. The women in Yada Yada come from a lot of different churches and might . . . I just don't want to offend anybody."

He shrugged. "Sure. I'll put it down in the basement."

"Uh . . . I already took it out to the garage."

His smile tightened. "Fine. Garage."

The tension between us had deflated somewhat but still hung there, like a helium party balloon hovering two feet off the floor. "Do you want to talk about the beer?" I asked.

"Not really," he said. "Maybe some other time."

I felt relieved. I didn't really want to talk about it now, either. But I didn't like the distance between us. Any crack, no matter how small, always felt like a huge canyon. "But . . . do you forgive me for yelling at you?"

"Yeah."

We sat on the steps a few more minutes, listening to the *thump, thump* of kids playing basketball in the alley beyond our garage, punctuated with the *caws* of several large black crows flying around a big elm one street over.

"I ran into Adele this afternoon—you know, the lady that squashed me like a bug the first night of our prayer group." I made my tone light, chatty. Maybe Denny and I just needed a bit of time to close the gap. "She has a beauty shop right on Clark Street—I didn't realize it was so close."

"That where you got your nails done?"

"Yeah. Feet, too." I giggled and pulled off one shoe and sock. "Whaddya think?"

I was relieved to see Denny grin as I wiggled my coral-tipped toes. "You sat still long enough for someone to give you a pedicure? Your mom always said she couldn't even play 'This little piggy went to market' without you screeching bloody murder."

"It wasn't easy. In fact—"

The back screen door banged open. "Mom. Dad. I'm back. When's supper? Somebody from Habitat for Humanity is going to talk to us tonight about the Mexico trip. Do you realize we leave in exactly one month?"

I made a face at Denny. Oh well. I had a lot to do to get ready for the party tomorrow anyway. I'd find some other time to tell him how freaked I got about that pedicure—and not because I was ticklish, either.

"Edesa get on the train okay?" I asked, rising reluctantly and following Josh back into the kitchen.

"Yeah. I hung around by the ticket booth till a southbound train came. Didn't hear any screams, so I'm pretty sure she got on okay."

"Oh, get out of here," I said, snapping him with a dishtowel. "I take it back. Set the table."

I pulled some catfish fillets out of the freezer and popped them into the microwave to defrost. Through the screen door I could see Denny still sitting on the back porch steps. Probably wishing he had one of those beers I'd hidden in the garage . . .

Stop it, Jodi. Drop it till you have time to talk.

24

Thank You, God," I murmured, pulling open the blind on the bedroom window the next morning and seeing blue sky above the garage roof. The prospect of having all twelve members of Yada Yada plus assorted husbands *and* children underfoot in the house if it rained today had filled me with anxiety, akin to the claustrophobia I'd felt the time I got stuck in an elevator with ten other sweaty people.

But blue sky and sunshine . . . that would help a lot. Our backyard wasn't very big—I could probably count the blades of grass —but at least Denny could grill the chicken out there and any husbands who came along could yak outside while Yada Yada had our prayer time together in the front room.

Kids, hmm. Maybe Josh and Amanda could haul them down to the lake and fly a kite or something. Didn't we have a kite somewhere?

Unfortunately, that was the extent of my prayer time that

morning. *I'll make it up to You, Jesus,* I promised, flitting from room to room like film footage that's been speeded up, munching a bagel while picking up magazines, shoes, schoolbooks, mail, and anything else that gave our house that "lived-in look." At least Avis would make sure we got prayer time at the party this afternoon . . . that would have to do.

I ended up making everybody wait in the car as I ran back to the house to set out a gallon glass jar filled with water and tea bags for "sun tea." When I climbed back into the car Denny said, "Relax, Jodi. It's going to be great. I'm looking forward to meeting the rest of Yada Yada. But . . ." He gravely fingered one of my earlobes. ". . . is this a new style? You're only wearing one earring."

BESIDES THE FACT THAT Denny saved me from looking foolish two Sundays in a row, his good-natured laughter as I ran back into the house for the missing earring had felt like a soothing ointment on the raw place between us. We walked up the stairs at Uptown hand in hand while Josh parked the minivan this time.

"Wonder if anybody from Yada Yada will come to church this morning?" I whispered, glancing about the upstairs sanctuary. I checked out the third row. "Whoa, you mean we got here before Stu this time?" My day was picking up.

"Mom, look! It's Edesa!" Amanda made a beeline for a couple of women whose backs were turned toward us, and sure enough,

Edesa turned around and gave her a big hug. I could see her introducing Delores and Emerald to my daughter.

I pulled Denny in their direction. "Delores!" I gave the shorter
woman a hug and bestowed one on Emerald, too. "I didn't really think
you'd be able to come to church as well as the party this afternoon."

Delores's round face dimpled. "Good excuse to have a girls day
out." She rolled her eyes and tapped the side of her head with her
finger. "My Ricardo *with* a job is a trial to live with. Unemployed?
He is driving me—" She drew little circles at her temple with her
finger.

We laughed but couldn't talk more because Avis was giving
the call to worship. Some people moved over a couple of chairs so
we could have seats together. I noticed Emerald, her jet black hair
caught back from her face with a baby blue ribbon, jockeying for
position between Edesa and Amanda. What a cutie.

We were singing the second song when I felt a poke in my ribs
from the row behind me. "Hey, girl," came a loud whisper. "Why
didn't you save me a seat?"

I'm sure I grinned from ear to ear. "Florida!" I whispered and
gave her an awkward hug over the back of my chair. She was
dressed in black slacks and a loose-belted tunic—rose on black—
and her hair was different. The crown of little beaded braids had
given way to a cascade of shiny finger curls slicked back from her
forehead with tiny combs. Chris and Cedric, looking manly in
their khaki slacks and open-necked dress shirts, both gave me a
little wave. No Carl though. Denny might be odd man out at this
party, after all.

That was all from Yada Yada who came to Uptown Community that morning, but it was a start on our "church visitation." I wasn't too surprised that others hadn't made it—after all, Adele had "MaDear" to worry about, and Chanda was a single mom with three kids. Probably getting a babysitter—or mother-sitter—for one afternoon was challenging enough. I was surprised about Stu, though. She had come again last week and talked like she'd be here this morning.

The service was nice, pretty typical for Uptown. From time to time I glanced sideways at Edesa and Delores, wondering how our medley of contemporary worship songs—sincere, but rather monotone in intensity, accompanied by a few hand clappers—compared to worship at their Church of the Holy Spirit. It would be fun to visit a Spanish-speaking church. I ought to go when Amanda could go with me.

During announcements, the teen group asked members of Uptown Community to sponsor work projects for the teens the first three Saturdays in June to earn the remaining money for the mission trip. It hadn't really hit me yet that both my kids were going off U.S. soil for ten days . . . without me. As people gathered around the teens to pray for them, I felt strangely warmed to hear Florida's familiar, "Thank ya, *Jesus!*" and "You are *so good,* Jesus!" join Avis's regular affirmations.

Our visitors had come by public transportation, so I got together with Avis right after service to work out rides to my house. Delores and Edesa wanted to run by Dominick's to pick up some potato salad; Avis said she'd take them so we Baxters could get home to get the grill going. That left Florida and her boys to ride with us.

I saw Pastor Clark talking to Florida and making a fuss over Chris and Cedric. *That's nice,* I thought. Pastor Clark carried a vision for more diversity in the congregation. Maybe he was trying to recruit them. But finally we all made it out the door and piled in the minivan that Josh had waiting—double-parked—in front of Uptown's storefront.

"Didn't know this was yours and Avis's church, Jodi," Florida said, followed by a stern, "Get that seatbelt fastened, Cedric; don't you be fussin' 'bout it."

"Yeah. Almost a year now—well, last summer. That's how I met Avis and found out about the job at Bethune Elementary."

"Ain't that somethin'," Florida murmured as we pulled away, which I thought was odd. She couldn't have been *that* impressed.

BY THE TIME AVIS ARRIVED with her carload and a pan of hot macaroni and cheese, it was almost one-thirty and Chanda and Adele had just arrived, bearing a couple of bags of chips and a big pot of greens respectively. "Get that mac 'n' cheese in the oven," Adele ordered, charging into the kitchen. She put her own pot of greens on top of the stove and turned the flame on low. "Nothin' worse than cold mac 'n' cheese."

For a flicker of a second my territorial instincts rose up: *You may be the boss of your salon, Adele Skuggs, but this is my kitchen . . .*

but instead I tried to make conversation. "Where's your mother today, Adele?" I *was* curious. What did one *do* with someone suffering from Alzheimer's like MaDear, who was always looking to "escape" with her walker?

"My sister takes her on Sundays. Gives me a day off." She seemed to notice the others who'd come in with Avis for the first time. "Hey, Edesa . . . Delores. Oh, my . . . this your baby? How ya doin', honey? How's José doin'?" Chatting all at once, the little group threaded itself through the back door.

"Amanda's out there somewhere, Emerald!" I called after them.

Chanda George had disappeared into the bathroom the moment she walked in the front door. Coming into the kitchen now, she caught sight of others in the backyard and made a beeline for the screen door, giving me a polite nod in passing. Then, as if on second thought, she stopped and enveloped a startled Avis in a big hug.

"That was interesting," Avis murmured a few minutes later as the two of us set things out on the dining room table, buffet style. "Maybe getting everybody in the prayer group together is as important for Chanda as for Florida."

"You think?" I hadn't thought much about Miss Lottery Ticket since the conference—Chanda didn't have e-mail, so we hadn't really communicated. I really had no idea what her life was like . . . single mom, three kids, cleaning houses for a living. Did we have *anything* in common? But I did appreciate that she had made an effort to come out on a Sunday afternoon—*sans* kids, thank goodness—to Florida's party.

Avis was staring at me, an amused smile on her face.

"What?"

She pointed. "Your nails. I thought there was something different about you today, but I didn't know what. You did your nails."

"Nope. Got them done. At Adele's salon." I waved my fingers under her nose, enjoying the "oh *really*" look on her face. I'd wondered if anyone would notice.

Josh and Amanda had Florida's boys and Emerald in the alley, shooting hoops against a neighbor's garage, while most of the women flirted with Denny, who was manning the grill. Okay, they weren't really flirting, but he was the only man present and was being his charming self, which meant giving each new arrival a big welcoming smile and talking like they were old friends. I knew I could count on Denny to help put people at ease.

The doorbell rang as Avis and I set out the last of the red-and-white paper plates and matching napkins and cold cups on a folding card table in the dining room. "I'll get it," I said, hustling down the hall and pulling open the front door.

"Nony!" I shrieked, and gave her a big hug—before realizing that an absolutely gorgeous hunk of a man stood just behind her, six feet three if he was an inch. His skin was nutmeg, a spicy complement to Nony's darker skin, with deep-set eyes, a perfectly trimmed moustache and goatee, and—good grief!—dimples.

"Hi, Jodi," Nony said, dressed as usual in a beautiful African thing—a royal blue dress with slits up the side, embroidered all around the neck and wide sleeves with a silvery design. "This is my husband, Mark, and . . ." She reached around behind her husband

and pulled out two shy boys, each one holding a couple of liters of soda pop. "Marcus," she said, tapping the slightly taller one, "and Michael." Spitting images of their father.

"Come in, come in!" I beamed, awed by this beautiful little family. "Everyone's out in the backyard. The guy in the apron manning the grill is my husband, Denny. He will be so glad you showed up, Mark—so far he's been the only male at this hen party. If you don't count kids, I mean."

Mark shook my hand warmly and gave a slight bow. "Delighted to meet you, Jodi Baxter." I felt like Anna in *The King and I*. Yes, I could imagine this man was a professor at Northwestern University.

"Is Hoshi coming?" I asked.

Nony shook her head. "Can't. Writing a history paper." She gave her husband a look. "*Some* professors expect way too much research."

"Oh, I'm sorry. Tell her we missed her . . . Oh. There's a chest of ice on the back porch for that pop," I said to Nony's boys . . . just as I noticed a bunch more heads bobbing up the porch steps behind the Sisulu-Smiths. I stepped aside as Nony ushered her family toward the back of the house then returned to the open front door to welcome the new arrivals.

Yo-Yo! Followed by Ruth and Ben, carrying a big paper bag that said "the Bagel Bakery." And lurking at the bottom of the steps, Yo-Yo's two teenage stepbrothers, whose slouch and averted eyes made it clear that they wished they were someplace else.

"Ohmigosh!" I said, dishing out hugs once more. "I didn't know if you guys were coming! Ben . . . Denny will be delighted.

Three husbands ought to be enough for this crowd, don't you think?"

"Yes, plenty," Ruth said. "They can do the dishes while we talk. No?"

Laughing, I gave her a big hug. "I am *so* glad you came, Ruth. You have no idea," I whispered in her ear.

She waved me away like a pesky mosquito. "What's not to come? You have food, we eat. We are women, we talk. The party is Yada Yada, we pray." But something in her voice made me think her bravado functioned more as an internal pep talk. Frankly, I suspected we had Yo-Yo to thank for getting them all here.

I hustled the latest arrivals out to the backyard—which seemed tinier by the minute—and for a few minutes hugs, squeals, greetings, and introductions degenerated into a general hubbub. I called Josh from the alley, who—if he was surprised at the growing number of kids, hid it well—managed to coax Yo-Yo's brothers, Jerry and Pete, to play three-on-three in the alley.

Well, that's everybody, I thought. Everybody except Hoshi . . . and Stu.

I snuck away, hunted up Stu's number on the Yada Yada list, and called. Three rings, then an answering machine picked up. I hung up without leaving a message.

Strange.

25

Florida seemed to be having a great time. "That man of yours sure can barbecue some gooood chicken," she conceded to me, her plate piled high with blistered chicken, macaroni and cheese, greens, potato salad, and chips, before moving on to trade good-natured insults with Adele and Chanda, laughing and talking. I noticed she hadn't taken any of the potato kugel Yo-Yo and Ruth had brought from the Bagel Bakery. Shouldn't read anything into that, I told myself; she didn't go for the "yuppie" food at the hotel, either.

Watching the steady stream of nine kids—most of them hollow-leg boys—going in and out of the house with copious amounts of food, I began to worry about dessert. Stu was supposed to bring it . . . what did I have to substitute if she didn't show up? A quick inventory of the kitchen came up with two partially eaten half-gallons of ice cream and an unopened package of store-bought cookies. That would have to do.

On the way back out to the backyard, I snatched the camp brochure I'd put out on the counter to show to Nony. She was chatting with Avis but excused herself when I waved the brochure at her and pantomimed, *For you.*

"Didn't mean to interrupt," I apologized. "Just didn't want to forget to give this to you—you asked about a Christian camp on the e-loop, remember?"

"Oh, yes. Let me see."

Nony took the large brochure I handed to her and opened it up, disclosing a colorful display of photographs of kids zipping down a water slide, made up in clown faces, doing crafts, and riding horseback, sprinkled amid descriptions of the different age groups and specialty camps. "My kids have attended this camp for years," I put in. "They love it! It's got all sorts of great activities—parasailing, canoe trips, a ropes course, even a horsemanship camp—on top of the regular stuff. And they bring in lots of popular youth speakers. Amanda would probably be going this summer, except she's going on a teen mission trip to Mexico, and the dates conflict." I lowered my voice in that parent-to-parent confidential tone. "Good thing. No way we could afford both in one summer."

Nony studied the brochure for a moment or two longer, then folded it up and handed it back to me. "Thank you, Jodi."

"Oh, you can keep that."

Nony shook her head. "One look at that brochure and my kids would say, 'No way.'"

I felt like I'd been slapped. She must have seen me jerk because she added, "The pictures. Not a single black face in the whole brochure. Except one picture, and they're *all* black in that one."

I blinked. Really? I was sure I'd seen African-American kids at the camp when we took our kids or picked them up at the camp. At least one or two, anyway. "I'm sure they'd be wel—"

"It's not just that, Jodi," Nony said, not unkindly. "Look." She pointed to the one picture that showed several grinning dark faces just above a camp week described as "Urban Camp." "See that description? 'Underprivileged' . . . 'inner city' . . . 'scholarships.' That's the impression given by this brochure—that black kids are underprivileged, all live in the inner city, need scholarships, and come to this particular week of camp. Mark would have a fit."

A hot flash of embarrassment crept up my neck. What a dork I was! I should have noticed . . . but I had to admit, it hadn't even crossed my mind.

As if to soften the sting, Nony gave me a kiss on the cheek. "It's all right, Jodi. I appreciate you thinking of the boys." She retrieved her plate and moved off, as regal in our puny backyard as if it were a marble courtyard.

I retreated to the kitchen to stash the brochure . . . and started to feel defensive. I'd extended an invitation to share *my* world and been rebuffed. For that matter, how could this camp—an outstanding Christian camp in my opinion, at least up until the last five minutes—include any pictures of black middle-class kids having fun at camp . . . if they didn't *go?*

I wanted to go somewhere and stick a pillow over my head. *Suck it up, Jodi. You're the hostess of this party, remember?* I put the ice cream, a scooper, and the cookies on a tray then stood at the back door another moment or two, working up courage to go back outside and mingle, not knowing when I'd make a fool of myself again.

Standing at the back door, I had a sudden revelation. If all the kids in those pictures had been black, would Amanda or Josh think that camp was intended for them? Would *I* want them to be "token white kids," just to integrate the place?

No. I wasn't that noble. Sure, I'd welcome a healthy mix of kids, as I was sure Nony would, too. But, just like Nony, I'd mostly want my kids not to feel different, to feel like they *belonged*.

DENNY CLANGED HIS BARBECUE UTENSILS together. "Hey, everybody!" The general hubbub died down, and even the kids stopped slurping ice cream long enough to stare at my husband, who stood on the steps of the back porch in his silly apron.

"I've been forewarned," he said gravely, "that the Yada Yada Prayer Group plans to get together all by themselves right after we finish eating . . . leaving the gentlemen, by the way, to clean up—"

"What about these kids?" Ben Garfield glowered at Jerry and Pete, trying to look tough.

"No, no!" howled Yo-Yo's brothers. "We can't clean up. Josh is taking us to the lake to play volleyball!" The other kids lustily joined in the general protest.

Denny clanged his utensils together again. "All right, all right. Just put your own trash in that big trash can there, and it'll be half-done. But wait! Wait!" He held up the barbecue tongs as the kids made a mad rush for the trash can, intent on taking the promised hike down to the lakeshore. The hubbub settled once more.

Denny turned to Florida. "Before Yada Yada steals you away, we want to acknowledge our guest of honor, Florida Hickman, who is, I believe, 'five years saved and five years sober'! Let's give it up for Sister Florida!"

As cheers and clapping and laughter erupted, Denny hopped down and gallantly escorted Florida to the top step. "Speech! Speech!"

I grinned as Florida looked around the yard, tears sparkling in her deep brown eyes. This was perfect. Denny always did have a gift for the dramatic.

For a few moments, Florida didn't speak, her emotions doing a little dance between her big smile and the tears that threatened to flow. But as the happy clamor subsided, she lifted her chin. "There's only one guest of honor here—and that's Jesus. 'Cause if it weren't for Jesus—oh, Lord! If it weren't for Jesus—" She stopped and closed her eyes as the tears finally fell. She shook her head from side to side . . . but in a few moments opened her eyes again. "If it weren't for Jesus, I'd still be a mess for sure, still out on the street, still doing drugs, still stopping cars in the middle of the street, begging anyone and everyone for money for my next fix. But—praise Jesus!—He . . ."

My mouth slowly fell open. Florida went on talking, still giving God praise, but I no longer heard the words. My mind had stuck on the last thing she said: *stopping cars in the middle of the street, begging anyone and everyone for money . . .*

An old memory, a rainy day, way back when the kids were little, a wild woman stopping my car . . . could that have been *Florida?* Immediately, common sense told me that there must be thousands of drug addicts in Chicago. The odds that Florida and I had run into each other ten, maybe twelve years ago . . . impossible. We didn't even live in Chicago back then. Denny used to volunteer at Uptown sometimes, but Chicago was a big city—

". . . Uptown Community Church," Florida was saying. "Ain't God got a sense of humor, bringing me and the boys to that church today, the day y'all picked for my sobriety party? But it was one of the storefront churches I used to hit up for handouts. Didn't even remember the name, not until I walked in there this morning and saw the pastor—what's his name? Pastor Clark . . . right. He tried to get me straightened out a couple times, but I wasn't ready. Wasn't ready till they took my babies . . ."

Oh God. That was Florida.

"Jesus!" a piercing voice cried, yanking me back to the present. It was Chanda, shaking her head and waving one hand in the air. "Jesus!"

"Hallelujah! Glory!" Delores started clapping, and others joined in. A little way behind the others, Avis walked back and forth on the grass, head thrown back, lips moving in praise.

Still stunned at the revelation that our paths had crossed once before, I wanted to grab Florida, say something. But she stood on the back steps, one arm lifted heavenward, her voice rising over all the others: *"Thank* ya, Jesus! *Thank* ya!"

Looked like we were getting ready to have church right there in the Baxter backyard.

THE KIDS FINALLY ESCAPED under the supervision of Josh and Pete as the "oldest," volleyball in hand. Yada Yada moved into the living room, glasses of pop and iced tea in hand. (Though I'd been informed by Florida that adding sugar to cold iced tea just didn't do justice to the "real thing." "Girl, ya gotta add the sugar while the tea is *hot.* Ain't nobody ever told you how to make real 'sweet tea'—like they do down South?") The front windows were open and I'd put a fan in one, pulling a nice breeze from the open back door. Somehow, all ten of us found a perch, either on the couch or chairs or pillows on the floor.

"You got a real nice house, Sista Jodee," Chanda said. It was the first thing she'd said to me all afternoon.

"Nice nails, too," Adele quipped.

"Yeah. Look at you," said Yo-Yo, settling on the floor in front of Ruth.

At any other time, I would have enjoyed "joining the club" of nail-painted women. And it was the perfect time to give Adele and her salon the credit. But I didn't want to lose what had just happened in a flurry of small talk. "I gotta tell you guys . . . Florida and I met before. Twelve years ago."

The room was suddenly silent, and nine pairs of eyes looked at me.

"I . . . I didn't realize it until just now . . . out in the back-yard! But, Florida, when you mentioned that you used to stop by Uptown Community to get a handout—"

Florida pulled back behind her stare. "Thought you and Denny have only been at Uptown since last summer."

"That's true! But before that, Denny had been volunteering there for half a zillion years, even when we were living in Downers Grove. The first time I drove into the city to pick him up . . . a woman jumped out in front of my car—Good Lord! Scared me half to death. It was raining, too. I could have hit her!—but all she wanted was some money. To feed her kids, she said. I didn't know what to do. At first, I told her to go to Uptown—they could help her. She said she'd been there, done that. But . . ." I tried to make eye contact with Florida, but she was leaning forward, hands clasped on her knees, her eyes focused on her hands. ". . . that's why I think it was you."

I couldn't tell what Florida was thinking. But a lump was growing in my throat. "Never in all my wildest dreams did I think God would put *that woman* in my hotel room at the women's conference . . . put her in my prayer group . . . in my home . . . in my life . . . as my friend."

"Glory," someone breathed. Probably Avis. But I kept my eyes on Florida.

She finally looked up. "So, what did you do—back then, I mean?"

"You don't remember?" I waited to see a slight shake of her head. "Well, I was going to take you to the grocery store to buy you some food and diapers—that's what you said you needed."

"Did you?"

"No." I dropped my eyes. "On the way we stopped at the church and . . . you were gone when I got back to the car."

"Stopped at the church to check me out?"

I swallowed. *Bingo.* I nodded.

Florida's face crumpled. "I don't remember it—stopped a lot of cars during that time." Her voice was hushed as though uncomfortable with the idea that one of the women in this room—the women who knew the Florida who was "saved, sober, and sanctified"—had met the "other" Florida.

"*I* think this is incredible." Delores broke the tension. "Don't you see? God had a plan all along to bring all of us together—and maybe it started that day when Florida and Jodi met by accident."

"Get out!" Yo-Yo arched back. "That was just coincidence, right?"

"There are no coincidences with God, Yo-Yo," said Avis.

"What's that mean?" Yo-Yo pressed. "God's got some big *reason* Florida hit up Jodi for money years ago? Some big *reason* this bunch of women got number twenty-six on their gold sticker at that conference?"

"Maybe." Avis smiled.

"'Fear not, for I have redeemed you; I have called you by name; you are mine,'" Nony quoted, flipping through her Bible. "Where's that passage, Avis?"

"Wait a minute," said Yo-Yo. "Don't go throwing Bible verses around. What's this name business? I mean, God calling us by name."

"Names have meaning," Edesa suggested.

"Yeah, right. Yo-Yo . . . a spinning toy going nowhere," Yo-Yo muttered.

"Here it is." Avis had her Bible open. "Isaiah forty-three: 'Thus says the Lord, who created you . . . "Fear not, for I have redeemed you; I have called you by your name; you are Mine. When you pass through the waters, I will be with you; and through the rivers, they shall not overflow you. When you walk through the fire, you shall not be burned, nor shall the flame scorch you. For I am the Lord your God, the Holy One of Israel, your Savior"' . . ." She looked up. "That's a good passage for this celebration."

"For Florida, yes. Praise God! But I was also thinking," Nony murmured, "about what Delores said about God calling us together as a group . . . and planning it a long time ago . . . and giving us a *name.*"

Delores got so excited she was practically bouncing on the couch beside Florida. "*Gloria a Dios!* Ruth, what did you say 'Yada Yada' meant—that Hebrew meaning?"

"Never heard what *that* was all about." Chanda pulled a face.

Ruth looked taken aback, as if she had not planned to speak. "What am I, a dictionary?" But she dug around in her purse, finally pulled out a square of paper, and unfolded it. "All right. Yada Yada like we've been spelling it—without an *h* on the end—means 'to perceive, to understand . . . to be known, to make oneself known.'" She frowned and read farther in the tiny text on the photocopied page. "'Often used to describe God's knowledge of man.'"

"And women," Adele sniffed.

"*Sí, sí,*" Delores said impatiently. "Don't you see? Jodi and Florida had absolutely nothing—nada—in common when that drug addict stopped that car. They didn't know each other, they didn't understand each other, they didn't think they'd ever see each other again—"

"You sayin' God knew?" Yo-Yo still looked doubtful.

"That's it," said Avis. "God knew them, He knew you, He knew each one of us back then—and wanted all of us to know Him . . . and maybe wanted us to know each other, too."

"For real?" Chanda's eyes were big. "You be sayin' that God planned all along for these here sistas to get together? And named us, too?"

I wasn't sure how all this fit together with the fact that I had "met" Florida for ten minutes twelve years ago . . . though it seemed terribly significant *somehow.* I still couldn't read Florida, though, what she thought about it. I wanted to get up and just give her a hug, let her know I was glad we'd met, glad God brought us back together again.

Nony was smiling and waving her Bible. "Don't know why God calling us by name shouldn't apply to a group as well as individuals. We *thought* we made up a name for this group just off the cuff—but look what it turned out to be. God's name for us."

"That's it. What's the other meaning of Yada Yada, Ruth?" Delores pressed.

"Yadah Yadah with an *h*? Hmm . . ." Ruth peered again at the tiny print, moving it to arm's length. "Yadah Yadah means—

among other things—to praise, to sing, to give thanks. It says here—"

The doorbell rang. Ruth stopped and looked up.

Rats, I thought. *Wish Denny would get it.* But Denny was in the backyard and probably didn't hear it. "Go on, Ruth, I'll get it." I stepped over Yo-Yo and Edesa, who were sitting on the floor and headed for the front door. Behind me I heard Ruth finish, "It says here, 'an expression of thanks to God by way of praising.'"

I pulled open the door. Stu was standing on the other side of the screen, her long hair tucked behind one ear, showing off the little row of earrings, and holding a nine-by-eleven pan of something. Dessert. *A little late,* I huffed to myself.

"Hi, Jodi. Everybody here?" Stu pulled open the screen door and practically charged past me into the living room.

"Hey, Stu. Get mugged on the way?" cracked Yo-Yo.

A few others started to call out greetings, but Stu held up her hand like a traffic cop. "Sorry I'm late. But I've got news." She paused, looking around the room, her eyes finally falling on Florida.

"I found Carla."

26

Stu's announcement surged from person to person like a slow-motion shock wave and pulled Florida off the couch. "You . . . found my baby?" Disbelief and hope, fear and longing tangled themselves around those words.

"Pretty sure. Everything seems to—"

Adele's big frame rose up from the La-Z-Boy like a protective mother bear. "Don't do this, Leslie Stuart, not unless you *know*—"

"Wait. Please. Listen to me." Stu shoved the pan of dessert into my hands and moved to Florida's side. She took the dark, trembling hands in her own and lowered Florida to the couch cushions, kneeling down beside her. "They don't know exactly how it happened, *how* Carla's foster family got lost in the system, but my contact at DCFS thinks the original social worker quit or got fired and Carla's files got lost, or misfiled, or something. That's why they couldn't find any record of her when you went back."

"Sounds like DCFS, all right," Adele muttered, and sat back down.

By now all of us were glued to Stu's words.

"But . . . there's a family with a foster child who recently applied to adopt the little girl, and DCFS can't find any of *her* records. That tipped off my friend, who had copies of your papers, Florida . . . and the facts fit: first name, date of birth, date taken into custody by DCFS, all that kind of stuff. He's pretty sure it's your Carla."

"You mean . . . the family didn't steal her? Or run off to some other state? Or . . . or hurt my baby?" The struggle to let go of her fears was written all over Florida's face.

Stu shook her head. "No. Don't think so. This family applied to adopt her, after all. They'd have to stand up to some scrutiny. And . . . probably means they love her. Enough to want to keep her."

The word "adopt" finally sank into Florida's awareness. "Keep her? But . . . no, no! I want my baby back. Now that she's found, I want my baby back!" She made an attempt to stand up, but Stu's firm grip on her hands kept her in her seat.

"Don't worry, Florida," Stu said patiently. "They've only applied for adoption. Nothing's final. Once DCFS matches up the paperwork, your own application to get your daughter back will certainly affect the adoption process. The fact that your husband and sons are back with you? Definitely a plus factor."

"*Sí, sí.*" Delores, who was sitting beside Florida on the couch, put an arm around her shoulder comfortingly. "*Muy bueno.* And we pray."

"Are the foster parents white? Or black?" Chanda's question interrupted the flow of encouragement like an open manhole that one had to dodge in the middle of the street.

Stu shrugged. "I don't know. Does it matter?"

"Matter!" Adele jumped in, screeching to a halt right in front of the yawning manhole. "White folks think they can raise black kids color-blind. But most of 'em don't know a whit about preparing a black child for life in this society. Huh." She folded her arms across the wide span of her bosom. "Takes more'n love or money or good intentions. Black kids need identity, the strength of they own kind. What else gonna—"

Stu stood up. "I disagree. There're too many kids wasting away in the foster care system—most of them children of color—to get all self-righteous about what color an adoptive family should be. We need more people wanting to adopt, period."

"Why don't you adopt, then?" Chanda asked.

I felt slightly smug that Stu was on the hot seat after riding in on her white horse to save the day. Adele had a point, of course, but to be honest, I agreed with Stu. I probably would've been rendered speechless by Chanda's challenge, though, but Stu lifted her chin. "I've thought about it. Seriously."

"Want a couple of teenage boys?" Yo-Yo snickered. "I need a break."

"Ah . . . this might make a good discussion at another time," Avis said. "But right now it's a moot point, since, as Stu says, we don't know. The important thing is . . . Carla was lost, but now she's found. What an answer to our prayers! We need to give some glory to God!" She stood up—I think it's against Avis's nature to praise God sitting down. "Glory to You, Jesus! Glory!"

Florida's tense body gradually melted against Delores's arm around her shoulder. "Yes . . . Yes! Thank ya, Jesus. Thank ya! *Thank* ya! You're a *good* God!"

Others began to join in the prayer and praise. I thought *hallelujah,* too—hallelujah that Avis had the wits to derail *that* discussion. I wanted to join in the praise and prayer, too—if Carla really had been found, that was worth shouting about!—but I was still standing in the doorway, holding Stu's nine-by-eleven pan. I slipped out to the kitchen and set it on the counter. Maybe it would keep the kids busy if they got back before Yada Yada was done.

The praise from the living room could be heard clear out in the kitchen—maybe even out in the backyard. I peeked in Stu's pan—yum, lemon bars—then glanced out the screen door. Denny, Mark Smith, and Ben Garfield had parked three lawn chairs in the shade of the garage. They looked relaxed, friendly. Sure were a funny trio. Denny, the all-american-guy high school coach . . . Mark, the svelte college professor, tall, dark, *and* handsome . . . and Ben, short, stocky, a shock of wavy silver hair, and features that could make him a stand-in for Itzhak Perlman if he played the violin. I could hear Ben's guttural guffaw as he raised a bottle to his lips.

Bottle? I squinted and peered intently through the screen door. Had Ben brought some beer to the party? Hadn't noticed any when they came in. Which meant—

I did a quick double-check of the other guys. Both Denny and

Mark held red plastic cups. I glared through the screen door. *That better be iced tea in that red cup, Denny Baxter—*

"Jodi?"

Startled, I turned to see Ruth standing behind me. Her face was red, her eyes bleary, and she was holding a tissue to her nose.

"Ruth! Are you all—"

"Need to get Ben . . . need to go." Ruth's voice wavered.

"Ruth . . . wait." I put my hands on her shoulders and could feel her trembling beneath my fingers. "Ruth, tell me what's wrong."

She began to cry in earnest then, stifling the sobs in an effort to be quiet. I pulled her into my arms, pulling past her resistance, pressing our heads together cheek to cheek, and just held her while she cried. A movement behind Ruth caught my eye, and I saw Avis hesitate in the doorway between the dining room and kitchen. I crooked a finger at her to come in.

After a minute or two, Ruth quieted and pulled back from my embrace, fumbling for a tissue and blowing her nose in a healthy snort. Avis came closer. "Ruth?"

Ruth turned her head. "I'm all right. Just need to leave . . . I'll get Ben—"

I was about to say, *You can't go! Then Yo-Yo will have to go, and her brothers aren't even back from the lake yet* . . . but Avis cut to the chase.

"Ruth, you've got a load as big as a dump truck on your shoulders. Let us help you carry it. Isn't that why God put this group together?"

Ruth just shook her head as fresh tears spilled down her cheeks.

"It has something to do with Florida and finding Carla . . . doesn't it." It was a statement, not a question. Avis put a firm arm around Ruth, who mopped her blotchy face and allowed herself to be walked back toward the living room. "Come on. Let's face into it. After all . . ." Avis gave Ruth's shoulder a tender shake. ". . . you're the one who told us Yada Yada means 'to be known, to make yourself known.'"

The group had gathered around Florida on the couch, their hands laid on her knees, her shoulders, her head as first one, then another, continued the prayers for Carla, for strength in the waiting, for a speedy reunion of Florida's family. Avis led Ruth back to her chair and waited quietly with her until there was a lull in the spoken prayers, even as various ones were murmuring, "Have mercy, Jesus" or, "Bless You, God."

I probably would have said a big "Amen!" at that point, bringing the prayer time to an end so Ruth could share whatever it was that was eating her up. I was afraid that if we didn't hurry, she would change her mind and leave. But Avis just turned the prayers.

"Father God, You have loved us so much . . . loved us in spite of all our imperfections. You sent Jesus and covered all our sins with His blood . . ." A general chorus of *thank Yous* and *hallelujahs* filled in the blanks. "Thank You for bringing Yada Yada together and allowing us to pray for one another. Thank You for answering those prayers, for sparing José's life, for finding Carla . . ."

The rest of the group pitched in. "Yes, You did!" "Thank ya!" "You're a good God!"

"Now give us that same kind of love for one another . . . give us ears to hear and hearts that are open to bear each other's burdens as we listen to our sister Ruth."

That took everyone by surprise. Eyes popped open as the women realized Avis meant it literally. I caught a few looks that said, *What's goin' on?* passing between folks as they took their seats.

"There's joy in this room because of the news Stu brought us," Avis said, "but there's also pain. One doesn't cancel the other out—we need to be able to bear both sorrow and joy at the same time." She lifted her eyebrows at the still-blotchy-faced woman beside her. "Ruth?"

For a moment, Ruth just shook her head and blew her nose, and I thought she couldn't do it. But then her voice croaked, "I . . . I wanted to leave, not spoil the celebration. But a mother hen, she is." Ruth jerked a shaky thumb at Avis. "Oh, Florida, of course you want your daughter back, and . . . and I want that for you. Yes, I do. But . . . but . . ." The tears started fresh.

"But what? What kind of 'but' you talkin' 'bout?" Florida's voice had an edge. Avis's prayer about "bearing each other's burdens" was going to be a hard sell if it had anything to do with not getting Carla back.

Ruth squeezed her eyes shut. Couldn't blame her. Maybe it would be easier to talk if she didn't have to look at the ring of skeptical faces.

"The family that's been raising Carla for . . . what? five . . . six years? I can't help thinking about *them.*" It was a good thing Ruth's eyes were closed, because Florida's eyes narrowed. Avis simply raised her hand to cut off any comments. "Because that's me," Ruth wailed. *"Me."*

More looks passed around the circle as Ruth took a big, shuddering breath. What in the world did she mean? When Ruth spoke again, her voice had lowered almost to a whisper and I had to lean forward to hear her. "A foster mother I was, years ago . . . three times I've been married and no kids. So my second husband and I, we decided enough of this moping! We'll adopt a kid through Jewish family services. Huh. But that process dragged on and on, so we went to DCFS and took a foster child, a beautiful little girl . . . mixed she was—Asian and black and maybe something else— and we had her for five years. Five years! And we loved her so much . . . and we wanted to adopt her. Nothing from her mother or father for five years—not a word! And all of a sudden, her daddy shows up and wants his 'baby girl' back. And they took her . . . they *took* her . . ."

The room was deathly silent except for Ruth's gut-wrenching wails. Yo-Yo was staring at her friend, open-mouthed. Avis simply held up her hand as if to say, *Just hold the comments and hear her out.* And, eyes still squeezed shut, Ruth's sobs finally quieted and she spoke again.

"Tore us apart, it did. My husband and I . . . we didn't make it. I . . . he . . ." Ruth seemed to sink into the memory, not crying this time, just revisiting the pain that drove them apart.

The room was hushed for a long time. Then Yo-Yo blurted, "But you and Ben—you practically took my brothers in while I was doin' time. And you smother-mother me, too, for that matter. Pretty good parents, if ya ask me."

Ruth opened her eyes and smiled at Yo-Yo in spite of her

dripping nose. "Yes, my Ben. Number Three. Helped me move on, Ben did. *And* meeting you and Jesus in the Cook County Jail. I thought I'd put it all behind me . . . until . . ." Ruth studied her lap, where she had shredded at least three soggy tissues. "Until Carla."

Florida leaned forward. "I'm gonna get Carla back, do you understand? Ain't gonna make no apologies for that. And I don't wanna feel sorry for the foster family that has to give her up. Does that make us enemies, Ruth?"

Ruth jerked her head up. "No! No . . . I'm sorry. So sorry. I shouldn't have—"

"Yes, you should," Avis said firmly. "Florida's story is her story . . . and Ruth's story is her story. A good reminder that *every* story has two sides, maybe more. And there's no way we can be a prayer group if we don't know each other's stories." She reached over and laid a hand on Ruth's knee. "Ruth, remember praying with Delores at the conference? All we knew was that José had been shot. Didn't know why . . . didn't know what. Some of us probably thought he was gangbanging, just didn't want to say it."

Ouch. Avis got me there.

"But did that stop us from praying? No, because Delores's pain became our pain. And we're praying with Florida, because she's our sister and God put us together in Yada Yada to stand with each other. If Yada Yada had existed when you were going through the fire, we would have prayed with you, too. It's not up to *us* to make the difficult decisions like King Solomon. What are we going to do, cut the baby in half?"

"Cut the baby in half? *What* are you talking about, Avis?" Yo-Yo sputtered.

The tension buckled and broke into laughter. Avis smiled. "Tell you later, Yo-Yo. All I want to say is, if the Yada Yada Prayer Group means anything at all, it means standing with each other *no matter what.*"

27

*D*enny and I stood on the front porch saying good-bye to our guests as Yada Yada, long-suffering spouses, empty dishes, and assorted offspring straggled out of the door. Emerald Enriquez had a hard time letting go of Amanda and made Edesa *promise* she could come with her the next time she gave Amanda a Spanish lesson. Yo-Yo's stepbrothers kick-boxed with the other boys on the sidewalk until Ben Garfield pulled up in the car he'd had to park two blocks away—and even then he had to yell, "Get in the car *now* or you'll walk home!"

Florida turned down Denny's offer to walk her and her boys to the el. "We'll be fine—don'tcha worry none. Delores, Edesa, and Emerald have to catch the train, too." She patted him on the arm, like some granny thanking an overzealous Boy Scout. "But that's very sweet, Denny." Florida cast me an impish eye. "Better hold on to your man, Jodi Baxter. Ya don't want ta train 'im this well then lose 'im to some hungry hussy."

Everyone in earshot laughed as Denny turned red . . . but remembering the comment later, it seemed an odd thing to say, teasing another woman that she might lose her husband to some "hussy." I mean, *ouch*. After all, we didn't really know everybody's story in Yada Yada when it came to men. Who had fathered Chanda's three kids? Had Adele ever been married? Ruth was on number three! Even Avis's love life was still a mystery.

Not that I was worried about Denny.

Avis was the last to leave, cradling her empty pan. "You two need any more help cleaning up?"

"Nah. We'll just let Willie Wonka lick the rest of the dishes." Denny's smirk lasted only a brief second. "But seriously . . . what happened in there? Ben heard his wife wailing, and I practically had to tackle him to keep him from ripping in there."

Avis leaned back against the porch railing and nodded at me to go ahead. Briefly I tried to tell Denny how Florida's search for her missing daughter had stirred up a lot of painful memories for Ruth, who'd been a foster parent wanting to adopt, but the child had been taken away from her. "When Stu showed up and said that Carla had been found—"

"Found!" Denny's jaw dropped. "Florida's daughter has been found? Why didn't you say something?"

Avis shook her head. "Sorry. We couldn't. The kids came back, and Florida didn't want to get Chris and Cedric's hopes up before she could check it out. And since it's a holiday weekend, she's going to have to wait till Tuesday."

"Whew." Denny sank down onto the top step. "That's huge.

But what about Florida and Ruth? I can only imagine . . . *sheesh.*"

I hadn't even had time to process for myself what had happened in my living room. Part of me wanted to just *think* about it for a while before trying to explain it. But Avis was studying a jet's contrail overhead, as though waiting for me to respond.

"Well, yeah. They both felt pretty raw . . . but Avis kept us from making it a 'foster care issue' and focused on what Ruth and Florida both needed in the painful situations they're in."

Avis shook her head. "Not me. That was God, no doubt about it. If I'd stopped to think about it, I would have hightailed it before putting myself between two she-bears with their fur up!"

Okay, so God deserved the credit. But I'd been awed by the simple truth Avis had spoken into the group, diffusing Florida's pointed challenge *("Does that make us enemies, Ruth?")* and enabling the rest of us to love both of them.

We had cried and prayed and hugged each of them and prayed some more. But the best moment for me was when Ruth reached out her hand to Florida and said, *"The wall I put between us . . . I am sorry. Can you forgive?"* And Florida, hesitating only a moment, had said, *"Guess I'd be poundin' new nails into the cross if I didn't forgive you, after all the forgivin' God's had to do for this sinner."* And she'd taken Ruth's hand and pulled her into an embrace.

We *really* had started having church then, but a few minutes later the kids arrived back from the lakefront, barging through the front door—all nine of them—and then standing in the doorway gawking at their mothers praising and crying and praying. Chanda had gotten so excited she'd started jumping up and down.

I'd reluctantly peeled myself away from the "party" and shooed the younger set toward the kitchen, where I let them dig into Stu's lemon bars and told them to hustle out to the back-yard. When Avis closed out Yada Yada ten minutes later and we drifted toward the back of the house, the lemon bars were gone. Only crumbs.

Didn't matter though. We'd been having a feast.

EVEN AVIS WAS GONE NOW. We let Josh drive Amanda to youth group at church, and Denny bagged the last of the trash while I put away leftovers and filled the dishwasher.

"So, did I overhear Yada Yada deciding to get together regu-larly after this?" Denny asked, lugging a bulging plastic trash bag through the kitchen, followed by an ever-hopeful Willie Wonka, who so far had not gotten to lick any dishes.

"Uh-huh. Chanda complained that not everybody got to share stuff for prayer today, so couldn't we meet again real soon? Several folks work on Saturday, so we're going to try every two weeks on Sunday—like five to seven. Might visit each other's churches now and then, too." I noticed Denny's puckered lips. "What? Will the car be a problem?"

His lips unpuckered. "Nope. Gotta get the kids to youth group but . . . okay, I kinda hate to give you up Sunday evenings when the kids are gone. Especially now that summer's just around the corner. That's been our special time, walking to the lake, stopping for coffee . . . you know. But if it's just every other week . . ." He shrugged. "Guess I can deal with it."

I followed him out the screen door as he headed for the trash can in the alley. I probably should have talked it over with Denny first before agreeing to meet with Yada Yada on a regular basis. But I'd been so glad the others wanted to, I hadn't even thought about it. I think everybody realized we couldn't "yada yada" in *either* sense—"becoming known" or "giving thanks to God by praising"—unless we actually met face to face.

"Bring that recycling bin, will ya?" Denny called back over his shoulder.

I bent down to pick up the blue recycling bin on the back porch, overflowing with empty liters of pop and tin cans . . . and two brown bottles. Beer bottles. So my eyes hadn't been fooling me when I'd looked out the screen door. I looked after Denny, who had disappeared behind the garage. Should I—?

I felt torn. I didn't really want to get into a fuss with Denny after such an amazing afternoon. On the other hand, I couldn't just ignore it, could I? There they were, sitting right in the recycle bin. And I had specifically *told* Denny I didn't want any beer at this party.

I picked up the blue bin. We met on the sidewalk as he came back toward the house. I stood in the way.

"Denny? I thought we had an understanding—no beer at this party. *Especially* at this party." I held out the recycling bin.

Denny puckered his lips again and looked aside, as though

studying our neighbors' fence. For a moment I thought he wasn't going to answer. But he turned back, his gray eyes flickering with ill-concealed impatience. "Jodi, I will tell you exactly what happened. But I'm getting tired of you questioning me like I'm a sneaky teenager." He took the recycling bin and walked it out through the back gate, then came back empty-handed.

"Ben Garfield came to this party. Remember Ben? Short Jewish guy who likes his beer."

I felt annoyed at his smart-aleck tone but kept my mouth shut.

"Mark and Ben and I are making small talk in the backyard while you and . . . and your Yada Yada thing"—he waved his hand in little circles toward the house—"go inside and do your stuff. And Ben asks, 'Say, Denny. Got any beer?' Just like that. And as it happens, I *do* have some beer. It's sitting out in the garage where my wife hid it. I didn't bring it up, I didn't put it out, but the guy asked for it. So what was I supposed to do, Jodi?"

This time I was the one who studied the neighbors' fence.

Denny shrugged. "So I told him, yeah, but it's not cold. Thought that might be the end of it, but Ben says, 'Stick a couple in the ice chest, will ya?' So I went to the garage, got a couple of beers, and stuck them in the ice chest. For Ben, Jodi."

Okay, so it wasn't Denny's idea. I should have dropped it right there. But I still felt betrayed. "What about Mark?"

"What about Mark?"

"What's Mark going to think? You didn't offer him one, did you?" My voice was rising and my temperature, too, imagining Mark telling Nony on the way home that Jodi's husband kept a stash of beer in the garage. "What about the kids? Did they see you drinking?"

Denny's eyes darkened, and he put his hands on his hips. "Last question, Jodi. *Ben* offered Mark one of the beers and Mark said, 'No thanks.' Simple as that. And yes, Ben was still drinking the second beer when all the kids came back. Nobody blinked an eye. Now . . . are we done here?"

No, I thought, *we're not done here. This wouldn't even be an issue if you hadn't bought those six-packs in the first place.* But Denny had already gone back into the house.

WHAT SHOULD HAVE BEEN a pleasant, peaceful Sunday evening after successfully pulling off Florida's sobriety party turned instead into Denny and me giving each other the silent treatment. I felt discouraged, like walking on a treadmill and getting nowhere. We had to talk about this sometime. What was with Denny, anyway? Why couldn't we talk about it without him getting all huffy? Or maybe I was the one who got huffy. But he *knew* this was a sore point for me. My parents would think we were on the road to perdition if they ever knew we had beer in the house with their grandchildren.

With Denny nursing his anger in front of the living room TV, I cast about for something to keep me busy. I supposed I *could* get a head start on those annoying construction-paper flowers to decorate my classroom for Parents Day . . . or make some baked beans for the picnic we'd been invited to tomorrow afternoon by some Uptown families who were barbecuing at Lighthouse Beach. But I didn't feel like it. Tomorrow was soon enough.

Ah. I spied the overflowing hamper in the bathroom. Hadn't touched the laundry all weekend. The perfect mindless task. Maybe I'd even do the kids' laundry—they deserved *something* for being such great party hosts for the Yada Yada kids all afternoon.

Dragging the laundry baskets from each bedroom into the dining room, I started sorting, wishing I was sorting wood and metal so I could drown out the canned TV laughter from some dumb "reality show" in the front room. I threw dark wash-and-wear into one pile *(bam! bam!* they'd go) . . . light-colored stuff into another *(crash!)* . . . bras, slips, and blouses into a cold-water pile *(bang!)*. . . jeans with sweats *(boom!)*—

Okay, I was angry. But the afternoon felt spoiled, like the yellowed underarms of my favorite white T-shirt. I tossed it in the pile of light stuff. There were other things I'd really wanted to tell Denny about what had happened that afternoon, like discovering that Florida and I had run into each other (almost literally!) twelve years ago. That still boggled my mind. *Couldn't* be just a coincidence . . . could it? I mean, not if I truly believed God was in charge of all our comings and goings. So what did it mean, that Florida had come back into my life, a totally changed person?

I tossed a pair of Josh's sweatpants onto the pile of jeans then picked them back up to remove a paper sticking out of one of the pockets. Why couldn't he remember to empty his pockets before he threw his clothes in the laundry? How many times had we had to tape dollar bills together or iron school papers—or worse, ruined a whole load with a renegade ballpoint pen?

I yanked the folded paper from the pocket and unfolded it. Stylized yellow butterflies rode a swirl of brilliant colors from top to bottom, advertising something about a "Teen Rave." What in the world was a teen rave? Sitting down on the floor in the middle of the piles of laundry, I studied the copy separated by the lemon yellow butterflies. "Teen Club! . . . Dance! . . . Alcohol Free! . . . No One Over 17 Admitted! . . . Fun! . . . Teens Only! . . . Rockin'! . . ."

I looked at the sweatpants. Josh had been wearing those sweats when he and the other kids went to the lake this afternoon. Did he actually think we'd let him go to a teen dance club? "Alcohol free" sounded good, but "No one *over* 17 admitted"? What—no chaperones? Red flags went up all over the place with *that* little tidbit. Where did he pick this up, anyway?

Stomping feet on the back porch brought Willie Wonka's nails clicking down the hallway from the living room toward the back door. Couldn't have heard it—must have felt the floor shaking. The dog paused, confused by the piles of laundry between him and his goal, then he executed a few awkward leaps and met Josh and Amanda at the back door.

28

*W*onka!" Amanda draped herself all over the chocolate Lab, just like she'd been doing ever since she was a three-year-old.

"Hey, Mom." Josh paused at the doorway between kitchen and dining room. "Doing laundry? On Sunday?"

I waved the flyer at him. "What's this?" I pasted on a smile.

"Oh. That." Josh shrugged and started to pick his way through the piles of clothes on the floor. "Just something Pete gave me."

"Pete?"

He sighed patiently. "Pete Spencer—Yo-Yo's brother."

"Yeah," Amanda butted in, holding one end of Willie Wonka's old knotted play sock and pulling him into the dining room, his teeth clamped on the other end. "Pete asked Josh and me to go to this teen dance club thing next weekend. He said it's really fun . . . no alcohol allowed . . . a place high school kids can go to have fun."

My anxiety level pushed up into the orange zone. Amanda had been invited, too? She was only fourteen!

"Josh, hold it." My son was about to disappear down the hall toward his bedroom. "It says 'No one over seventeen allowed.' That means there's no adult supervision."

Josh actually rolled his eyes at me. "No, Mother. The club owners are adults—gotta be, right? They *say* that so the place won't be crashed by college kids and party types." He looked down on me from his five feet eleven. "I thought you'd want us to go."

"*Want* you to! Why?"

"Because it's Pete asking us to go."

"But you hardly know Pete! And he's had a very rough life— his mom's an addict, his sister was in jail. I mean, kids like that easily get caught up in smoking or drinking or doing drugs, and I don't want—"

"Mom." Josh's voice took on a weary tone, as though explaining something to a child. "This Yada Yada thing today? They were *your* friends. You acted like you wanted us to be friends with their kids, right? So . . . we're just trying to be friends." He threw up his hands, turned, and disappeared into his room. At that moment he looked just like his father.

"Yeah, Mom," Amanda echoed. "Besides, Florida smokes and she's *your* friend. She was smoking right here."

"What do you mean?" Of course I knew Florida smoked, but I hadn't noticed her "dipping out for a cig" today.

"Out front—you know, when we were all eating in the back. Yo-Yo too."

Oh, great. Just great. I wanted to be friends with these women in Yada Yada. I really did. But I hadn't counted on what kinds of things my kids might pick up from the lifestyles of such a diverse group.

"Well, you're right," I said. "But those are habits they picked up before—" But Amanda and Willie Wonka were already tussling their way down the hall toward the living room.

Grrr. Why did I keep ending up on the losing end of arguments in this house? But I still felt uneasy about that flyer. I needed to talk with Denny . . . when we were talking again, that is.

I tossed the flyer on the dining room table and took the first load down to the basement. At least the washing machine was free. In fact, I hadn't seen our upstairs neighbors all weekend. Maybe they'd gone out of town for the holiday. I kinda wished they'd seen our multicultural backyard party today . . . maybe they wouldn't be so standoffish.

Upstairs I heard the phone ringing, then Amanda's voice a moment later. "Mo-om! It's for you!" I hustled up the basement stairs and picked up the kitchen extension.

"This is Jodi."

"Sista Jodee?" The Jamaican accent on the other end could be only one person.

"Oh!" I tried not to sound surprised. "Hi, Chanda."

"Sista Jodee?" The voice on the other end hesitated.

What did she want? Did she leave something at my house this afternoon? "I'm here, Chanda. What is it?" I heard a snuffling noise, like she might be crying.

"Sista Jodee, I got somethin' for Yada Yada to pray about, but

. . . I don't have a computer. Could you send it to other people by e-mail? I can't wait till our next meeting."

Couldn't help feeling good that Chanda had called *me*. "Sure, Chanda. I'll get a pencil . . . okay, go ahead."

Again I waited through some snuffling. When she did speak her voice was so quiet I missed what she said. "Try again, Chanda. I can barely hear you," I said, plugging my other ear.

"I . . . found a lump in my breast," she whispered from the other end. "I'm so scared, Sista Jodee. My mother, she died from breast cancer. What if . . . what if I got it too?"

I FELT OVERWHELMED by Chanda's phone call. No wonder she'd acted like a scared rabbit when she first got here today . . . and no wonder she'd been so eager to have Yada Yada meet again. Without being able to get in on the e-mail loop, she was pretty isolated from the prayer group except for one-on-one phone calls. And who did she know well enough in the group to just call and talk? Adele? Maybe, maybe not.

The TV was still going in the living room. Sounded like the whole family was in there now, laughing at some show. I was tempted to join them, to just let everything be *okay*. I even took a few steps in that direction, and then stopped. I did promise Chanda I'd send her prayer request on the e-loop. And—I groaned—I still had all this laundry to do.

I was still sitting at the computer when I heard the TV go off and a noisy threesome tromping down the hall. "'Night, Amanda! 'Night, Josh!" I called.

"'Night, Mom," they called back, disappearing into their caves—though I knew good and well they'd stay up late listening to music or reading or talking on the phone, because they could sleep in tomorrow. The teenage version of Memorial Day.

I sensed Denny standing in the hallway behind me, watching my back. Half-turning my head I said, "Denny?"

"Yeah?"

I turned and faced him. He looked so boyish standing there in his jeans, hands in his pockets. I knew he hated the distance that came between us when we quarreled, hated it as much as I did. "I . . . wanted to say thanks for everything you did today to help pull off Florida's party. Grilling, cleaning up . . . but mostly just liking my friends and showing it."

Denny hunched his shoulders and propped himself against the open archway between dining room and hallway. "Don't know if Nony said anything when you guys were meeting today, but sounds like she's putting a lot of pressure on Mark to emigrate to South Africa. But from what Mark says, it just ain't gonna happen. No way does he want to raise his sons in Africa."

"No . . . she didn't say anything today. But I'm not surprised." This wasn't what I wanted to talk about.

"I'd still like to hear more about how Stu 'found' Carla. What in the heck does that mean?"

"Sure." I drew a breath. "Wanna talk now?"

He peered at me for a long moment. He knew good and well

what I really wanted to talk about. "Tell you what . . . we both got a day off tomorrow. We'll talk then, okay?"

I tried not to let my disappointment show. But he was probably right—tomorrow would be better. We were both tired now. "I've got to spend some time at school getting ready for Parents Day this week," I reminded him. "And we're meeting the Whittakers and the Browns at Lighthouse Beach around four for a picnic."

"We'll make time," he promised. "Coming to bed?"

"Yeah. Give me a minute."

I turned back to the computer and stared at the e-mail message on the screen I'd been writing . . .

To: Yada Yada
From: BaxterBears@wahoo.com
Subject: Prayer Request from Chanda

It was GREAT to see everybody this afternoon. (We missed you, Hoshi!) What a fantastic way to celebrate Florida's five years of sobriety!

Chanda called this evening with a prayer request: She discovered a lump in her breast (last week?) and is really scared. Her mother died of breast cancer. She really wants our prayers. Don't think she's seen a doctor yet. She could use lots of encouragement.

Florida and Stu, please keep us up to date on what happens next, now that Carla is found. (Like Avis said, what an answer to prayer! I'm still praising the Lord!) We still need to pray, right?

Just a reminder to mark your calendars for two weeks from today. Adele said we could meet at her house that Sunday, five o'clock.

I'd been kinda surprised when Adele volunteered to host the next get-together of Yada Yada. 'Course we weren't going to do a party—just prayer. Still, I hadn't expected Adele to be the first volunteer.

I moved my cursor to "send," then hesitated. *". . . still praising the Lord"?* Hardly. I mean, yeah, *theoretically* I was still praising the Lord that Carla had been found. But I hadn't been doing any *actual* praising since Avis had said the last "Amen." And *"We still need to pray, right?"* Right. I seemed to recall promising God that morning that I'd "make it up to Him" when I hit the floor running with everything I had to do to get ready for church and Florida's party. But somehow it was easier to *talk* about praying for all these requests than actually *praying.*

I deleted the "still praising the Lord" phrase, hit "send," and shut down the computer.

I'd pray tomorrow. I really would.

29

*D*enny and I finally talked. Not exactly sure we came out at the same place, but at least we talked. I woke up early enough on Memorial Day to get some quiet time in the living room with my coffee, Willie Wonka, and Jesus. That was a good start. For a while I just soaked up the pleasure of not having to rush out of the house on a Monday morning and let myself fantasize about the day school would be out. Frankly, I could hardly wait. My first year teaching in a Chicago public school was hardly the high point of my teaching career—even with a good principal like Avis. Part of me longed for the third grade class I'd taught in Downers Grove, where everybody spoke standard English, and I only had to deal with thirty different personalities, not thirty different cultures.

I wasn't sure I was ever going to "get it." Frankly, I dreaded starting over again next fall with an entirely new class. A lot of the kids were sweet, but it only took one eight-year-old thug-in-the-making to ruin it for everyone, including me.

But I prayed. Prayed for Chanda and the fear she was dealing with, and that she'd suck up the courage to get to a doctor. Prayed for Ruth, for the loss of the little girl she'd hoped to adopt but instead lost forever. Prayed for Florida, that she could be reunited with Carla as soon as possible. Prayed for Carla, who hadn't seen her mommy in five years. *(Five years . . .* I couldn't even imagine not seeing Amanda for five years.) I even prayed for the foster family who would have to give her up.

And I prayed for Denny and me, that we could get over this little hump. *I mean, Jesus, we've been married almost twenty years— twenty good years—and we have learned to work out a lot of differences. How come we're suddenly tripping over this?*

I spent several hours at school, along with quite a few other teachers taking advantage of the holiday to decorate our classrooms, and felt pretty ready for the Parents Day coming up on Friday . . . providing Kevin kept his pencil to himself and didn't vandalize anybody's work, or we didn't have a bomb threat or something.

Denny and Josh were over at Touhy Park shooting baskets when I got home, and by the time they got home and showered, it was time to pack up the bratwurst, buns, charcoal, lighter fluid, and the hot beans I'd left baking in the oven and head for Lighthouse Beach.

So it was almost eight o'clock that evening before Denny and I had a chance to take a walk, leaving Amanda and Josh, over their protests about "homework," to clean up the picnic stuff. We walked hand in hand down Lunt Avenue toward Sheridan Road and ended up at Panini Panini sidewalk café, where we ordered iced coffee— decaf.

I told Denny everything Stu had told us about tracking down a foster child they thought was Carla. "That's gotta be tough," he said, twisting his iced coffee around and around on the round glass tabletop. "Tough for the family who's been taking care of her for five years, tough for Carla, tough for Florida who's been working so hard to put her life together again."

I pulled out the flyer Yo-Yo's brother had given to Josh and Amanda. "What do you think of this?" I asked, not wanting to wave all my red flags yet, since I didn't really have much ground to stick them in.

He gave it a good once over. "Hmm. I don't think so—not till we know a lot more about what goes on at these teen raves. So for this coming Saturday, anyway, it's out."

I gaped at him in happy relief. How did Denny do that? Yes or no—bam, that's it. Well, I'd let *him* tell Josh and Amanda.

We were silent for a while, slurping our iced coffees till we were sucking air at the bottom. After getting Denny's agreement on the teen rave thing, I hated bringing up a sore point. Maybe, like he said, I was making too big a deal over the whole thing. And I *could* take responsibility for jumping all over him.

I set down my plastic cup. "Denny? About yesterday . . . I really do see that you felt caught in the middle between Ben Garfield and me about the beer. And I'm sorry that I made it such a big issue . . ."

He tore his eyes away from the assorted species of humanity walking by the sidewalk café in everything from sloppy sandals to combat boots. "Okay, thanks. I appreciate your saying that."

"But I'm still confused about why you bought all that beer in the first place."

A finger tapped impatiently. "I thought we went over that."

"I know, but . . . " I'd thought of another point in my favor. "I mean, after your dad's heart attack last year, doesn't it make sense not to drink at all? I mean, that stuff tends to run in families."

He shrugged slightly. "Actually, there are a lot of studies that say a moderate amount of alcohol is good for your heart."

"But . . ." Frustration began to lick at the edges of our conversation. "It's not just that. We've got teenagers who are very impressionable. And what if we offend some of our new friends who got saved out of all sorts of addictions?"

He seemed to be studying my face. "That's really it, isn't it? It would embarrass you if your new friends saw a bottle of wine or some beer at our house."

"No! I . . ." I stopped. *Be honest, Jodi.* "Okay, yeah. I . . . I just don't want anybody to be offended, or think—"

"—or think your husband's a lush." Denny looked at me hard. Then, to my surprise, he leaned forward and took my hands. "Jodi. We've been married almost twenty years. Have I *ever* gotten drunk? Or abused alcohol in any way?"

I looked down at our entwined hands. "No, but . . ." Why couldn't he just not do it because I didn't want him to?

We sat in silence for a few moments as twilight settled over the city and the streetlights came on. The evening was warm and, if anything, the cars and foot traffic going up and down Sheridan Road grew thicker, like the ants that had found our picnic that afternoon.

Denny sighed. "Look, Jodi. It really bugs me the way you've been jumping all over me. Like you don't trust me. And I don't think I've given you any reason to do that. But let's call a truce. I won't stuff the refrigerator with beer, and I promise to be very circumspect when it comes to your friends. And *you* promise to give me the benefit of the doubt, okay? Romans fourteen, remember?"

I nodded grudgingly. Pastor Clark had given a good teaching last month from the fourteenth chapter of Romans on "Christian freedom" in what we eat and drink, while also being careful not to be a stumbling block for others or cause them to sin. But surely that wasn't the *only* Scripture passage that might apply here.

"Okay, come on." Denny pulled me to my feet. "That waiter is giving us the evil eye. 'Vacate that table, you miserable penny pinchers, or order some actual food!'"

I laughed as he pulled me toward the intersection to cross with the light. "Oh, gosh, Denny, I forgot to tell you the most amazing thing. Remember that time I picked up a panhandler—eons ago—and you got mad at me for being so naive?"

THE NEXT TWO WEEKS seemed to pile up on each other, like a rug runner that kept bunching up instead of lying flat. Parents Day was a success, more or less, though for the life of me I couldn't figure out why a third of my parents didn't even show. But now that June was here, the school day consisted mostly of corralling thirty young prisoners who had suddenly smelled freedom. "Get back in your seat!" "No, you went to the bathroom ten minutes ago." "Because I said so, that's why." "No punching!" The worst part was enduring the sullen looks of my young charges who acted like I had denied them parole.

If I had my way, it'd be against the law to have school after Memorial Day. But so far the Chicago School Board hadn't asked my opinion.

Josh and Amanda got several calls from church members for the Saturday teen workdays—washing windows, childcare, painting a stairwell—so they actually had an excuse when Pete called to ask if they were coming to the teen rave. I wondered if Yo-Yo had given permission for him to go. On the other hand, she worked at the deli Saturday nights. Maybe she didn't know.

Stu came to church on Sunday, but she said the earliest appointment Florida could get with DCFS was next week. Personally, I'd hate to be the social worker who told Florida she had to wait. Probably was walking around with a blistered ear.

I checked up on Yada Yada e-mail when I could. Lots more chatting since we'd met face to face at Florida's party. Even Ruth sent an e-mail telling Chanda to get her behind to the doctor right now or she'd come over and take her herself. I hit "reply" and reminded Ruth that Chanda didn't *have* e-mail, and she'd have to use the phone to threaten her.

Had to laugh, though. If we weren't careful, Ruth would smother-mother the lot of us. But I was so glad God had steered Yada Yada through *that* minefield.

Hoshi was still anxious about her parents' visit . . . Ricardo Enriquez still hadn't found a job—or Florida's husband, either, for that matter . . . Nony wanted Yada Yada to visit her church in Evanston—the Worship Center, or something like that—but said we could decide on a date when we got together at Adele's . . .

By the time the second Sunday of June rolled around, I was eager to see everybody in Yada Yada again—not to mention I could use some prayer-and-praise encouragement to make it through the last week of school. How did Avis keep her poise through all the ruckus? Teachers were harried, parents were complaining about grades, a fifth grader even had to go to the hospital because a classmate shot her in the eye with a rubber band and a paper clip!

Adele's apartment was practically close enough to walk to—only about ten blocks from our house—but Denny said, no, he wanted me to take the car and not be walking alone on the streets, especially coming home. Things were good with Denny and me since our talk—at least the "beer discussion" seemed to have dissipated.

I called up Avis and asked if she'd like a ride—one less parking place to have to find. As I packed my Bible and notebook into my tote bag, I noticed I still had the old flyer about the teen rave stuck in there. I was about to throw it out, then left it on the off chance I'd get a minute to ask Yo-Yo what she knew about these raves, since I could almost bet the subject would come up again.

It wasn't easy finding a parking place near Adele's apartment building on a Sunday afternoon. In fact, Avis and I circled the block at least two times hoping someone would pull out and leave us a space. Finally pulled into a lot that said, "For customers only! All others will be towed!" and crossed our fingers. Only had to walk two blocks to get to Adele's building.

We arrived at 5:10, afraid we were late. But Avis and I were actually the first ones. I sipped the glass of lemonade Adele pushed into my hand, and Avis admired Adele's collection of "All God's Children" figurines, while the others straggled in over the next thirty minutes. Couldn't really blame them—most had farther to come, and some, like Florida, didn't even have a car.

Adele's first-floor apartment seemed dark, and I realized all the blinds were pulled, even though it was still daylight. I had the urge to run from room to room, pulling up all the blinds and opening the windows, but I drowned the urge with more lemonade and joined Avis by the glass cabinet that held the cute collection of African-American figures. But finally everyone arrived who was coming, even Hoshi this time, who got a ride with Nony. Delores was on duty at the hospital, but Stu had picked up Edesa since she had to drive in on the Eisenhower Expressway from Oak Park anyway. I certainly hoped Stu's fancy silver Celica wouldn't be missing its hubcaps when we got done here today.

In my eagerness to give Florida a big hug, I knocked over the glass of lemonade I'd set on the floor, and it spilled all over my tote bag. "Better that than Adele's rug," Florida snickered under her breath, fishing out my Bible, notebook, keys, and wallet from the wet bag while I ran to find some paper towels in Adele's kitchen. When I came back to the living room, she was pulling out the now-soggy flyer.

"Hate to tell ya, Baxter," she teased, waving it around, "but you're over seventeen. If you're into Ecstasy, you'll have to get it at a forty-something rave."

I stopped, the wad of paper towels still in my hand. "What do you mean, Ecstasy?" Florida rolled her eyes. "Oh, girl, it's there right under your nose. Look." She shoved the flyer in front of my face. "See all those yellow butterflies? Yellow Butterfly—that's the street name for one kind of the Ecstasy drug. Red Camel . . . Boogie Nights . . . Cloud 9 . . . some others, too." She took the paper towels out of my hand and started to mop up the spilled lemonade. "You savin' that flyer for some reason?"

30

I was so shaken by Florida's casual drop that street drugs were being advertised in the flyer Pete had given my kids that I sat in a stupor for the next ten minutes, only vaguely aware that Avis had gently prodded the group past yakking all at once to starting our prayer time with some Scripture. I couldn't believe I even *discussed* whether Josh and Amanda should go to that teen rave. *But how was I to know, God? Do I have to be a recovering junkie to be aware of what's going on out there?*

I glanced at Yo-Yo, who sat slouched in her usual position, feet straight out, hands stuffed in the pockets of her boxy overalls. Why did she keep coming to Yada Yada anyway? After all, she wasn't even a Christian . . . well, at least she wasn't sure about "this Jesus stuff." But did she approve of these teen rave things her brother was going to? She was his guardian, for heaven's sake!

"Jodi!" An elbow in my side and Florida's hiss got my attention. "You okay? You whiter than Whitey right now."

I glanced at her sidelong. "Yeah, I'm okay," I whispered back. Then I giggled. "Whiter than Whitey, huh?" and she started to laugh, too. "Could be my problem," I added.

Avis looked up from her Bible and peered at us over the top of her reading glasses. But we both put on straight faces so she continued reading. "Seek the Lord while he may be found; call on him while he is near. Let the wicked forsake his way and the evil man his thoughts. Let him turn to the Lord, and he will have mercy on him, and to our God, for he will freely pardon. 'For my thoughts are not your thoughts, neither are your ways my ways,' declares the Lord. 'As the heavens are higher than the earth, so are my ways higher than your ways and my thoughts than your thoughts.'" Avis closed her Bible. "From Isaiah, chapter fifty-five," she said.

"Can I see that?" Yo-Yo said, actually sitting up and peering at the Bible next to her in Ruth's lap. "You mean God might go away and not be able to be found?"

I carefully peeled apart some pages in my Bible still clinging together with lemonade. Isaiah 55 was one of my favorite passages: *"Come, all you who are thirsty, come to the waters; and you who have no money, come, buy and eat. . . ."*

"I think the main point of the chapter," I pitched in, "is that God *can* be found now. Look at all the invitations—'come' . . . 'come to me' . . . 'seek' . . . 'call on him' . . . 'turn to the Lord.'"

"And all the promises if we do," Nony added. "'Buy wine and milk without money' . . . 'eat what is good' . . . 'your soul will delight in the richest fare' . . . 'he has endowed you with splendor.'"

"Wait, wait." Yo-Yo leaned forward. "Talk plain English, will ya? I don't get all this water and wine and milk stuff."

"Those are just figures of speech," Avis explained, "meaning God wants to fill our lives with good things, like giving water to a thirsty person, or food to someone who's hungry."

"Oh, Lord. Ain't that the truth." Florida punched the air. "Thank ya, Jesus."

"So how do you get all that good stuff?" Yo-Yo wanted to know. "I mean, coming to God—is that like coming to this prayer group? Or going to church and listening to God-talk?"

I felt a twinge of conscience for my ricocheting thoughts just a few minutes ago, questioning why Yo-Yo was even coming to the prayer group. Her presence had been suddenly threatening to me because of her brothers, because they'd come to my home and brought their damnable flyer with them . . . but here she was, basically asking how to come to God!

"I talk; you don't listen." Ruth wagged her head. "I told you already, you must believe Jesus is the promised Messiah."

Edesa nodded. "And accept Him as your personal Savior."

"What's that song Donnie McClurkin sings?" Adele snapped her fingers and burst out Jamaican style, "'Born, born, born again, yuh must be born again . . .'"

"Arrrgh!" Yo-Yo exploded. "There you go, using all those bozo buttons. You think people know what they mean, but *I don't get it.*"

I was intrigued. I'd grown up all my life with those "bozo buttons," as Yo-Yo called them. How did you break it down for someone like Yo-Yo who wasn't familiar with religious shorthand?

"It ain't that hard, girl," said Florida. "Remember Bob Dylan?—nah, you too young. But he had a song . . . 'Ya gotta serve somebody—might be the devil, might be the Lord, but ya gotta serve somebody'—or somethin' like that. Ya just gotta make a decision: Ya gonna sit on the fence? Or give your life to Jesus twenty-four seven—all day, every day. And if anybody asks ya what your religion is, you say, 'I'm a follower of Jesus Christ.' "

"Twenty-four seven?" Hoshi looked confused. "Is that what I should tell my parents when they come?"

"No, Hoshi." Avis tried to hide a smile. "Just tell them the last part—you're a follower of Jesus Christ."

"I get it." Yo-Yo sat back. "Okay. Let me think about that."

Avis nodded. "Do you have a Bible, Yo-Yo? I can give you some good scriptures to read."

"Nah. I tried reading the Bible. But it's too hard."

"Don't worry. We'll get you a modern translation—" She smiled at the face Yo-Yo made. "Sorry. A Bible in plain English."

"Okay."

"But Hoshi reminded us of one of the things we need to pray about—telling her parents that she has become 'a follower of Jesus Christ.' When are they coming, Hoshi?"

"First weeks August. Very short time."

"Any news about Carla . . . Florida? Stu?"

Both shook their heads. "Had me a meeting with DCFS last week," Florida said. "I think next time somebody needs to go with me so I don't lose my temper. Oh, girl, when they told me they were 'looking into it,' I let them have a piece of my mind. Ten, *twenty* pieces. Losing Carla's paperwork? Gimme a break! They better look into it *fast.*"

"I'm sorry, Florida," Stu said. "I'll try to go with you next time if I can."

"All right. We need to keep those prayers going." Avis glanced around the group. "Chanda, we've been praying for you since you put your prayer request on the e-loop. Any . . . news? Have you been to the doctor?"

Everybody looked at Chanda. As usual, she'd been sitting mute, her gray skirt and dark top blending into the dusky color of the room. Her hands started twisting the handkerchief she held in her lap. "Uh- huh, I did go, Friday . . . Ruth kept calling me up till I made an appointment at the St. Francis Clinic. But I don't got no insurance. Don't know how I'm going to pay for it—not 'less my numbers win."

Oh, brother. Not likely, I thought.

"The doctor, what did he say?" Ruth prodded.

"She. Doctor was a she, which helped some. She said it felt like a cyst thing. But she wants to stick a needle in it to make sure, and wants me to get one o' those mammogram things." Chanda's eyes filled, and her hands twisted the handkerchief tighter. "Oh God, I'm scared. Even if it's not . . . not . . . you know . . . I heard those mammogram machines flatten your breast like a pancake and it *hurts.* And I'm scared of needles. Even in my arm! But in my . . . in my . . . ?"

"Oh, honey." Adele rolled her eyes. "You can do it. You a normal size. Now, me? They hardly know what to do with these things." She spread her arms and puffed out her large bosom. Thank goodness I wasn't the only one who laughed.

"The aspiration they do with the needle's not so bad." Avis chimed in gently. "Really. One of us will go with you to hold your hand."

"What do you mean, not so bad? How do you know, Sista Avis?" Chanda looked doubtful.

Avis was silent for a moment, as though she hadn't intended to go this far, and suddenly the group seemed to hold its collective breath. Then she said quietly, "Because I've been through the whole nine yards."

Chanda's eyes widened. "You had breast cancer? Did you . . . did they take . . . ?"

Involuntarily ten pairs of eyes strayed to Avis's chest. She always wore loose-fitting things—tunics, big stylish tops in bold prints. Did that mean—?

"Whoa! Slow down, everybody." Avis shook her head. "No, I did not have a mastectomy. I did have a lumpectomy, because I did have cancer—but they found it early. It hadn't spread anyplace else. But even that . . ." Avis's mouth twitched, almost smiled.

"What!" several people cried together. All of us had a morbid fascination with this conversation. Avis, of all people! She'd told us more about herself in the last sixty seconds than I'd figured out in the last ten months.

"It's nothing, just . . ." Avis's shoulders started to shake, and her smile grew bigger. Good grief, she was laughing.

"What?" a few more people begged.

"It's not funny," Chanda sniffed.

"No, no, it's not funny. I'm sorry, Chanda. It's just that . . ." Avis shook her head, still grinning at her private joke.

"You better tell us, Avis Johnson," Florida said, "or we all be thinkin' you crazy."

"Already thinkin' that," Adele muttered.

That was the truth. This wasn't like Avis at all.

"All right." Avis tried to control herself. "Like I said, I had a lumpectomy, and they only took about one-fourth of my breast. Which I'm grateful for, believe me. But . . . to be honest, when I looked in the mirror, I still felt deformed. And I was worried . . ." She blinked rapidly, as though fighting some lurking tears. " . . . worried my husband might think so, too. I didn't want him looking at me, afraid of what he was thinking about my body—even though he kept assuring me it made no difference to him."

So there is *a Mr. Avis! Or was.* I was dying of curiosity. Why hadn't she ever talked about him before?

"Of course I had to go for all these checkups, and the next time I had a mammogram, the technician put these two little black plastic dots on either side of the scar so it would show up in the x-ray picture. And when I looked down at my breast . . ." Avis's shoulders started to shake again as she tried to control her laughter. " . . . it seemed like this little old man with no teeth was looking back up at me—you know . . . the puckered scar, the two little black eyes, and this protruding dark nose . . ."

Florida laughed right out loud. "Oh, girl, I can just *see* it!" And by that time, all the rest of us were cracking up.

"What did you *do?*" Nony said, grinning as big as the rest of us.

"Well, I started laughing—laughing so hard I could hardly stop. And the technician, she looks at me like I'm crazy. So I told her—"

"You told her?" Adele sputtered. "You *was* crazy, girl."

"Yes, she did look at me funny—especially when I asked her if she would just leave the two little black dots so I could show my husband."

At this, we all howled.

"You didn't!" Chanda eyes popped.

Avis got out a tissue from her purse and wiped her eyes. "I did. When he got home from work, I made him sit down on the couch, and I unbuttoned my blouse—"

"You go, girl!" Adele shouted.

"—and showed him the little old man with no teeth . . ." She could hardly go on, she was laughing so hard. But finally she gasped, "And we had the best laugh we'd had in a *looong* time."

So did Yada Yada. It took us a good five minutes to pick ourselves up and resume some semblance of order. But when we did, Ruth bluntly asked the question that was burning in my mind and probably everyone else's.

"Your husband, where is he now?"

Avis took a long shuddering breath and was quiet for a moment or two. When she spoke her voice had dropped, and she spoke almost reverently. "That's the hard part. He died two years later . . . from cancer."

31

Whew. Finding out that Avis had had breast cancer and that her husband had died of cancer was *huge*. Who would have known, as serene as she always seemed and so ready to "give glory to God" in every situation? Her hilarious story about visualizing "the little man with no teeth" on her "deformed breast" seemed so out of character for Avis . . . and yet, maybe not.

"Laughing together was so healing for Conrad and me!" she told us. "In fact, it helped prepare us for what lay ahead when he was diagnosed with pancreatic cancer. They couldn't operate— the cancer was too far advanced by the time he was diagnosed. But God showed us that even in the midst of a crisis, we can look for His gifts of joy and peace." She shook her head, half-smiling at the memory. "He wouldn't let our daughters be all sad and gloomy around him, even at the end, when he was bedridden and in a lot of pain. He'd crack jokes and tease them . . . and I'm so grateful.

Their memories of their dad are happy ones right up to the end, even though they miss him terribly. I'm only sorry he never met his namesake . . . Conrad Johnson the third." She threw up a hand. "Don't get me started on the grandbabies! I think maybe it's time to pray for Chanda."

And pray we did, gathering around our sister who cleaned houses on the North Shore, praying with many voices for healing. As part of the prayer, both Avis and Nony read a whole litany of "healing scriptures," claiming God's promises for health and wholeness for Chanda. I certainly believed God could heal, but I wasn't always comfortable thanking God in advance, like we *knew* for sure that's what He was going to do. In fact, I felt a little confused; Avis's husband had died, hadn't he? It was a little easier for me to pray that Chanda would experience God's peace in the middle of the uncertainty and that she could trust that God loved her and was working out His purposes in her life.

While we were still praying, the door buzzer sounded. "Ain't time yet," I heard Adele mutter, but she padded silently in her slippers for the front door. Shrill voices from the stairway took shape as Adele opened the door.

"Don't know this place! Take me home!"

"MaDear, you *are* home. Here's Adele—see?"

"Adele who?"

We heard Adele's sharp voice. "Sassy, you wasn't s'posed to come till eight. I got company."

"I know, I know. But . . . had to bring her home. She . . . never mind. Talk later. But I gotta go now. 'Bye, MaDear. Don't be mad, Adele. I'll call you." And footsteps retreated down the short flight leading out the front door of the apartment building.

The apartment door closed and Adele appeared back in her front room carrying a walker folded flat in one hand and dragging MaDear by the hand with her other. "Sit here," she commanded, lowering the elderly woman into the dining room chair she'd been sitting in earlier. "Shh, now. We're praying."

"Oh. Praying." Out of the corner of my eye I saw MaDear press her hands flat together in front of her sunken bosom and squeeze her eyes shut. "Yessuh, Jesus . . . thanks ya, Jesus . . . 'Alle-*lu*-jah . . . Yessuh, yessuh . . ."

Adele started to rejoin the group praying around Chanda, but Avis moved over to the little woman in the dining room chair and began to pray. The rest of the group followed her, several kneeling down in front of the chair, others taking MaDear's hands and holding them, and began to pray for Adele's mother as if she'd been there the whole time. MaDear's eyes opened and she looked from face to face, a smile beginning to soften the birdlike face.

"Adele? Adele? We having a party?" she said in her throaty voice.

"Sure we are, MaDear." Adele's own voice sounded husky.

Yada Yada prayed for MaDear for several minutes, then we drifted back to our places with the last few "Bless the Lords." Edesa opted for sitting on the floor with Yo-Yo so Adele could have her chair.

As the room quieted, Avis raised her eyebrows. "Anything else before we close out today?"

"What about you, Jodi?" Florida spoke up. "You always so busy keepin' everybody connected. What can we pray 'bout for you?"

Her question took me off guard. "Oh, well, I don't know . . . nothing really." That sounded lame, and I knew it.

"Maybe Jodi doesn't need our prayers." Adele's statement sounded more like a challenge.

"Of course I do," I tossed back. Where did she get off saying something like that? Every time I thought Adele and I were breaking ground, it felt like she broke the shovel over my head. "I *would* appreciate prayer for my kids . . . Josh and Amanda are going to Mexico on a mission trip the end of this month—a youth group thing. But I have to admit I'm anxious. All the terrorist threats . . . the turmoil in the Middle East . . . heightened security. It's not easy letting them go out of the country right now." *There*, I thought.

Avis nodded. "Of course. Anyone else?"

"Well, uh . . ." Yo-Yo scratched the back of her short, stand-up hair. "You all good at prayin', I know that. So maybe you can pray for me about this Jesus thing. You know, deciding to be a Jesus follower or however you said it, Florida."

Nony literally leaped out of her chair. "Halle*lu*jah!" she shouted. Adele's living room erupted with "Glory to God!" and "Praise Jesus!" Yo-Yo wanted to be a Christian! Now *that* was worth shouting about.

Yo-Yo stuck her hands in her pockets and hunched her shoulders till she could get a word in edgewise. "You guys finished? 'Cause it ain't like there's anything to shout about yet. I done some stuff . . . stuff I ain't proud of. What's God gonna say about that?"

I NEVER DID GET TO TALK TO YO-YO that evening about the teen rave flyer, but it seemed like a downer after the way we ended Yada Yada at Adele's apartment. I mentally made a note to call her sometime before we met again in two weeks, which Nony offered to host at her house in Evanston, just north of the city. "You're all invited to visit our church that Sunday, too, if you'd like," Nony had said. "Easy to find . . . the Worship Center on Dempster, just west of Dodge. Doesn't look like a church, though. We meet in a warehouse."

"Well, Jodi and Avis's church meets in a storefront," Edesa had joked. "Maybe you'll have to wait till Yada Yada comes to Iglesia del Espíritu Santo to visit a *real* church."

Avis was ecstatic on the way home. "You know, it was really Yo-Yo who encouraged us to hang in there with each other after the conference—to keep praying for Delores and José, remember? And, thanks to you, you got us all connected by e-mail. Maybe she didn't know it, but it was God's plan all along for us to hang in there for Yo-Yo, too, don't you think?"

"Absolutely." I laughed. "Avis, I am so high, I don't even think the car tires are touching the ground."

"Here." She fished around in her big purse and pulled out a CD. "Stick that in your CD player." In a few moments the car was filled with a mixture of gospel and praise and worship music.

I pulled up in front of Avis's apartment building and spied a parking space not far away. It gave me an idea. "Avis, could I come up for a few minutes? I'd like to see a picture of your husband . . .

if you don't mind. After the story you told tonight, I'd like to meet him because . . . that's part of you I didn't know about."

She hesitated just a millisecond. "Sure. Come on up."

I parked the car—thanking God for the mini-miracle of a parking space on the street at that time of evening—and followed Avis up to her second-floor apartment. It was . . . just like Avis. Elegant art prints on the walls, shiny wood floors—shoes off at the door, please—with bright-colored area rugs, beige-and-black furniture, bookcases filled with hardcover books, and silk flowers in curved opaque vases. Colorful translucent drapes were caught back from windows that boasted Venetian blinds, turned just so to let the light in and keep prying eyes from below out.

"It's beautiful, Avis," I breathed.

She walked over to a low bookcase, the top of which was covered with framed photographs, and picked up a five-by-seven silver frame. "This is Conrad."

The picture was actually Avis and Conrad, standing by the railing of a ship, his arm clutching her close. They were both wearing white slacks and marine blue shirts, setting off the rich deep color of their skin. Avis was laughing, holding on to a long headscarf that was blowing in the wind. Conrad was grinning at her, obviously thinking he was the luckiest man in the world.

"That was our twentieth anniversary," she said. "We took a cruise to the Caribbean. Our first and last." She pointed out the rest of the photographs. "Those are the three girls—Charette, Rochelle, and Natasha. Charette and Rochelle are married. This one is Charette's twins, Tabitha and Toby, last Christmas. And this . . ." She picked up a portrait of a toddler with loose black curls all over his head, grinning happily. ". . . is Conrad Johnson the third. Rochelle's baby. She gave the baby 'Johnson' as his middle name so he could carry his granddaddy's name."

"And Natasha?"

"She's in grad school at the University of Michigan. Comes home once in a blue moon."

I looked at the photo of Avis and Conrad on the cruise ship a long time, then finally set it down. "I wish I'd known him." I turned to her. "Why haven't you ever mentioned him before? He seems like a wonderful man."

Avis sat down on the love seat along the front windows, her gaze on the big elms lining the street. "Because . . . I miss him. It's not easy to talk about him. It's easier . . ." She hesitated. ". . . easier to just praise God for the good years we had, for giving him to me long enough to raise our girls." She turned away from the window. "But if you want to know the truth, Jodi, it's not easy to be around married couples. That's one reason I turned down your invitation to dinner, because I knew when I got home, I'd probably tear my hair out, I'd feel so lonely. I didn't mean to be rude, but . . ." She shrugged.

Avis . . . lonely? Tearing her hair out? I was trying to absorb this new picture of the calm, self-assured Avis Johnson, principal of Mary McLeod Bethune Elementary School, the praise and worship leader at Uptown Community Church, whose joy spilled over to the rest of us, helping us white folks worship, helping us be thankful.

"I'm so sorry, Avis. I didn't know." It was getting darker outside, and I really needed to get going. "How do you do it—keep going, I mean. You always seem so happy."

"I *am* happy. Really. As long as I keep my focus in the right place—right on Jesus and all the good things God has done for me. Or Satan rushes right in and makes me start feeling sorry for myself." She gave me a hug. "Thanks, Jodi . . . thanks for wanting to 'meet' Conrad. I think he'd like you, too."

THE DIGITAL CLOCK ON THE DASH glowed 8:13 as I turned on the ignition. Ohmigosh, I was supposed to pick up Josh and Amanda from youth group on my way home, and I totally forgot! I was sure they'd be home by now anyway, but just in case I drove down Morse Avenue past Uptown's storefront exterior . . . no lights.

Okay, so I blew it. We'd have to work out the Sunday night car thing on the nights Yada Yada wanted to meet. But I couldn't feel bad; the whole evening had been incredible. I reached over and turned up the volume on the CD player—and smiled. Avis had forgotten her CD.

I was halfway to the house from the garage before I noticed Denny sitting by himself on the back steps. "Hi! I'm home."

"Uh-huh. Heard you before I saw you."

"Heard me?—no, you didn't! The music wasn't that loud . . . was it?"

"Uh-huh. That loud." But he reached up and pulled me down on the step beside him. Twilight had settled over the neighborhood, smudging the row of garages along the alley into a gray base that sprouted a silhouette of treetops and power lines against the cobalt blue of the sky. Only then did I notice that he was balancing a bottle with one hand on his knee.

Well, what of it. We'd talked about it and called a truce. He'd asked me to trust him, and so I would.

"Um, sorry I'm late. Did the kids get home okay?"

"Yeah, they got a ride. But your name is mud."

"Oh dear." I sighed. "I better go apologize." I started to get up, but he pulled me back.

"Don't go. Not yet."

I waited, but he said nothing more. We sat in a circle of silence, hearing only the hum of traffic over on Sheridan Road and the muted squeal of an el train. I began to feel anxious; how long had Denny been sitting out here like this? I'd expected to find him in front of the TV watching baseball.

"Denny? Is something wrong?"

He took a big breath and let it out slowly. "The school board hasn't renewed my contract yet for next year."

"Hasn't . . . what does that mean?"

"Nothing yet. But they're talking budget cuts. And you know how it is: Last to come, first to go."

"Oh, Denny." I put my arm around his broad back and laid my head on his shoulder. "Oh, Denny . . . I'm so sorry." But for one brief second it tickled my fancy like good news. Maybe we'd move back to Downers Grove, pick up our life where'd we'd left off a year ago. Our old neighborhood, our old jobs, our old church . . .

But I knew that's not what Denny wanted. He'd had tenure at his job in Downers Grove, and he had taken the risk of moving into the city because he felt that's what God wanted him to do.

And Yada Yada . . . I suddenly realized I didn't want my old life. Not if it didn't include Yada Yada. Whatever my "destiny" was—as Evangelist Olivia Mitchell had put it—it had something to do with Yada Yada. We'd only been a prayer group for barely two months, and already it had been a roller coaster ride that left me breathless. Shaken up. Energized.

Wanting more.

32

But the idea of moving back to Downers Grove kept niggling at the edges of my thoughts, especially when I told Denny about the "yellow butterflies" on the flyer being a code for Ecstasy drugs at these teen raves. "I don't know, Denny," I said a couple of hours later as I turned back the handmade quilt covering our bed and crawled in. "This stuff scares me. Maybe we should have waited till the kids are out of high school and *then* moved to Rogers Park." My finger traced the circles of the "wedding ring" quilt my mother had made for us when we got married. Quilting . . . did anybody do that anymore? It seemed so quaint, so honorable, the stitches of a simpler life. Unfortunately, Amanda wouldn't get such a gift from my hands. Maybe I should give her this one . . .

Denny cut the bedside light and crawled in beside me, pulling me close, my head on his chest and our legs entwined. "Maybe. But we're fooling ourselves if we think our kids wouldn't face similar challenges out in the 'burbs. Drugs, sex, guns . . . they're everywhere. Remember Columbine? Safe town, safe school—or so everyone thought."

I shivered against the warmth of Denny's bare chest. I didn't want to think about Columbine. "What are we going to do, Denny?" I whispered into the dark. "About your job, I mean."

"Nothing yet. Pray, I guess. Hey—get Yada Yada praying. That ought to shake up the heavenlies."

FRANKLY, WE DIDN'T HAVE MUCH TIME to think *or* pray all that week, except on the run. Since it was the last week of school for all four of us, the kids had exams, Denny had to turn in phys. ed. grades and attend end-of-year award ceremonies for the different sports programs, and I had to give the bad news to three parents that their offspring would have to repeat third grade or get special tutoring this summer to bring their reading and math skills up to fourth-grade level. One parent did not take this well and accused me of everything from being a racist to committing "gross emotional abuse" for "letting" her child fail.

I wanted to go nose to nose with this outraged mother and tell her I would be more than happy to pass her child on to fourth grade because *I didn't want to have to suffer her kid in my class one more minute, much less another whole year!* But I didn't. She would, I said calmly, have to take up her complaints with Ms. Johnson.

On the last day of school, I used the money I'd collected from the Darn Lucky Box to buy Ho-Hos for my class, and gave back everybody's "lost" items who hadn't bothered—or been able—to redeem them with the requisite quarter.

When I got home, Amanda waved her report card under my nose. She'd passed Spanish! We celebrated by taking the kids out for pizza at Gullivers on Howard Street—Chicago pizza at its best, in our opinion. We might get an argument from friends who swore by Gino's or Giordano's or Carmen's . . . but let any visitor mention California pizza, or even New York pizza, and we united with one voice: *Any* Chicago pizzeria beat out the competition by a long shot.

Gullivers not only had great pizza, but it was practically a museum of Victorian chandeliers, antique wall mirrors, old paintings in ornamental frames, brass lamps in every shape and size, even marble busts and nymph-like maidens. The weather was nice enough that, we could have eaten in the inner courtyard, but we elected to sit in a booth, its thick wooden table polished dark and smooth by many arms and elbows. Denny slid in beside Amanda, and Josh beside me.

We had finished sharing the hot breadsticks and large Italian salad—"Ewww!" Amanda cried, throwing all the anchovies on Denny's plate—and had just started in on the large sausage pizza with mushrooms and black olives, when Denny brought up the yellow butterflies. "Did either of you know drugs would be available at that teen rave?"

Amanda's mouth fell open. "No! That's stupid! Why would they advertise it as 'alcohol free' and then sell drugs?"

"Good question," I muttered.

"Josh?"

Josh shook his head with a nonchalant shrug. "No . . . but I'm not really surprised."

"But you were actually thinking about going!" I protested.

"Hellooo. Mom, I see guys dealin' drugs all the time. If you want a guarantee that no drugs would show up *anywhere* I go, I'd have to join a monastery or somethin'."

I raised my eyebrows at Denny. *Say something!*

"Point taken," Denny said patiently. "But if kids get caught dealing drugs at school, they get busted. It's illegal. It's against the rules. The school works hard to keep drugs out. Even if it 'happens,' that *is* different from an event that blatantly sells drugs to teenagers. So, just to be clear: The answer is already 'no' to any party, social activity, or event that isn't supervised by responsible adults committed to a zero-tolerance policy when it comes to alcohol and drugs for underage kids."

"That wouldn't keep me from getting drugs if I wanted to." Josh tilted his chin defiantly.

I nearly choked on my pizza.

"*Chill,* Mom. I'm not going to pop some stupid Ecstasy pill or start doin' drugs. That's just my point. You guys sound like you don't trust us. It's my own *decision* that keeps me from messin' with drugs—not your rules."

I just stared at Josh, then at Denny, then at the pizza crust on my plate. I did trust my kids . . . didn't I? But I didn't trust the world "out there." They were still *kids,* after all!

"We do trust you, Josh." Denny's tone was gentle. "Amanda, too. We're proud of you both. But we're your parents, and we have a responsibility to put guidelines on what we feel is appropriate or not appropriate. At the same time, you're absolutely right. We can't protect you from everything—especially at your age, Josh. You're almost an adult, and bottom line? It is the decisions *you* make, the ones that come from within, that determine the way you will go."

Well, okay. That's a good speech from someone who was Mr. Party Animal in college. "Sometimes people make the wrong decisions." I kept my eyes on my plate, moving a piece of sausage around with my fork. "And some decisions have terrible consequences."

From the corner of my eye, I could tell Denny had leveled his gaze across the table at me. "Yes, people do make mistakes, Jodi. But sometimes that's part of the learning process."

Amanda sucked out the last of her soda. "Dad, can we get another pitcher of root beer? And about the party stuff . . . does that mean you don't want us to be friends with Pete and Jerry?"

"Yes, root beer . . . and yes, friends. But how about on your terms? Like inviting them to some of the youth activities at Uptown. Or a day at Great America or something."

Had to hand it to Denny. Frankly, I'd been thinking, *Friends? You gotta be kidding!* But that was a good idea, a Jesus idea, inviting Yo-Yo's brothers to stuff . . . maybe Chris Hickman, too, Florida's oldest. I didn't get the impression that Florida had found a regular church yet.

I just hoped my kids wouldn't get rebuffed like I had when I gave Nony that camp brochure.

JOSH AND AMANDA had another full day Saturday doing work projects to raise money for the mission trip. Hmm. We might have to pay our own kids to get the Baxter windows washed this year. But while they were gone, I decided to give Yo-Yo a call and just be straight up about the reen rave flyer—parent to parent. Besides, I'd been meaning to tell her she could borrow one of my modern English Bibles—or I'd give it to her, for that matter.

Yo-Yo picked up on the second ring. "Yeah?"

"Yo-Yo? It's me, Jodi."

"Oh, hey, Jodi. Whassup?"

I told her I had a "plain English" Bible she could have. "Okay. That's cool. Thanks, Jodi."

"Um . . . Yo-Yo?" Why was I such a big chicken about this? "Have you seen those flyers about teen raves—just for teenagers seventeen and under?"

"Yeah. I've seen 'em around."

"Did you know Pete gave one to Josh and Amanda and invited them to come?"

"*Pete* did?" The string of swear words that followed took me aback.

"I'm sure he was just trying to be friendly," I hastened to say. "But Florida clued us in on the yellow butterflies—"

"Jesus!"

I hesitated. I was pretty sure she wasn't calling on Jesus.

"Look, Yo-Yo, I'm not trying to get Pete in trouble or anything. We didn't let our kids go. Maybe Pete didn't go, either; I don't really know. Just wondered if you knew about it, and since both our kids—well, our kids and your brother—were talking about it, just wanted to compare notes, see what you think."

"He's busted; that's what I think." She expelled a long sigh. "But I gotta work evenings . . . it's hard keepin' an eye on what he's doin', 'specially Saturday night."

"Yeah, I know. We all gotta pray for our kids."

Yo-Yo laughed. "Guess I gotta get on the main line now, huh? Like all the rest o' you. Hey . . . you gonna visit Nony's church next week? Ruth and me was thinkin' of comin'—if I can get off Sunday. I'm tryin' to change my day off, but they ain't too happy about it."

As I hung up, I noticed my manicure was looking a little worse for wear. Rats. Guess there was no way it'd last long enough for the visit to Nony's church.

33

nly two weeks till the Uptown Community youth group left on their trip to Mexico, building houses with Habitat for Humanity. But now that school was out, we all slowed down in the Baxter household. Denny had been hired to coach some of the summer park leagues—not much money, but it helped, and he liked coaching the younger kids. Amanda had gotten hired as a "mother's helper" half-days for an Uptown mom who worked at home, so she was raking in the money big time. Josh wasn't so lucky. The ten-day mission trip made it difficult to pick up a summer job, so Denny put him to work painting the garage.

As for me, I had a list of "projects" as long as my arm that I wanted to do this summer. And for another thing, I'd promised God I'd be more faithful having a "quiet time" in the morning, to read my Bible and pray. But during my first "quiet time" of the summer, it occurred to me that that was an odd phrase. "Quiet time." That's what they called it at church camp when I was a kid, what every pastor or teen group leader or Bible study I'd ever been part of had called it—that, or "personal devotions."

No wonder I had never included out-loud praises to God in my devotions, or turned up the music and danced.

Denny and I had decided not to say anything to the kids about his job contract—not until we knew something for certain. So I hesitated to put that prayer request out on the e-loop, where Josh or Amanda might see it if any of the Yada Yada sisters commented on it by reply mail. We were meeting in less than a week anyway; I'd wait till then.

I checked e-mail from time to time but guessed the others in Yada Yada were like me. Now that we knew we were going to meet on a semiregular basis, fewer requests showed up on the e-list. But Chanda called me late in the week. She had an appointment for a mammogram the following Tuesday, and would I go with her? "Avis promised somebody would go with me," she pouted, "but everybody I've called so far got to work, and Avis doesn't return my calls. You done with school, though, right?"

I knew for a fact that Avis had gone to visit her grandkids this week, but she said she'd be back in time for Yada Yada on Sunday. But . . . this shouldn't have to fall on Avis's shoulders. "Sure, I could do that. Do you want me to pick you up?"

"That'd be great, Sista Jodee. That way I could take the babies. Didn't know where I was goin' to find a babysitter for them, anyway."

I smacked my forehead as I hung up. Taking care of Chanda's

"babies" was the last thing I wanted to do after so recently shedding myself of my thirty third-graders. *Calm down, Jodi. It's only a couple of hours. Just pack a bag of goodies, and you'll be fine.*

But Chanda's call reminded me that I hadn't heard anything from either Stu or Florida about what was happening in Carla's case, so finally I just picked up the phone.

"Girl, them people got so much red tape, I could plaster my walls with it," Florida steamed. "I gotta fill out half a zillion forms, take a drop, get a home visit . . . don't seem like no end to it."

I murmured something sympathetic, but frankly, I felt at a loss.

"Jodi . . . I *am* gonna get my girl back, ain't I?"

She was looking for reassurance from me? I wished Avis wasn't out of town, or that I could get Nony in on a conference call. But it was just me—me and whatever faith I could muster. Reaching deep, past my gutless human skepticism, I reached for the promises I *said* I believed.

"We gotta believe it, Florida. What's that thing you're always saying? God didn't bring you this far to leave you, right? Jesus said it only takes two to agree on something and 'it will be done for them by My Father in heaven.' And we're *all* standing together with you on this one."

"Where's it say that, Jodi?"

Oh, Lord. I knew lots of Scripture verses, just couldn't remember where to find them on demand. "I'll look it up and e-mail you the reference, okay?"

"Thanks, Jodi. See ya Sunday at Nony's. You goin' to her church in the mornin'?"

DENNY AND THE KIDS decided not to go with me to the Worship Center because Nony warned us that it sometimes ran "late-ish," and they all had stuff they wanted to do in the afternoon. We argued about who was going to get the car, but three to one beat me out (even though they *could* have walked to Morse Avenue— barely a mile). "Okay," I said, "but I need to be at Yada Yada by five o'clock. Get the car back in time—promise?"

Denny shrugged. "No problem." So I gave in and called Avis. No answer. Maybe she wasn't coming back till this afternoon. Who else lived close to me . . . Adele?

Rats. I'd rather not have to call her. But it didn't look like I had any choice. I dialed.

Adele picked me up in her Ford Escort at nine-thirty Sunday morning. We found the Worship Center in Evanston easily enough, but like Nony had said, it didn't *look* like a church. A plain building hunkered down in a small industrial strip on Dempster Street.

Inside, a young African-American woman with a pretty smile gave us both a big hug and handed us bulletins. Adele wasn't the "huggy" type, but she allowed it and we both made our way into the main room, which was two or three times bigger than Uptown's worship space, though rather cavernous and "warehousy." The chairs were nice, though. *Padded.* Uptown should take a clue. Banners hung up and down the two aisles, and the platform was decorated with big green plants and flowers and a nice backdrop that looked like it might once have been a theater prop in a Victorian play.

I thought the service had already begun, even though we got there before ten, which is when Nony said the service started, because several men and women were walking back and forth at the front, praying rather loudly. Adele and I sat about halfway back in the middle section, and I twisted around to see if I could spot Nony but didn't see anyone I recognized. But as the praise team filed up onto the platform and the musicians took their places, Ruth plopped down on the padded chair next to me.

"Where's Yo-Yo?" I whispered.

Ruth shook her head. "She asks; her boss says, 'What do you think this is, the Pope John deli? We *work* on Sunday." She patted my hand. "But she's coming to Yada Yada later on."

"Huh," I grunted. Now that Yo-Yo had become a Christian, working at a Jewish deli might be problematic as far as going to Sunday services.

Over the next half-hour, the Worship Center praise team launched into several vigorous praise songs, which were shown by overhead projector on the wall. We had to jockey a few seats down the row in order to see around one of the steel pillars that held up the roof. As we were singing something about "My miracle is coming . . . my breakthrough is on the way," I saw Nony and Mark come in with their two boys—along with Hoshi and a whole string of young adults who looked like university students. The Smiths all gave us big smiles but sat closer to the front. Mark, in a dark suit, looked even more handsome than I'd remembered. Nony was wearing a black slinky dress with a gauzy black-and-gold shawl over it and big gold earrings. Gosh, that woman knew how to dress, I thought enviously—though I knew the same outfit would look like a Halloween costume on me.

We'd been on our feet worshiping about half an hour when Florida pushed Chris and Cedric into the row in front of us, followed by Stu, who must have picked them up. Not a bad representation from Yada Yada, I thought.

Nony had said the vision of her nondenominational church was to be "a church of all nations," but except for half a dozen white folks and a few Hispanic and Asian folks, everyone else was black. Guess it wasn't any easier for an African-American church to attract people of other races than for a well-intentioned white church. It crossed my mind that if we merged Uptown Community and the Worship Center, *nobody* would have to feel like a minority.

We finally got to sit down as the worship leader called up Pastor Lyle Foster, who'd been sitting on the front row—and everybody stood up again and clapped and cheered. That blew my mind! I couldn't imagine Uptown cheering when Pastor Clark got up to preach, even though most people liked his teaching.

This ought to be good.

But if I thought it was time for the message, I had another think coming. "Pastor Lyle," though not a tall man, seemed to fill the stage with his energy. The next thing I knew he had begun to sing a song that he seemed to be making up on the spot; the instruments—a full set of drums, bongos, two saxophones, keyboard, and a tall, lovely woman on electric bass—picked it up quickly, and the praise team was backing him up like they'd known it all along. Several times in the next half-hour he said, "You all can sit down now," so of course I sat down. But it was like he was teasing, because thirty seconds later he and the musicians were off and running on another song.

We finally did sit down, but the pastor came off the platform and began walking around, followed by his elders or ministers—both men and women—laying his hands on people and praying for them. He called one woman out of her chair and prayed for her in the aisle, and *bam!* She fell backward and was caught by two strong men who laid her down gently as a woman covered her legs modestly with a burgundy-colored cloth.

All this seemed to be right up Adele's alley, because she was thanking God and praying in tongues all along.

They finally took an offering, dismissed the kids to "Youth Ministry," and I thought it was finally time for the sermon. But the pastor came off the platform again and asked a woman who'd been part of the praise team to come to the front. She looked to be thirty-five or so, maybe a single mom because the pastor started talking about how she was struggling to keep her head above water and make a home for her kids. Then he said, "The Spirit of God is telling me that we need to encourage this mother. I want ten people who have a twenty-dollar bill in their pocket to come up and bless our sister."

For a split second I thought, *Oh, how embarrassing! What if ten people don't go up?* But within thirty seconds, not only ten people went up, but fifteen . . . maybe twenty, or twenty-five! One of the ushers stood by and held a bucket, and when everyone had gone back to their seats, the pastor took the bucket and turned it upside down, raining money down over this woman's head, who by now was weeping and jumping and praising God.

34

*W*ow. Quite a service," I told Nony as we stood at the back of the church afterward. I had hardly noticed the time, though now my stomach was grumbling and my watch said 1:10. People streaming by stopped to welcome us "visitors" with outstretched hands, smiles, and hugs. During the announcement time, Nony had made us all stand and told her congregation that we were part of her prayer group from the Chicago Women's Conference and that we were visiting each other's churches.

"Well, you can stop right here," the pastor had joked. "See you all next week at ten o'clock sharp."

But right now I was anxious to get home, since in another four hours we'd be meeting at Nony's house for Yada Yada. I wondered what Stu would do, since she lived all the way in Oak Park—an hour from here on stop-and-go streets—and felt guilty, because I didn't really want to invite anyone to hang out at our house. But finally I asked if she needed a place to stay till Yada Yada met this evening and felt relieved when she said, no, she and Florida were going to hang out at the lake with the boys for a while then take them home and come back up to Evanston.

Well, she and Florida are getting thick, aren't they! I thought, caught between wanting to go home and chill for a few hours and wishing they'd invite me, too. But they didn't, so I left as I'd come, in Adele's car.

It was almost two o'clock when Adele dropped me off. "Thanks a lot for the ride, Adele." I peeked back into the window of her Ford Escort. I really should return the favor. "Do you want a ride this evening?"

Adele shook her head, chunky earrings swinging. "Tell you the truth, don't know if I'm gonna make it tonight."

"Oh." Adele didn't offer any explanation and just pulled away. I wondered what that meant for Chanda. As far as I knew, Chanda didn't have a car; didn't she usually come with Adele?

I felt annoyed. Did that mean I should pick up Chanda? I wasn't even sure where she lived, though I could easily look up her address on the Yada Yada list. Then, still standing on the sidewalk, I scolded myself. *There you go again, Jodi, thinking you have to make everything work out. Nobody asked you to pick up Chanda. If Chanda calls, fine. But until then, just leave it alone.*

Feeling better, I ran up the steps to the front door and let myself in with my key.

"Anybody home?" I called, but was only greeted with the *thump, thump, thump* of Willie Wonka's tail. He had positioned himself in the hallway where he could keep an eye on both ends of the house. Notes on the dining room table said Denny was playing softball with some of the guys . . . Josh was out on his bike doing the bike path along Lake Michigan . . . and Amanda had gone over to a friend's house from church and would go straight to youth group from there.

I was half-disappointed, half-glad. Disappointed because I was eager to tell Denny about the worship service this morning, wishing he'd gone with me . . . glad because I relished nobody needing anything from me for the next couple of hours.

I made a tuna sandwich, poured myself a glass of iced tea, and stretched out on the living room couch with a novel I'd been wanting to read. Willie Wonka plunked down with a *whumph!* alongside the couch and closed his eyes. Ah, this was what Sunday afternoons were supposed to be like.

But the temperature was rising, and soon the hot, muggy air felt like a sweating gorilla sitting on my chest. Peeling myself off the couch, I turned the fan in the front window on high and glanced at the sky. Enormous thunderheads billowed like neon white mushrooms above the building tops along Lunt Avenue. A storm was brewing. Well, let it. Maybe it would cool things off . . . though it would probably bring Denny and Josh home sooner than they'd like.

A CRACK OF THUNDER so loud it nearly split the house in two sent me flying off the couch like an electric shock. Where was I? . . . Why was it so dark? . . . It took a few seconds to realize I'd dozed off over my book.

I looked at my watch in the greenish gloom. Four-thirty! I should be leaving if I wanted to get to Yada Yada on time. "Denny?" I called out. No answer. Why wasn't he home? He'd promised!

Well, I'd get myself completely ready so I could dash when he got here with the car. No call from Chanda . . . that was good. I wouldn't have to take extra time picking her up. Hoped that meant she had a ride.

At twenty minutes to five, I was standing on the front porch, eyeing each car that came by with its headlights on. No rain yet, but flashes of lightning periodically lit up the brooding sky followed by grumbles of thunder.

I kept glancing at my watch: 4:45 . . . 4:50 . . . Where *was* Denny? He couldn't still be playing ball—not with the skies about to open the floodgates.

I'm not sure what made me go out to the garage, except it was five minutes to five, there was no sign of my husband, and I was mad. Leaving my tote bag with my Bible and notebook on the front porch, I covered the distance between front porch and garage in determined strides. The garage, of course, was empty. And so was the corner where I'd stashed the six-packs under the bushel basket.

"Hellooo!" Denny's voice wafted out the back door. "Car's out front."

I stormed into the house. Denny, his sweats covered with grass stains and mud streaks, was washing his hands at the kitchen sink. "You're late," I snapped. "Now I'll be late."

"Whoa!" He shook the water off his hands and reached for a hand towel. "You told me to have the car back by five o'clock." He pointed to the kitchen clock. "At the tone, it is now . . . five o'clock."

"Very funny. I said I had to *be there* by five. I should've left twenty minutes ago." I could smell the beer on his breath. "You've been drinking," I said flatly. "How many did you have?"

Denny's eyes narrowed. "Jodi, give it a *rest*, will ya?"

"You took the beer from the garage."

"So? You don't want it around the house. Might as well enjoy it with the guys." He threw the hand towel on the counter and headed for the shower. "Oh!" he tossed over his shoulder. "It looked like rain, so I took Larry home first."

"Oh, *right*." I followed Denny right on his heels. "You took Larry home first. You shouldn't even be driving, Denny Baxter."

Denny whirled at the bathroom door. "What is *that* supposed to mean?"

I crossed my arms and stared him down. "I can smell it on your breath. And if I can smell it, so could a cop! What if you'd had an accident? What if you got arrested on a DUI? What then, Denny? Your career as a coach would be over in a *blink*—not to mention any ministry with the guys at Uptown. Ever think of that, Denny? Huh?"

Denny was breathing hard, the muscles in his jaw pulsing.

The words kept coming. It was like I couldn't stop. I didn't even know whether I was mad or scared or worried or what. "And what about our reputation as a family? What about the kids? What about *me*? Don't you care?"

Denny snorted and leaned an arm on the doorpost. "Me? Nah. In fact, I did it on purpose. I said to myself, 'How can I make Jodi mad? I know, I'll give Larry a ride—that ought to waste ten minutes—and make Jodi late! And then, we'll get rip-roarin' drunk. That oughta be good for another ten.'" He rolled his eyes. "Sheesh!" Turning on his heel, he slammed the bathroom door behind him.

"Don't shut the door in my face!" I screamed. But the only sound on the other side of the door was the shower jets, turned on full force.

Shaking with anger, I glanced at my watch. Five-ten. Now I *really* was going to be late. I didn't even feel like going to Yada Yada . . . but no way did I want to just stand there being ignored, either. I stomped past Willie Wonka, who stood staring at me, tail hanging motionless, as I snatched up my tote bag on the front porch and headed for the minivan, which Denny had parked across the street.

Before I even got the door open, the clouds let loose.

By the time I got inside, slamming the door shut behind me, I was soaked.

"Oh, great," I seethed, turning on the ignition and flipping on the lights and windshield wipers. "This is just great. I'm going to look a mess."

I jerked the wheel and pulled the minivan out of the parking spot, slightly grazing the bumper of the car parked in front of me. Well, who cared. Not me. Denny shouldn't have parked so tight in that spot.

I clicked the wipers to their highest speed, but I still had a hard time seeing between the foggy windshield inside and the huge splats of rain coming fast and furious on the outside. But I navigated west toward Clark Street, the main drag that would take me north into Evanston.

Tears of frustration and anger rose to the surface. Why couldn't Denny just say, "I'm sorry" when he blew it instead of getting all defensive? I might still be late, but that certainly would've helped.

Not only that, but if I'd left *on time* I wouldn't have to drive in this deluge, either.

The windshield wipers chased the rain from side to side in a hopeless frenzy, but so far the downpour had showed no signs of slowing down. Had I even remembered to bring Nony's directions how to get to her house? They lived somewhere close to the university, in one of the north Evanston neighborhoods. It was going to be hard to see street signs and house numbers if the rain didn't break soon.

Clark Street was extra busy. A long row of headlights came toward me in the premature darkness; a long row of red taillights sparkled in the rain in front of me. Even as I gripped the steering wheel of the minivan, I tried to get a grip on my feelings. I didn't want to show up at Yada Yada mad as a wet hen and have to confess that Denny and I had just had a big fight about his drinking—what would that sound like? Besides, maybe it wasn't all Denny's fault. Had I just been mad at him for being late? Had I overreacted . . . again?

Up ahead, the next two lights turned green. Good. I'd make it through the first one for sure . . . could I make the next one at Howard Street, too? Howard was the east-west border between Chicago and Evanston, at which point Clark Street became

Chicago Avenue, a nice long stretch before another light. I pushed the accelerator slightly, keeping an eye on the speedometer to make sure it stayed near thirty miles per hour, even as the rain continued to hammer the roof.

The traffic moved steadily . . . I was going to make it . . . keep going, Jodi, don't slow down . . . just a couple more car lengths . . .

I was watching the light and didn't see the small hooded figure dash out into the street until I was almost upon it. "Oh God!" I yelled and stomped on the brake. I felt the car skid under me . . . in front of my headlights a face jerked my way—just a kid!

I jerked the wheel, but the car kept sliding sideways . . . I felt a sickening *thump* . . . "Noooooo!" I screamed, and only at the last second saw a pair of headlights heading straight for my driver's-side window—

35

I'm swimming . . . upward toward the light . . . all is silent around me, the silence of the ocean beneath the waves . . . but my lungs are bursting . . . pain wracks my side . . . I must break the surface and get a breath . . . but I can't move my arms . . . why can't I move? . . . voices . . . there are voices, but I don't know what they're saying . . . blurry faces above the water's surface . . . I must break through . . . must struggle to the top . . . must get a breath—

"She's coming around."

I hear the voice . . . close, so close, but just out of reach . . . the light behind my eyelids is bright . . . did I break the surface? . . . why does it hurt to breathe? . . . if I reach out my hands, will I be saved? . . . but, God, I can't move my arms!

"Jodi? Jodi Baxter? Can you open your eyes?"

With great effort, I managed to crack open my right eye—then closed it again against the bright light just inches from my face. But try as I would, I could not open my left eye.

"Jodi, can you hear me?" The voice was male. Insistent. Kind.

Yes! Yes, I can hear you! I tried to nod . . . but the most I could manage was a twitch. Panic rose in my throat like bile. Why couldn't I move my head? Why couldn't I move *period?*

A hand touched my arm. "Easy, Jodi," said the voice, "don't struggle. We've got you in a cervical collar and strapped to a backboard to keep you immobile—just until we can assess your injuries."

Injuries? What injuries? "What . . . where am I?" Was that croaking my voice? My lips felt dry and cracked, the words dry and cracked, too. Once again, I tried to open my eyes and found myself staring with one eye at a bright light at the end of a long metal arm.

A masked face moved between me and the light and looked down. The masculine voice behind the mask said, "Jodi, I am Doctor Lewinski, St. Francis Hospital. You've been in a car accident. We've called your husband—he'll be here soon. But we're going to take you to get some x-rays, okay? Can you tell me what hurts?"

What hurts? I wanted to take a deep breath, but anything beyond tiny, rapid breaths sent fire shooting across my chest. "Chest . . . side," I croaked. I forced my mind to roam over my body, trying to pinpoint the pain. "And . . . my leg . . . thigh . . ."

"Okay, good girl. We're going to take care of that . . . just hang on. We'll get those x-rays so we know what we're dealing with."

"JODI? Jodi, it's Denny."

The familiar voice pulled me once more through the fog into

the light. I willed both eyes to open. Denny's face hovered close to mine. Seeing the crinkles at the corners of his eyes, feeling his breath on my skin, sent a tear sliding down my cheek. "Denny . . ."

"That's one heck of a shiner you got there, babe." I could hear both tenderness and terror in his voice.

"Denny . . . what—?"

"Shh, shh, don't talk. Just want you to know I'm here."

I closed my eyes. Everything was going to be all right. Denny was here.

"MR. AND MRS. BAXTER?" A tallish man with close-cropped brown hair and angular features parted the curtain and came into the narrow examining space. "I'm Doctor Lewinski, chief resident of the ER." Through my cracked lids I saw the doctor—*sans* mask—shake Denny's hand. "We've got some good news."

Good news . . . good news, he said . . .

Dr. Lewinski consulted the clipboard he held in one hand. "Jodi's CAT scan shows no epidural or subdural hematoma, in spite of the nasty knock she got on the left side of her head. X-ray of her spine is normal, which is why we took her off the board and got rid of the collar."

I felt Denny grope for my hand and squeeze.

"Also, no collapsed lung—which can easily happen if a broken rib punctures the lung."

"Broken rib . . ." Denny sounded dazed.

"Several. That's giving her the most pain right now. But the left femur x-ray shows a midshaft fracture. We've got it splinted and wrapped in cold packs to keep the swelling down, but we'll have to put a rod in there, as soon as we're sure she's stabilized. And . . ." The doctor paused.

"And?" Denny repeated. I could hear the fear creep back into his voice.

"The CAT scan of her abdomen shows a badly ruptured spleen. We may be able to treat it without surgery as long as she's stable."

"What about . . . the cut on her head, and all the swelling? You know, her eye . . ."

"Superficial. A few stitches, mostly in the hairline—you won't even be able to see the scar."

Through my half-opened eyes, I watched Dr. Lewinski walk around the end of the bed and come close to me. "Don't mean to talk about you in third person, Mrs. Baxter—may I call you Jodi? Once the swelling goes down, you'll have a beaut of a black eye, but that'll go away in a week or two . . . Oh, by the way. You have visitors." He nodded soberly and headed for the door. "I'll send them in—but only for a few minutes."

My fingers curled around Denny's hand. *Don't leave me . . . don't leave me.*

"Mom!" Amanda's voice bounced into the room just ahead of her distraught face. "Ohmigosh! Dad—what happened? Mom?"

I could see Josh, tall and grim-faced, right behind his sister.

"Mom? What happened?" Amanda asked again.

I searched for words. "I . . . don't know . . . don't remember."

"But there's cops—"

"Not now, Amanda." Denny's voice was suddenly sharp. "Just give your mom some love, and we can talk later. The doctor was just here . . . good news! Mostly."

Amanda opened her mouth, but a shake of Denny's head shut it again. She bent over the railing and kissed me gently on the right side of my face. "Oh, Mom, get better real quick, okay?"

Wordlessly, Josh bent over the bed and kissed me on the forehead. My mouth twitched in an attempt to smile. He smelled like Denny's aftershave. Josh straightened and jerked a thumb toward the door. "Avis is here. C'mon, Amanda." He and Amanda disappeared out of my vision.

I tried to turn my head, but the movement created a stabbing pain near my left eye. "Avis?" I croaked. *How did Avis—?*

A commotion somewhere outside the curtain stirred up like a pot coming to boil. Voices argued; grew louder. Denny bent close to my ear and started talking rapidly. "Avis called me, worried because you didn't show up at Nony's—only seconds after I got a call from the hospital. I called Pastor Clark and he brought me straight to the hospital. Avis picked up the kids at youth group."

Avis drifted into my view, clutching her big Bible. "Hey, sister." She went around the bed and took my fingers, avoiding the tubes taped to the back of my hand. Her touch was gentle, her face calm. "Why didn't you just tell us you wanted Yada Yada to meet at St. Francis?"

I stared at her face, confused. I had no idea what she was talking about.

Avis smiled gently. "Sorry. Lame joke. But Yada Yada is here, praying in the waiting room. Pastor Clark, too." She looked at Denny. "Denny, you okay?"

The churning voices outside formed words, invading our curtained space. "Where is he? Where's my baby? I want to see my baby!"

I searched for Denny's eyes. "Is . . . someone's baby sick?" I managed.

Denny just shook his head, avoiding my eyes. "You stay here, Avis. I'm going to go see the kids a moment." I felt his fingers leave my hand.

Avis paged through her Bible. "Satan gave you a good lick, sister, but we're not going to just stand by while he messes with you. Here, listen to Psalm 103 . . . 'Praise the Lord, O my soul, all my inmost being, praise his holy name. Praise the Lord, O my soul, and forget not all his benefits—who forgives all your sins and heals all your diseases, who redeems your life from the pit and crowns you with love and compassion—"

"What do you mean, *dead?*" One voice outside rose above the others to a shriek. *"Not my baby! Not my baby! Oh God, no-ooooo."*

My fingers groped for Avis's hand. "What's . . . happening out there?"

"No, you keep listening to me, Jodi. 'The Lord is compassionate and gracious, slow to anger, abounding in love. He will not always accuse, nor will he harbor his anger forever—'"

"Who killed him? *Who killed him!*" I turned my face toward the screams, ignoring the shooting pain in my head. "Tell me who! . . . He's going to jail for this! He's going to pay!"

Avis's voice clothed the naked screams, pulling me back into the sound of her voice. "'He does not treat us as our sins deserve or repay us according to our iniquities. For as high as the heavens are above the earth, so great is his love. . . .'"

I tried to concentrate on the words she was reading. But I felt strange . . . lightheaded. I heard a sound behind my head. *Beep . . . beep . . . beep . . .*

A nurse swept the curtain aside, checking the machines just out of my sight. "Ma'am, you need to leave," she said to Avis. "Now." She swept out again, calling, "Dr. Lewinski? Get Dr. Lewinski, stat, in Number Seven!"

"Hold on to Jesus, Jodi." Avis's dark eyes locked on to mine. "He who is for you is stronger than he who is against you." And then she was gone.

My breaths were coming fast and shallow. "Avis? *Avis!* . . . Denny! I want Denny!"

36

I *was swimming again . . . swimming forward . . . but the water*
was loud, drumming on my head . . . something was holding
me back, clutching my middle in a viselike grip . . . Oh God, it
hurt . . .

Swipe, swipe . . . swipe, swipe . . . windshield wipers swept the
water from before my eyes . . . follow the red lights . . . bright lights
coming toward me . . .

A face! . . . a brown face in the water . . . lit up bright . . . lit up
scared . . . lit up—

I forced my eyes open. I felt sick as a dog. Immediately Denny's
face filled the space in front of my own. "You're awake." A smile
crinkled his gray eyes. "Doc says surgery went smooth as glass—
but you're going to have to stay a few days."

Pincers with jagged teeth seemed to grasp my whole left side,
from my ribs down to my leg. I fought a wave of nausea. A tube
hung out of my nose, taped to my face. "Hurts," I moaned.

"I know, babe. You're going to be okay, though. Just hang on."

I was vaguely aware when I got wheeled through the halls . . . an elevator . . . more halls . . . into a room. The bare walls were blue . . . no, gray . . . something. Tall ceilings, tall windows . . . like a reformatory or convent.

I dozed, fighting nausea every time I awoke. People came in and out . . . Dr. Lewinski . . . Pastor Clark . . . a male nurse . . . Nony and Mark . . . Piecing together different comments, I realized I was minus one mangled spleen and had a metal rod holding my left femur together.

"Where are . . . kids?" I asked Denny at one point.

"Avis took them home. Edesa is going to stay at the house with them. Josh is okay, but Amanda . . . well, she'll be all right with Edesa there." He brushed the hair from my forehead. "They love you, you know. They're worried . . . your folks, too. They'd be here in a millisecond, but your mom's had a bad chest cold and her doctor's worried about pneumonia. I told 'em to stay put; we'd take care of you."

I squirmed under his intense gaze. "I must look awful." I couldn't look good and feel this awful.

"You're alive. You look beautiful to me."

THAT FACE! . . . *the arms flailing . . . lit up bright . . . lit up scared . . .*

I opened my eyes. The pain had dulled. The nausea diminished.

Denny was asleep in a chair in the corner, one leg over the arm of the chair, his head slumped at an uncomfortable angle. A shadow of a beard covered his chin and jawline. I watched him, remembering . . .

We'd had a fight . . . I was late. Late and mad. It was raining—no, pouring. The kind of rain that flooded the sewers and left small lakes at every street corner. And dark too early. I was trying to make the green light, trying to hurry . . .

Denny stirred and stretched. "Hey, babe. How you feel?"

I took several slow breaths. It hurt, but I had to get some air. "I remember the accident."

Immediately Denny was at my side. "Don't think about it, Jodi. Right now you just gotta get—"

"A boy, he . . . he ran right in front of my car. It was raining. I could hardly see. I tried to stop . . . I jerked the wheel. That's . . . all I remember."

"That's okay, honey. We don't have to talk about this now." Denny fussed with my blankets and pointed to a basket of flowers on the windowsill. "Look. They're from Yada Yada—well, Stu sent them for everybody, I think."

I didn't see the flowers. I didn't see anything. *Only the face, the flailing arms . . .*

Another wave of nausea brought a vile taste into my mouth and I retched, but only spittle came dribbling out. Denny grabbed a tissue and dabbed at my mouth. "You okay?"

I focused on his eyes. "Denny . . . what about the boy? Is he . . . okay?"

Denny looked away.

"Tell me!"

Denny shook his head. "No. He . . . died last night."

I heard Denny's words, but they didn't compute at first. *Died? The boy died?* But as the words sank in, they flowed like ice water into my veins.

"I . . . hit him?"

Denny nodded, tears wetting his cheeks. "That's what they're saying. Nothing's for sure yet, not until they investigate—"

"They who?" My voice came out in a whisper.

"Uh . . . the police. When you're better they want to talk to you . . ."

I think Denny said more words, but it was like a dream and far away. *The boy . . . I hit him . . . I killed him . . . I killed a boy . . . somebody's child . . . killed him! Killed!*

I heard a scream, a scream piercing the blueness of the room, ripping it like fingernails on skin . . . I heard Denny's voice from far away . . . *"Don't, Jodi, don't!"* . . . footsteps came running . . . hands held me down . . .

The scream was my own.

WHEN I AWOKE, I couldn't remember where I was. What day was it? Why was I here? A blue room . . . bags of clear fluid hanging on a pole with long skinny tubes taped to my hands . . . my hands—tied by strips of cloth to the bedrails . . . why?

And then it all came back to me like getting smashed in the gut by a heavyweight boxer . . .

I screwed my eyes shut, trying to shut it out.

A car accident. I'd killed somebody. Killed . . . a boy.

The wail started in my aching gut and burst from my mouth. "Oh God, no-oo-ooo!"

"Jodi? I'm right here, girl." A cool hand touched my face, brushed the tears from my cheeks. I opened my eyes. Bright sunshine streaming in the tall window created a halo of light around Florida's dark face and tiny ringlets.

I groaned and turned my face away. *Oh God, does everybody know?* "Please! Pull the blinds."

"But the sun is shining! And look at all these flowers that keep coming in." She peered at the little cards. "Denny's folks . . . couple of families from Uptown Community—"

"I want it dark!" I snapped. I wanted to yell, *I don't want flowers, either! Don't people know I killed somebody? They oughta send the flowers to his funeral!*

"You gotta get a grip, girl, else they gonna leave you tied up so's you don't pull out all these tubes."

I refused to look at her. "Just . . . go away."

"Huh. You got some attitude there. Well, it won't work with me. I'm gone . . . all the way to this here chair." The room darkened, then I heard the plastic cushion on the corner chair *wheeze* as she plopped down.

I kept my eyes shut. Maybe she'd think I was asleep and leave. But I heard her humming and filing her nails.

Finally, I opened my eyes. "Where's Denny?" I whispered.

"Comin'. Avis, too. They gotta be here by ten o'clock. But

your man needed some sleep. He's been here nonstop since Sunday night."

I mulled on that for a moment. *Why ten o'clock?* Then it occurred to me that I didn't even know what day it was. "What's today?"

Florida got up out of the chair, came over to the side of the hospital bed, and looked me up and down. "Tuesday mornin'. When the sedation wears off, Doc says you can get up and walk a bit today—test out that walker over there."

She had to be kidding. "Don't feel like it," I mumbled. Tuesday . . . Tuesday . . . I was supposed to do something on Tuesday. But for the life of me, I couldn't remember what.

"Gotta. Doc says he'll take that tube outta your nose when you pass some gas."

I glared at her. "Why is the doctor telling *you* anything?"

Even in the now-shaded room, I could tell Florida was grinning ear to ear. "Told him I was family. The look on his face was priceless."

Oh, right. Like he believed her. I started to turn my head away again, then turned back. "Why ten o'clock?"

She shrugged. "Police want to talk to you, ask you about the accident. Denny said they had to wait till he could be here."

My lip trembled, and I started to cry. "I-I'm scared, Florida."

"Hey. Sure you scared. But it's gonna be all right. Police gotta do they job. They gotta talk to everybody when there's an accident—including you."

She thinks she knows what I did. Oh, God, if she really knew . . .

A middle-aged nurse I'd never seen before came in to take my vitals. "Good, you're awake, Mrs. Baxter. Can we take these off, now, hmm?" She looked at me over the tops of her glasses as if I were an erring child and proceeded to untie my wrists. I said nothing, just lay still and looked away.

Denny and Avis showed up shortly before ten. "My private taxi," he grinned, jerking a thumb at Avis, then leaned over the bed to give me a kiss.

I stared at the thin blanket making lumps and valleys over my body, gripping its edges in my fists. *Oh, right. I've also banged up the minivan, so now Denny has to bum rides from our friends.*

Avis touched my hand. "Yada Yada is praying around the clock for you, Jodi. Everybody sends their love."

Tears welled in my eyes, and I squeezed them shut. They could forget praying for me. They had *no idea* what they were praying about! Love me? Not if they knew. They should be mad—mad as hell! That would feel good. We could just yell at each other then. That's what I wanted to do . . . just yell! Yell bloody murder!

"Jodi?" Denny's voice broke into my stupor. "The, uh, police are here. They want to ask you some questions. Can you do that?"

"I don't know," I whispered, and started to cry.

"It's okay, honey. I'll help you."

I grasped the front of his sport shirt and pulled him close to me, "I don't want Avis and Florida here when the police . . ."

He turned and whispered something to Avis and Florida, who quietly left the room, passing two uniformed police officers who came in, holding their hats with the signature blue-checkered bands under their arms.

Déjà vu. Just a month ago, two Chicago policemen had come into José Enriquez's room, and Avis and I had tiptoed out. I'd wanted to hang back and listen then . . . were Avis and Florida listening just outside my door? *Go away!* I screamed at them in my mind.

"Mrs. Baxter?" The first police officer was African American, a good six feet and two hundred pounds, with a bull neck as wide as his ears. The other police officer was also male, but younger, thinner, with straight black hair, olive skin. Maybe Puerto Rican. "I'm Sergeant Shipp, and this is Officer Carillo."

I gripped Denny's hand. *It's not fair, God! Why can't I have that . . . that female officer with the ponytail who came to see José?* I hoped they'd ask me questions I could just answer yes or no. But Sergeant Shipp went digging. "Can you tell us what you remember about the accident?"

I looked frantically at Denny's face. He nodded at me encouragingly. "Just tell them what you told me yesterday, what you remembered."

I closed my eyes to see it again, but *the face* rose up so quickly, I quickly opened them. Breathing as deeply as my tightly bound ribs would allow, I told them about the heavy rain and the darkness . . . about the green light at Howard and Clark Streets . . . about the hooded figure that ran into the intersection in front of the minivan . . . stomping on the brake and jerking the wheel . . . about the bright headlights coming straight at me. "That's all I remember," I said weakly.

"Mrs. Baxter," the sergeant said, "you know by now that this accident involved a fatality. The young pedestrian died of injuries sustained when he was struck by a vehicle, possibly yours. Do you remember striking the young man?"

Panic began to rise in my throat, but Denny broke in. "Sergeant Shipp, are you saying there's a question about *which* vehicle struck the boy? If so, then I don't believe my wife is required to answer that question."

Sergeant Shipp snapped his notebook shut. "All right. That'll be all for now, Mrs. Baxter." The two men made for the door, but Sergeant Shipp beckoned for Denny to follow them. In the doorway, the officer lowered his voice, but it still carried into the room. "Mr. Baxter, we have at least three witnesses who are saying it was your wife's vehicle that struck the boy, and there are conflicting reports about who had the green light. The state's attorney is prepared to press charges."

"What—what charges?"

"Vehicular manslaughter. With or without gross negligence."

"But . . . it was an *accident*. It was raining. The boy ran out into traffic—"

"That may well be, Mr. Baxter. But my advice to you? Get a lawyer."

37

enny!" I grabbed my husband's hand as he returned to my bedside. "What did he mean, vehicular manslaughter with—?"

Denny put a finger to my mouth. "Don't worry, babe. Don't worry. The family is naturally upset and wanting to blame somebody. This isn't going to go anywhere."

I stared at Denny's face, reading the twitch in his jaw, the reluctance to look me straight in the eye . . . *Oh God! Oh God! This can't be happening!*

I looked away. "What's his name?"

"Who? The officer?"

I swallowed with difficulty. "The boy."

"Jodi, don't—"

"What's his *name?*"

Denny sighed. "Jamal Wilkins."

Jamal Wilkins . . . somebody's child . . . no more.

"How old was he?"

"Jodi, don't torture yourself like this!"

"Tell me!"

Denny sighed again. "Thirteen." He wandered over to the window and pulled the cord opening the blind so he could look out. "His friends say they were trying to cross the street to get under the overpass to get out of the rain. Jamal had his sweatshirt hood up and didn't see . . ."

The overpass that took the commuter train tracks over Howard Street into Evanston. Just a few more yards to safety and shelter.

Denny turned. "Should I go tell Avis and Florida they can come back in now?"

I shook my head. "No, please . . . tell them I'm sorry, but I want to rest."

Rest. That was a good one. I wasn't sure I would ever be able to close my eyes again without seeing that face.

BUT I DID SLEEP—slept as much as I could so I didn't have to think or talk. And each morning when I woke up, somebody from Yada Yada was already in the hospital room—usually Avis or Nony, walking around the room praying over me, over the machines, over the doctors. Even Yo-Yo showed up one morning, slouching in the corner chair in her typical pose. Like everybody else, she had opened the louvered blinds to let in the sun, and like every other morning, I wearily asked her to close them.

The light seemed obscene somehow, given the circumstances.

The nurses made me get out of bed and walk a little farther each day, using a walker. I felt like a prisoner of war, dressed in a humiliating gown that wouldn't stay closed in the back, hobbling on one good leg and an old-lady walker, with a nurse-guard trailing me, pushing the ever-present pole of liquid goodies to make sure I didn't run for it.

Denny went back to work on Wednesday—he'd already missed two days of his new summer job—but I didn't lack for visitors. Besides Pastor Clark's daily visit, Delores, Edesa, Stu, and Ruth all popped in at various visiting hours. Somebody in Yada Yada had probably made a "Visit Jodi" list, and I didn't need three guesses to know who.

Adele had showed up at noon on Wednesday, bringing with her a huge tube of hand cream with aloe. "I had two cancellations in a row," she announced, as though needing a reason to be there in the middle of the day. She picked up one of my hands and examined it critically. "Hmm. Gotta do something about these chicken claws." She squirted a huge gob of cream into her palm and worked it into the chapped skin of my hands, around the tape and tubes connecting me to the IV pole. I felt awkward with her massaging my neglected hands, but it felt so good and comforting that I didn't want her to stop—ever. It was the first time in five days that I felt like a woman.

To my surprise, I'd liked Adele's visit. She didn't try to talk to me or cheer me up; just rubbed my hands, layer after layer of thick hand cream. "Thank you," I whispered as she stepped away from the bed to make room for a male nurse who came in with a large paper cup with a plastic lid and straw.

"Let's get that tube out of your nose." The young man grasped the nasogastric tube that had been pumping fluid from my stomach. "Now, when I pull on this, I want you to cough. Okay?" Round glasses perched on his rather thin nose were topped by a shock of limp brown hair, making him look like a grown-up Harry Potter. He pulled, and I coughed . . . again and again. Felt like kicks in my side as the tube slowly emerged.

"Heard you passed gas this morning, Mrs. Baxter." He acted as if he was making casual conversation.

I rolled my eyes. "Oh brother." I could hear Adele snickering in the background.

The nurse was unperturbed. "Now that we've passed that milestone, Doc says to try some ginger ale today." He handed me the paper cup with the straw. "But go easy . . . only little sips."

I took a sip, then another. It tasted so good. I hadn't realized how parched my mouth and throat were for real liquid. I took a bigger sip . . . and suddenly it all came back up and then some, splatting all over the bed and the nurse's clean white tunic.

He stared at me as if I'd done it on purpose. "The basin, Mrs. Baxter. You're supposed to use the basin." A big sigh. "Guess we're going to have to change this bed again." He snatched the paper cup and took it with him as he headed for the door.

"Sorry," I squeaked, lying back weakly on the upraised bed. Did he have any *idea* how much it hurt to throw up when you had a big incision in your belly and five broken ribs?

The moment he was gone, Adele appeared at the side of the bed with a warm wet washcloth for my face. "That boy needs a stronger stomach if he's gonna be any kind o' *nurse,"* she muttered, barely concealing a grin.

DENNY AND THE KIDS usually appeared about suppertime and stayed a couple of hours in the evening. I was glad to see Josh and Amanda, but I desperately wanted some time alone to talk with Denny about what the police officer had said. We didn't know a lawyer—and couldn't afford one even if we did! What were we going to do? But no one was telling me anything.

Not that I had the courage to ask. I clung to the veneer of normalcy, the stream of nurses and visitors popping in and out like pinballs, the annoying shots and medications in little plastic cups, trips to the bathroom to see if I could "go," even the hated walks down the corridor with the back of my gown flapping. I was even glad when the night staff woke me up at intervals to take my vitals—anything to keep the nightmare of *that face,* lit up in my headlights, from taking over my sanity.

When the kids arrived on Thursday evening, Amanda eyed the "supper" tray of Jell-O and clear liquids an aide brought in. "Can't you eat any real food yet? It's been four days!"

I sighed. "My abdomen is still bloated. Dr. Lewinski calls it 'post-op ileus'—doc-talk for saying that my intestines are in shock and can't handle solid food yet."

Amanda looked anxiously at her father then back to me. "But when are they going to let you come home?"

"I don't know—I was hoping by this weekend." I reached out a hand to my daughter. "Gotta see you off to Mexico on Sunday." I tried on a smile.

"Uh, Mom." Josh cleared his throat. "We've been talking to Dad and thinking maybe we shouldn't go—not with you banged up like this. I mean, Dad's gotta work, and you're gonna need somebody to take care of you when you get home."

I stared at my children. I wanted to hug them, bawl all over their shoulders, thank them over and over for thinking of me. Yes, yes, I needed them, wanted them, didn't want them to go away to Mexico with its dirt roads and crazy bus drivers and unsafe water and terrorists just waiting to sneak over the border—

"No. Absolutely not."

"No? Why not? Look at you, Mom!"

I had looked at me in the bathroom mirror, and it wasn't pretty. "Because you two have looked forward to this trip for six months, and you've worked hard to earn the money, and it'll be a great experience, and you're going. I'm not dead, and by all accounts I'm going to recover and be back nagging you to death about cleaning your rooms."

Denny couldn't repress a smile. "I knew your mother wouldn't go for it."

"But who's going to take care of you, Mom?"

I rolled my eyes. "I'm *supposed* to get up and get around. At least at home I can wear some decent clothes so I don't shock

Willie Wonka. See those crutches?" An aide had brought in a pair of elbow crutches for me to use to avoid hurting my cracked ribs. "By the time you get back from Mexico, I'm going to challenge you to a three-legged footrace."

By this time my husband and kids were laughing. Amanda leaned over and gave me a hug. "Thanks, Mom." She pulled back and studied my face. "But . . . are you sure? Because we really would be willing to stay."

"Absolutely sure."

The three of them left in high spirits. Mom was practically her old self again. She wanted them to go. Everything was going to be all right.

I watched the heavy door shut behind them, feeling heavy with guilt. They thought I was being wonderful and selfless. They had no idea how selfish I was being. I knew their offer to give up the trip and stay home "to take care of Mom" was sincere . . . but they would resent it. Resent *me*. Maybe even hate me for being so stupid and careless to have an accident, to ruin our car, and ruin their Mexico trip on top of it.

I couldn't bear it. Somewhere out there was a family who already hated me because I had taken away their son, their "baby." "Taken away?"—huh. Killed him. *Bam!*—like that. They wanted me in court, probably wanted me in jail . . . maybe wanted to ruin *my* family.

Great silent sobs welled up inside me, each one painful as they fought against my broken ribs and sore abdomen. Hot tears spilled down my face, and my nose started to run. I couldn't reach a tissue, so I just blew my nose on the bedsheet . . . but the tears wouldn't stop.

"Oh God! God!" I wailed out loud. "Where are You? Why did You let this happen? I don't care how banged up I am—but why did You let that boy die? Everything would be okay if he just wasn't *dead!* And Jesus isn't walking around Chicago these days raising dead boys back to life, is He! . . . *Is He!*"

The last two words were practically a scream, but the door stayed closed, and no visitors or nurses or aides came tripping in. I was alone . . . utterly abandoned and alone. Giving in to the fear and grief and confusion that were my life, I cried and cried and cried.

38

*D*r. Lewinski discharged me on Sunday. Guess I'd peed and pooped to the staff's satisfaction, because they started to give me real food the last two days and sent me home with a long list of instructions of what I could and couldn't (mostly couldn't) do for the next six weeks. "We'll need a follow-up x-ray on that leg and start you on some physical therapy," the doc said.

Denny picked me up in an old car that looked like something from Rent-a-Wreck. Somebody at Uptown was loaning it to us until the insurance paid up and we could get another car—but the insurance wasn't paying anything till they found out whether I was liable.

Guilty until proven innocent . . . now I knew what *that* felt like. But the loaner was okay if we didn't want to actually go anywhere— and it looked like I would be staying put for a while.

I got home in time to hug Amanda and Josh good-bye before they left in the church van for O'Hare Airport, where they would be boarding Mexicana Airlines for Mexico City. I hunched over my elbow crutches, looking at the two large duffel bags in the hallway, packed, zipped, locked, and ready. "I . . . wasn't here to help you get ready."

"Oh, Mom! Don't apologize! Edesa came over and helped us pack—except she made me and Josh wash our own clothes. Fold 'em, too." Amanda grinned, proud of herself. "But she knew just what to take for weather south of the border."

I wasn't apologizing, I thought mournfully. *I'm sad for me, that I missed it.*

And then it was another round of hugs and kisses and pats for Willie Wonka . . . and they were gone.

After waving good-bye from the front porch, Denny held the screen door for me. "Honey, let's get you in bed. You hungry? I could make you some tea and toast. And it's about time for your meds."

"Okay. Thanks." My whole midsection hurt, and I could hardly wait for the codeine-induced relief they'd sent home with me.

Denny turned back the wedding ring quilt on our bed, collected all the pillows from the kids' rooms to prop me up, and made sure I got in bed without falling over. Then he headed for the kitchen. I stared at the wedding ring quilt . . . and for the first time since the accident realized my long recovery was going to be hard on Denny, too. No sex, no cuddling, no fooling around.

Neither one of us had talked about the fight we'd had just before the accident. In a way it wasn't important, given the really big stuff we were dealing with now . . .

Or was it?

Willie Wonka pushed his nose over the side of the bed and tried to lick my hand, which was still bruised from the IV. I idly stroked his silky ears, but my thoughts were elsewhere, going backward, back to last Sunday night . . .

Denny had gotten home late. I'd said I had to be at Yada Yada "by five o'clock." He got the car home "by five o'clock" . . . so, okay, maybe that was a misunderstanding. I cringed, remembering how apoplectic I'd been that he made me late. I should probably apologize—

But wait a minute. Denny had been drinking; I had smelled it on his breath. Sure, I could apologize for the misunderstanding about the time—but what about *that?* Still . . . I couldn't very well say anything now, could I, since *I* was the one in deep doo-doo. He could throw it right back at me and get off clean as a whistle. After all, he wasn't the one who . . .

He wasn't the one who . . .

A horrible realization pushed itself into my consciousness. I'd accused Denny of being a danger behind the wheel—but *I* was the one who had been drunk on anger, driving hard, driving mad—

No! I couldn't think like that. It was an accident! It wasn't my fault! *It wasn't my fault!*

DENNY HAD BOUGHT A CELL PHONE and told me to call him immediately if I needed anything. He seemed really worried about going off to work and leaving me alone, but it was a relief. Small talk was hard for me when my whole world seemed like it was spinning out of control. After a week of doctors and nurses, being poked, prodded, and paraded, good ol' Willie Wonka was about the right kind of company I needed: practically deaf, undemanding, just there.

But around noon I heard a voice holler, "Hello? Jodi?"

I was lying in my darkened bedroom, not reading, not thinking, just in a kind of numb stupor. But I roused myself on one elbow. "Who's there?"

Footsteps came down the hallway. "Avis! I brought supper." The footsteps diverted through the dining room to the kitchen. A few minutes later she pushed open the half-closed bedroom door. "You okay?"

I *had* been, thank you. "Yeah, I'm okay. How'd you get in?"

She came in all the way and sat on the end of the bed. She was dressed casually, in white summer slacks, a blousy pale green top, and white thong sandals that stood out against her rich brown skin, even in the dim light. "Denny didn't tell you? He gave me a key, asked me to check up on you while he was at work."

"Ah." I fiddled with the quilt over my legs, conscious of my still bruised face and limp nightshirt. "Thanks for bringing us supper."

She waved a hand. "It's just mac 'n' cheese. One of the few things I can cook—everything else I touch turns out raw or charred!" She chuckled. "Just don't tell Yo-Yo."

I tried to smile, but I wasn't very good at it.

Avis dug around in her big leather purse. "Look, I brought you some CDs to listen to. Especially when you're home alone, it'll be good to fill your days with praise." She looked at me closely. "You're going to need some Word you can draw on, Jodi, when the going gets tough . . . oh! And I brought you this." She pulled a piece of paper out of her Bible. "It's a list of healing scriptures. When you don't know what to pray—" She waved the piece of paper. "—pray these. Especially Psalm 103, the one I circled. That one's for you, Jodi."

She stood up. "Want me to put it with your Bible?"

"Uh, sure. It's in my tote bag somewhere . . ." My tote bag had been in the now-wrecked minivan. "I'll have to ask Denny. Maybe he knows where it is."

"Okay. Want me to put one of these on now?" She held up one of the CDs.

"Uh, no, that's okay. I . . . think I'm going to sleep now for a while."

She knew I was stalling. But we both let my lame excuse stand. She came over and put both the piece of paper and the CDs in my lap. "Jodi, I don't know why God is taking you through this valley, this 'valley of the shadow of death,' but He's got a reason. A big reason. Go *through*, sister . . . go through."

A few minutes later, I heard the front door close, and all was quiet.

Yea, though I walk through the valley of the shadow of death, I will fear no evil . . .

How many times in my life had I repeated Psalm 23, feeling safe and secure, like that little lamb in the Sunday school pictures being carried by the Good Shepherd? But I had never really thought about what it meant to "walk through the valley of the shadow of death," and I *was* afraid.

AVIS'S PAN OF MACARONI AND CHEESE was so huge, Denny and I figured it would probably feed us for the rest of the week. But after reheating some for lunch the next day, I decided to freeze the rest and bring it out when the kids got home from Mexico.

I sat at the dining room table, blinds darkened, my crutches propped on a nearby chair, picking at my lunch and thinking about what Denny had said last night. He'd been very quiet when he came home from work—not at all like Denny, who was usually full of funny stories about the kids he was coaching in the summer park program . . .

"I talked to a lawyer last week—"

"What lawyer? We don't have a lawyer."

"We have one now. Stu gave me a couple of names of lawyers who handle cases like this."

I'd pressed my lips into a thin line. That meant Stu knew why we needed a lawyer.

"He called me today on the cell, wants to talk to you before the arraignment—"

"Arraignment?" My heart seemed to skip a beat. *"What does that mean?"*

"Like a hearing where the charges are read and bail is set. William Farrell—our lawyer—says it's routine; you don't have to appear, especially not in your condition. The defense lawyer is given a copy of the charges by the state's attorney's office, then a preliminary hearing is set. Maybe even next week."

Next week? I could feel my heart beating rapidly. So they really were going to press charges; I really was going to have to go to court.

"Why didn't he call and tell me?" I hadn't meant for my tone to be so challenging, but that's the way it came out.

Denny hid his exasperation well. *"Because you've just been through a terrible ordeal, and I don't want the lawyer or anyone else calling out of the blue upsetting you about this!"*

"I'm upset already." Tears had brimmed in my eyes and splashed down into Avis's macaroni and cheese.

Denny had reached out his hand and closed it over my own. *"I know, honey. Let's just talk to the lawyer tonight and let him take it from there. Maybe you won't even have to go."*

Not have to go? I'd clutched at the hope. *"But . . . it's my life they'll be talking about. Don't I get to say anything? Tell my story?"*

"I don't know, Jodi. This is new for me too. We just need to pray about it and ask others to be praying."

"I don't want other people praying about it!" I'd wailed. *"I don't want everybody knowing I'm being charged with . . . with vehicular manslaughter, or whatever he called it."*

I don't know how long I'd been sitting there toying with my food, going over the talk with William J. Farrell, Esquire, in our living room last evening, when I heard the front door being opened and another "Hellooo! Sista Jodee?"

That didn't sound like Avis. A Jamaican accent, more like . . . "Chanda!"

Chanda stood in the archway of the dining room, loaded to the gills with a bucket, a mop, rags, spray plastic bottles, and aerosol cans. "What in the world?"

She held up a key and grinned apologetically. "Don' mean to scare you. Denny gave it to me. But you never mind. I be blessed quiet—'cept when I vacuum. You got a vacuum?"

"Oh, Chanda." What was Denny thinking? We had a zillion hospital bills we hadn't even seen yet! "Denny shouldn't have asked—"

"'E didn't ask. I just tol' the mon I was comin'."

Chanda . . . something about Chanda. Suddenly I remembered. *That* was what I was supposed to do last Tuesday—take Chanda to get her mammogram. And I hadn't once thought to ask anybody what the outcome was.

"Last Tuesday . . . I'm so sorry I couldn't take you to your doctor's appointment. Did you find another way?"

"Oh, sure. Avis took me."

"And—?"

"T'ot you'd never ask. Got a mammogram, got a biopsy of that ol' lump." A wide smile took over her face, making her almost . . . pretty. "No cancer! Hallelujah, Jesus! No cancer!" Chanda dropped the bucket and mop and did a little shuffle dance right there in the archway.

"That's wonderful, Chanda. I'm so glad."

Chanda wheezed and fanned her face. "Given me history, it's a *miracle.* Now if I could just win the Big Lotto to pay off those doctor bills . . ." She picked up the bucket and headed for the kitchen. "All right if I use this sink?"

Oh, help. She really is going to clean my house. If I didn't feel completely useless before, I certainly did now.

I turned in my chair so I could see her through the kitchen

door. "Chanda?" Did I dare say anything? "Chanda, why don't you quit playing the lottery and buy some medical insurance with that money? Just a suggestion—but I wish you'd think about it."

"Oh. That's what I plan to do. Soon as I get me some winnings, I'm goin' to buy life insurance, medical insurance, a car, and take the kids to Disney World!" Chanda poured some liquid in the bucket and turned on the water in the sink.

Well, at least she didn't get mad at me for asking. I watched her start in on the kitchen—the sink was full of breakfast dishes—then hobbled back to my bedroom. How embarrassing to have one of your friends cleaning your house. I cringed; the bathroom was the pits, though I couldn't blame Denny and the kids with the crazy week they'd had. We ought to pay her something—she did it for a living, for goodness' sake!—but she'd probably feel insulted if we did, since it was her idea.

Why was everyone being so darn nice to me? I didn't deserve it. It'd be easier if they all just left me alone.

I took another pain pill and lay on the bed in the darkened bedroom, listening to the faint sounds of Chanda singing "Winna Mon" in that patois accent of hers, water running, huffs and thumps and chairs scraping.

Jesus, You did a miracle for Chanda. Why can't You do a miracle for me?

But I knew there would be no miracle. Not for Jodi Baxter. A boy was dead because of me, and I would have to live with the consequences.

39

By the end of the week, I was weaning myself off the pain medication and getting around pretty well on the elbow crutches. My broken ribs and ten-inch abdominal incision only hurt when I took big breaths—or cried or laughed—so I generally put a lock on my feelings and moved through the days and nights in a sort of detached stupor.

The Fourth of July came and went without any help from us, though Denny had the day off and did the laundry, watered the lawn and wilting flowers, and grilled some salmon fillets.

I missed Josh and Amanda so much. Their absence felt like another huge hole in my gut, right next to where my spleen used to be. But I was glad they were gone, glad I didn't have to be cheerful for their sakes.

Denny was attentive, trying to anticipate what I needed before I even knew myself, but we didn't talk much about the upcoming preliminary hearing, which had been scheduled for the following

Monday. If I let myself think about it, I might just freak out. So we made small talk, watched TV in the evening, even held hands while Denny prayed for the kids, for the family that was grieving, and thanked God that I was healing . . . but things felt distant between us.

I knew what was wrong—everything was wrong!—but I didn't know how to fix it.

The doorbell rang late Friday afternoon. Grumbling, I pulled myself off the bed and hobbled down the hall in reasonably good time, considering, and hoped it wasn't someone who was going to mind me opening the door dressed only in one of Denny's extra-large T-shirts and a pair of slipper-mocs.

It was Florida, holding out a bag of sub sandwiches.

"So why don't you have a key?" I turned my crutches around and headed into the living room and the safety of the couch.

"Key? What you talkin' about, girl? I don't got no key to your house."

"Never mind. Just thought Denny handed out keys to everybody in Yada Yada." I lowered myself onto the couch, with my bum left leg stretched out and my right leg on the floor—which put my back to Florida coming behind me from the foyer. "Why aren't you at work?"

Florida moved to the overstuffed chair facing me on the other end of the couch. "Girl, don't mess with me. You know I work the early shift; I get off at three. Decided to come see you and bring you some supper. But I'm getting a little tired of the attitude."

I sighed. "I'm sorry, Florida. Really. I appreciate you and everybody else who's been checking up on me. But—"

"But what?"

Did I have to spell it out? I looked away, but my breathing got heavy, sending little jabs of pain shooting from my sore ribs. "You all act like I had a skiing accident or something. 'Oh, poor Jodi, let's bring her some flowers'. . . 'Hi, Jodi, here's some supper.' Chanda came and cleaned my house, for cryin' out loud."

"So? You got a problem with people doin' nice for you?"

I closed my eyes for a moment, trying to slow my breathing. When I felt in control again, I opened them. Florida was sitting on the chair, arms folded, eyeing me like some mama waiting to hear the big whopper her kid was about to tell her.

"Yeah," I blurted. "Because I don't deserve it! Everybody's acting like there isn't a dead kid who got hit by *my car,* whose parents are so angry at me that they want me in jail. I've even got a copy of the charges from the state's attorney's office: The State of Illinois versus Jodi Baxter. Vehicular manslaughter . . . or hadn't you heard? Oh. And nobody mentions the fact that the kid was African American and I'm *white*—but I wouldn't be surprised if his family tells the media that it was a . . . a hate crime, that I did it on purpose or something."

I shocked myself. Why was I saying all this? Why was I dumping on Florida, of all people? *Jodi, you're a real jerk. She just came by to see you, and you're blabbering like an idiot.*

Florida got up out of the chair. For a second I thought she was going to leave, and I couldn't blame her. I opened my mouth to apologize, to beg her forgiveness—but instead she stood over me, hand on one hip while she shook a finger in my face with the other.

"Suck it *up*, Jodi Baxter! What does *deserve* got to do with anything? You think the only reason you're my friend is because you *deserved* it?"

"No, no! That's not what I meant. It's just—"

"Oh, I get it. You think you done somethin' *so* bad God just can't forgive you. So you mopin' around, keepin' all you blinds dark, like life just came to a stop."

I squirmed, wishing she'd back off.

But she bent down closer to my face. "Well, what makes you think you deserved God's love *before* the accident? Huh?" She straightened and walked around the living room with its comfortable furniture, plants in the windows, and pictures on the wall. "Oh, you been blessed all right. Nice house, nice kids, good husband, good life . . . but don't take no credit for it. You was *born* middle-class. You was *born* white. You was *born* in a family that already knew God and raised you right. Them three right there gave you a leg up and a head start, while some of the rest of us are still strugglin' out of the starting gate."

I watched as she paused and shuffled through some of the CDs by the music cabinet. *Take credit for it? Sounds like she's blaming me for it.*

Florida turned. "Know what your problem is, Jodi Baxter? You don't want to accept that *you're just like me.* I didn't deserve God's love when I was strung out on drugs, now, did I? But the thing that turned me around? I discovered He loved me anyway. Jesus died on that bloody cross to save *me*—and look how far He's brought me! With all your blessings, all your middle-class-white-American privileges, you don't deserve God's love, either. But *you* seem to forget that He loves you *anyway*, that He saved you, and ain't nothin' you can do gonna change that."

"I know all that." I pouted.

"In you head maybe. But deep down inside, you ain't figured out yet what it means to be just a sinner, saved by grace."

She looked at the CD she'd picked up and had been waving in the air like a punctuation mark. "Where'd you get this?" She held it out toward me. Somebody named Donnie McClurkin.

"Uh, Avis brought it, I think."

"You listened to it? . . . Or this?" She waved another CD at me. I squinted. Clint Brown. I shook my head.

"Girl, you a sad case. Well, you *listen* for a change. Maybe God let you have this accident to get your attention."

Florida put the first disc in the CD player, punched the "on" button, and handed me the remote. "I gotta go have me a cig—" She fished a pack of cigarettes out of her purse, then laughed. "Yeah, God's brought me this far, but I still got a ways to go." She headed for the front porch. "But you—just listen."

I couldn't very well turn off the CD player with Florida sitting just outside on the front porch, having her "cig." So I lay on the couch as the gospel music filled the room. How often did I take the time to really *listen* to music? Usually it was just background noise while I cooked supper or watered my plants or prepared a school lesson.

I listened . . . and by the third song, I had forgotten everything but the words filling the room, filling my head, pushing deep down into the emptiness of my soul. "Just for me-ee," Donnie McClurkin sang, "just for me . . . Jesus came and did it just for me."

Oh God, do I really believe that? Even if there had been no Hitler or Ku Klux Klan or gang murders or drug lords or 9/11 . . . would Jesus still have had to die on the cross to cover my sins?

A voice seemed to shake up the inside of my head. *"You're missing the point, Jodi! Not 'would Jesus have had to?' . . . Jesus did do it . . . just for you. Because God so loved you, Jodi . . ."*

I'm not sure I heard many of the next few songs until the end, when another grabbed my attention.

We fall down, but we get up . . .
For a saint is just a sinner who fell down . . . and got up.

If Florida came back in, I never heard her because I was weeping.

AMANDA CALLED LONG DISTANCE Saturday afternoon. She'd bought a calling card with her own money and breathlessly tried to tell us in three minutes how much work they'd gotten done on the cement block home they were building with Habitat for Humanity in the Mezquital Valley. "And I'm learning lots of Spanish, Mom! It's so different here! I want to take conversational Spanish next year. Edesa would help me, I know! Oh—are you getting better, Mom?"

"I'm fine. Just stay safe and boil your drinking water!"

The front doorbell rang, and Denny, who'd been on the kitchen extension, went to answer it while I got in a few words with Josh, then said good-bye.

Denny poked his head into the living room, where I was stretched out on the couch with the cordless. "Company." He sounded peculiarly pleased about something but ducked down the hall.

"Hey, girl." I heard Florida's voice before I saw her. After the way I'd treated her yesterday, I could hardly believe she was back already. Good. I wanted to—

"Got somebody I want you to meet." Florida sashayed into the living room, holding the hand of a young girl who followed reluctantly, sucking on two fingers.

I thought my heart was going to stop beating. "Oh! Is this . . . Carla?" I looked back and forth from Florida to the child, as though seeing Florida at eight years old. All across the front of her head, Carla's hair had been braided in tiny cornrows held with little butterfly clips, looking for all the world like a little tiara, behind which sprang a wonderful mane of bushy black curls. She stared shyly at the braided rug on the floor, clinging to Florida's hand.

Florida beamed in the dim coolness of the living room, "Praise God Almighty! Jesus! Yes it is." She tugged the girl closer. "Carla, this is Sister Jodi . . . she's been praying for you."

My chin quivered. I hadn't prayed for Carla even once since the accident.

Carla pulled Florida down till her ear was level with the girl's stage whisper. "Why is she crying? An' she's got a big yellow eye."

Florida glanced at the tears spilling down my still bruised face and smiled. "She's crying because she's so happy to see you." Florida sat down on the overstuffed chair and pulled Carla into her lap. "We get visits to start with. Carla's staying with me an' the boys for the weekend."

I found my voice. "Oh, yes, Carla. I am *so* happy to see you. Your . . . mommy is my very good friend, so—" I had intended to say, "*—so I know we'll be good friends, too.*" But I was having a hard time pushing words past the huge lump in my throat.

Just then Stu bustled through the open front door and into the living room. "Finding a parking place in this neighborhood is like going to the dentist," she announced. "No, a tax audit. Whatever. *Irritating* would be too mild a word." She stood in the middle of my living room, looking me over. "So, Jodi. You got dressed today. Good for you. What do you think of our girl?" She beamed at Carla.

I reached for a tissue and blew my nose, hiding the smile that threatened to put a crack in my crisis mentality, letting in a tiny ray of hope. If God could turn it around for Florida after all she'd been through, then maybe, just maybe, God would get me through this mess, too.

40

*D*enny wanted me to go to church with him Sunday morning, but I couldn't face all the Uptown people yet—not to mention the flight of stairs up to the second-floor meeting room. I needed more time.

"You want me to stay home with you? You've been alone a lot this week." He truly seemed distressed about that.

"No, that's okay. Somebody ought to represent the Baxter family. And besides, then you can tell me about the service." This would be the third Sunday in a row I'd missed worship at Uptown, and I *would* like to go if I could be a fly on the wall and just take in the worship and singing and the sermon. But nobody was going to let me be invisible.

"Well, okay, if you're sure," Denny said reluctantly. "But how about if we get out and take a walk by the lake this afternoon. Maybe we'll drive up to Evanston's lakefront—they've got a lot of walking paths."

Evanston's lakefront. That sounded good. Not a chance in a million I'd run into anybody I knew up there.

But the moment I heard the garage door close and the old junker rattle down the alley, I had second thoughts about church. Maybe it was a bad idea not to go. At least I would have been distracted for a few hours. As it was, I couldn't avoid the terrifying reality that *tomorrow* was the preliminary hearing about the charges being brought against me.

I hobbled into the dining room on my crutches and looked at the computer. Hadn't checked e-mail since before the accident. Just couldn't deal with cute forwards, spam ads, or even what had been going on in cyberspace with Yada Yada. Now might be a good time, though. It was something to do.

But I felt overwhelmed at the long list of e-mails that loaded into the inbox after I'd logged on. Halfheartedly I scrolled down through the list. Just as I predicted: a lot of "Fwd Fwd Fwds" with "You gotta read this!" or "So true!" in the subject line. I didn't even have the energy to delete them. I scrolled past a scattering of messages from various members of Yada Yada . . . old friends in Downers Grove who'd heard about my accident . . . messages for Denny and Josh and Amanda . . .

But one subject line caught my attention: "Vehicular manslaughter." My mouth went dry. I checked the sender: William J. Farrell to Denny Baxter. As though pushed forward by an unseen force, I clicked on it twice to open it.

To: Denny Baxter

From: William J. Farrell, Attorney at Law
Subject: Vehicular manslaughter

Denny,

I'll try to answer your questions as briefly as possible:

<*Why vehicular manslaughter?*>

This is not a killing with "malice aforethought," therefore not murder.

<*What exactly are we facing here?*>

Vehicular manslaughter can be charged in two ways: with "gross negligence" or without it. The former is a felony. The latter is what we call a "wobbler," which means the prosecution has the choice whether to charge felony or misdemeanor.

Your wife has no priors and wasn't drinking, so I am confident that *at most* she might face a misdemeanor charge. Depending on the evidence, a misdemeanor charge—if convicted—can carry with it the possibility of jail time up to a year, and/or a fine and probation.

<*Does Jodi have to attend the preliminary hearing?*>

Usually, yes. But if she can't be there, I can get a continuance until she's more recovered. I haven't heard the state's attorney's actual evidence—that will happen

Monday. But I'm working on a number of fronts to counter whatever "evidence" they think they have. No matter what happens, we will, of course, plead Not Guilty.

<We won't have to post bail?>

No. The document Jodi signed releases her on her personal recognizance. Even the state's attorney doesn't think your wife is a flight risk.

I felt frozen to the chair, even though the temperature was already well into the eighties. How could words like "a killing" and "murder"—even "not murder"—be associated with *me*, Jodi Baxter? I'd only had one traffic ticket in my entire life, and that was years ago when I got stopped for having an expired registration tag.

I stared in disbelief at the message. Words like "if convicted" and "jail time" swam before my eyes. Suddenly, I felt desperate to get rid of it, make it go away. With shaking hand, I moved the cursor to "delete" then closed the window, shut down the computer . . . and as an added measure, squeezed my sore body around the side of the computer desk and pulled the plug.

Now I was sweating. I needed to lie down. I swung my crutches toward the living room and the comfort of the couch—but knew I had to fill my mind with something, or the words would taunt me, shout me down in the silence. I stopped by the music cabinet and picked up the other CD Avis had brought me. Clint Brown. Never heard of him. But I stuck the disc in the changer, took the remote and the CD insert with me, and collapsed on the couch.

I hit the "play" button.

The music filled the room, rolling around me, over me, through me. No cutesy songs. Every song was about Jesus, about resting in His presence, about finding "strength while I'm waiting," about Jesus being "my everything."

Florida had said, *"Listen!"* I listened. I wanted the lyrics to drown out the terrifying words still knocking around in my brain. *A killing . . . not murder . . . felony . . . misdemeanor . . . prison . . . fine . . . not guilty . . . guilty . . .*

I concentrated on the next song. "Where would I be? You only know . . ."

Did God know I would make such a mess of my life?

"I'm glad You see through eyes of love . . ."

Exactly what Florida had said.

The voice on the CD seemed to be singing from inside of me, capturing every thought, feeling, and dread of the past two horrible weeks.

"A hopeless case, an empty place . . ."

O yes, God! That's me, that's me!

". . . if not for grace."

My eyes, wet with tears of self-pity, flew open. I hit the "repeat" button and listened to the song again. There it was.

". . . if not for grace."

I played the song again . . . and again . . . and again.

". . . if not for grace."

348

SOMEONE FROM UPTOWN COMMUNITY sent home a wonderful Sunday dinner with Denny—chicken stew with dumplings along with homemade rolls, crunchy coleslaw, and peach cobbler for dessert. For the first time since the accident, I actually felt hungry.

Then, true to his word, Denny got me and my crutches in the candidate for Rent-a-Wreck and drove up to Evanston's lakefront, where we walked slowly along the jogging path for about half an hour then sat on a bench and gawked at all the bikers, in-line skaters, stroller pushers, and dog-walkers enjoying the lakefront park.

I told Denny I'd read the lawyer's e-mail. He looked pained. "I didn't mean for you to see that."

I took as deep a breath as my ribs would allow. "Can't hide my head in the sand forever, can I?"

The walk wore me out completely, and I practically collapsed into bed when we got back home around four o'clock and fell asleep. I had a dream that I was lying in a plain wooden coffin, but I wasn't dead, and the lid wasn't on. And stamped all around the outside of the wooden coffin was the same word again and again: Grace . . . Grace . . . Grace.

I woke with the dream still clear in my mind and lay there thinking about it. The funny thing was that in the dream I wasn't panicky, but I just lay in the coffin, peaceful-like.

As I lay on the bed in that twilight between sleep and being awake, I thought I heard voices . . . and laughter. Now I really was awake. Who on earth could be here?

I looked at the clock beside the bed. Five-thirty. Reluctantly, I swung my legs over the side of the bed and got my crutches. I didn't really want company. But I was curious. I hobbled down the hallway, but even before I got to the living room, I could pick out voices: Florida bragging on Carla while Delores kept exclaiming, "Oh! *Es* wonderful!" . . .

I stood in the archway leaning on my crutches, giving the living room a once-over. Practically everybody from Yada Yada was there . . . except Chanda and Edesa. And Stu. I cleared my throat. *"What* are you guys doing here?"

"Hey, Sleeping Beauty waketh!" Yo-Yo called out over the hubbub.

Yeah, right. Though I did look a little bit more like a normal human being today, after getting a shampoo from Denny last night. The bruising on my face was almost gone, too; I'd even put on a little makeup for our afternoon outing. And the denim skirt and sleeveless top I was wearing hid the scars on my leg and abdomen.

"Why aren't you home with Carla?" I growled at Florida.

"You think I'd be here messin' with Yada Yada if I still had Carla? Ha. I had to take her back by three this afternoon. If I was home, I'd just be blubberin' on my sleeve, so I might as well be here."

"It's the Sunday Yada Yada is scheduled to meet," Avis explained.

"Knew *you* wouldn't come out," Ruth butted in, "so . . . to you we brought the Yada Yada!"

Gosh, she looked smug. "Why didn't anyone tell me?" I asked, exuding patience.

"You? You would've said no; that's because why!"

"That's it" . . . "Got that right."

Florida snickered. "So we asked that soft-hearted husband of yours, who we got wound around our little fingers."

Figured. Wasn't Denny supposed to be protecting me from overstimulation? But I let slip a grin. I was glad to see everybody, in spite of myself. My sisters. All of them. Even Adele. A few weeks ago, I could never have imagined that this group of women—like so many pairs of crazy, colorful socks—would become the kick-off-your-shoes-and-let-it-all-hang out kind of girlfriends I desperately needed. Yet God put us together in time to help me through the most difficult days of my life.

Yo-Yo scrambled up. "Okay, everybody. Off the couch. Pegleg, here, needs a place to prop it up."

"No, no." I moved quickly toward a chair. "Just give me that footstool. I'll be fine."

"You sure?" But Yo-Yo dragged over the footstool, and I sat in one of the dining room chairs Helpful Denny must have carried in.

"We won't keep you long." Avis was sitting on one end of the couch with her big Bible in her lap. "But tonight seemed like a good night to keep you covered in prayer."

So. Everybody has probably heard about the preliminary hearing tomorrow. I sighed. Couldn't keep it under wraps forever. Well, they were here, and I certainly did need the prayer. I cast a glance at Adele filling the La-Z-Boy, remembering her comment: *"Maybe Jodi doesn't need our prayers."*

She'd been right. I hadn't felt any real *need* for Yada Yada's prayers, though I'd been willing to scratch out some prayer requests. But now . . . *Oh God, yes, yes, I desperately need their prayers big time—especially since I really don't have a clue how to pray right now.*

Avis opened her Bible. "Just wanted to share a short parable that Jesus told about how we should pray."

I didn't have my Bible, so I just listened as she read the familiar parable from Luke 18 about the two men who went to the temple to pray. The Pharisee—upright citizen, religious leader—stood tall and thanked God that he wasn't a sinner like other men. He didn't rob banks or commit adultery or plot evil. He wasn't even a lowlife like the tax collector standing nearby. And the things he *did* do! Why, he fasted (twice a week!) and was faithful to pay his tithes down to the penny.

But (Avis continued reading) the other man—a tax collector, generally assumed by everyone in that day and age to be padding his own pockets—bowed his head and beat on his chest in remorse, crying out, "God, have mercy on me, a sinner!"

Avis shut her Bible, but those last words rang in my ears: *"God, have mercy on me, a sinner!"*

Florida had said I didn't really know what it meant to be "just a sinner, saved by grace." Did she mean . . . I was like that self-inflated Pharisee? The realization was shocking. Everybody knew the Pharisees were self-righteous bad guys.

But it was true. I was proud. *Hey, God, it's me, Jodi the "good girl"! God, aren't You proud of me? I've been married almost twenty-years—unlike Ruth, who's on her third husband, or Chanda, who has kids by several daddies. And thank You for my kids, off on their mission trip to build houses for Mexico's poor—while Yo-Yo's brother is sneaking off to those teen raves and doing who knows what. You should be proud of me, God, because I know the Bible from cover to cover (even though I forget those pesky references). And don't forget, God, I've never done drugs like Florida or even smoked a lousy cigarette! Have never forged a check like Yo-Yo . . . or played the stupid lottery like Chanda. But I'm no fuddy-duddy, God—why I occasionally drink wine on special occasions, but of course I'd never get drunk . . .*

But Jesus had said that it was the *other* man, the one who *knew* he was "just a sinner," who went home forgiven.

That "other" Jodi, the one who's basically selfish and petty . . . who flies off the handle at her husband . . . who was "driving angry" a couple of weeks back . . . the one who was driving too fast for weather conditions . . . who hit a young kid . . . and killed him . . . killed him . . .

"Oh *God!* Have *mercy* on me! I'm just a sinner! Have *mercy!*"

I didn't even realize I'd cried those words aloud, except that everybody looked startled and stared at me. Both Avis and Florida moved quickly to my side and began to pray. I couldn't stop the tears, but they didn't stop the prayers. Someone stuck a tissue into my hand, and then I felt Yada Yada gathering around my chair, as first one hand and then another was laid on my stuck-out foot, my head, even a gentle hand touching my belly.

"*Thank* You, Father, for Your great mercy!"

"Thank ya, *Jesus!*"

"*Gracias,* Father God . . ."

Nony's voice rose above the rest, and I recognized the psalm Avis had pushed me to read. "Thank You, Father, that You are compassionate and gracious, slow to anger, abounding in love! You will not always accuse, nor will You harbor anger against us for-ever! You do not treat us as our sins deserve . . . so great is Your love for those who fear You—"

I heard a strange sound out in the hall. Others heard it, too, and glanced at one another. It sounded like Denny . . . weeping.

I suddenly felt afraid. Why was he crying? I didn't think I'd ever heard my husband sob like that. I wanted to get up and go to him, but I saw Florida leave the huddle around my chair and head for the hallway. In a moment, she was back, her arm around Denny, pulling him into the middle of the circle.

Denny fell to his knees beside my chair, head bowed, hands on his knees, and continued to weep. I felt confused, but I reached out and laid my hand on his hair. Soft dark hair, flecked with gray. Beneath my fingers, I could feel the heaving of his body . . .

After several moments, his sobs quieted, and he pulled out his handkerchief, wiped his face, blew his nose, and looked at me. Around us Yada Yada seemed to hold its collective breath.

"I . . . heard you cry out . . . for mercy." Denny reached for my hand. "But I'm the one who needs to ask forgiveness—from God and from you. Because—" He swallowed. "Because I *did* have too many beers the Sunday of the accident. Four to be exact. It was . . . . stupid. I was irritated that you'd gone off to visit Nony's church instead of coming to Uptown with the family, jealous that Yada Yada was taking up half of our Sunday evenings . . . and scared, too, scared that I was going to lose my job and that we'd made a big mistake moving into the city. So while I was out playing ball with the guys, I thought, *What the heck? What difference does it make? Live a little, Baxter.*"

"Uh-huh," Florida muttered. "Been there."

I couldn't believe Denny was spilling our business like this in front of other people—a bunch of women at that. But . . . maybe it felt safer than just talking to me.

"But I didn't mean to make you late, Jodi. I thought you said to have the car back by five o'clock—"

"I know, I know." I was shredding the tissue I'd been given into little pieces on my lap.

"But I did wait till the last minute. On purpose. I wanted to make you sweat—but still get the car back on time. But then you jumped all over me for making you late, and it made me mad. And it made me mad that you smelled beer on my breath and accused me of drinking too much . . . but—" His voice dropped to a whisper. "—you were right. I just couldn't admit it. Didn't want to admit it. Didn't want you to be right . . ."

The room was incredibly quiet. Denny seemed to have forgotten everyone else and just kept his eyes on me. "But when the hospital called and said you'd been in an accident, said there'd been a fatality, I was terrified, because . . . I knew it was my fault!"

"No, no, Denny!" I moaned. It wasn't fair, Denny taking all the blame. "I was angry. I was distracted. Too angry to be driving in that rainstorm." I could hardly believe what I was saying, admitting how wrong I'd been to be "driving angry." But for some reason it felt okay, even in front of Yada Yada. After all, I was "just a sinner"—just like everybody else. Except I was the last person to know it.

But it was like Denny hadn't even heard me. "Jodi, will you forgive me? I can hardly bear the suffering you're going through— not just the surgery and your leg. That's bad enough. But the *charges* they're bringing against you, the *hearing* tomorrow . . . I'm so sorry. So sorry."

Behind me I heard Florida mutter, "Oh God, if you ain't God all by Yourself. Glory!"

I couldn't say anything; the lump in my throat was too big. But Denny just wrapped his arms around me, and we cried together as Avis and Florida and Nony and the others started praising and shouting and crying and thanking God.

Don't know who put on the CD—probably Florida—but suddenly the song she'd made me listen to yesterday filled the room . . .

We fall down, but we get up . . .
For a saint is just a sinner who fell down . . . and got up.

41

I awoke Monday morning to sunshine trying to stick its fingers through the cracks in the miniblinds. The digital clock read only 5:32. But I knew I couldn't go back to sleep.

Today was the day of the preliminary hearing.

Denny was still asleep, rolled over on his side, just a sheet covering the foothills of his hip and shoulder. I reached out beneath the sheet to touch him, to rest my hand on the curve of his hip, then pulled back my hand. I didn't want to wake him—not just yet.

I lay quietly on my back, thinking about Yada Yada last night . . .

After Denny and I had quit crying on each other's shoulder, the group insisted that Denny stay. He'd settled down on the floor beside the footstool, his back leaning against my chair. Avis asked us straight out what was going to happen at the preliminary hearing the next day. Denny laid it all out, everything we knew.

"You scared, Jodi?" Yo-Yo never waited for niceties.

Nothing like ripping open my emotional walls. *"Terrified."* To my surprise, it felt so good to admit it. *"If I'm convicted even of a misdemeanor, it could still mean—"* I'd swallowed hard. *"—jail time."*

"Yeah?" said Yo-Yo. *"Well, you won't be the first person in this group who's spent time in jail, will ya? And . . . here I am."* She'd spread her arms out. *"Still in one piece. And wiser, too."*

"But . . . my kids." I was close to weeping again.

"Uh-uh." Avis had shaken her head emphatically. *"We are not going to go straight to the worst that could happen. What are we going to pray for, Hoshi?"*

Hoshi had been very quiet, as usual. But she'd perked up at Avis's question. *"A miracle."*

"Delores?"

"I pray that Jodi and Denny have God's peace, no matter what."

"Adele?"

Adele had shrugged. *"Might as well go for the gold . . . and pray that the charges would be dropped."*

Avis had seemed satisfied. *"All right. That's what we're going to pray for—a miracle, God's absolute peace, and that the charges will be dropped."*

"And that God will get all the glory," Nony had added.

And so they'd prayed, and toward the end it seemed like everybody was praying at the same time, just thanking God for His salvation, His mercy, His grace . . . and I realized after a while that it was no longer about *me.* Florida, Avis, Delores . . . each one was thanking God for His mercy and grace *toward herself . . .*

Willie Wonka's nails clicked on the floor as the dog came into the room and nuzzled Denny's hand hanging over the side of the bed. *Time to let me outside, people!* his eyes seemed to say.

Denny rolled over on his back then turned his head and looked at me. "You awake already, Jodi?"

"Um-hm."

"You okay?"

"Um-hm."

He rolled over onto his other side, facing me, and stroked my face, tracing the still tender scar under my bangs where my head had hit the side window. "What are you thinking?"

I was quiet a moment, relishing the gentle touch of his hand on my face. "I'm thinking I want to go to the hearing."

"What?" Denny sat up so fast he whipped the sheet off my prone body. "Jodi, you don't have to go—not till you've healed more. The lawyer said he could ask for a continuance."

"I know. But why wait? Maybe it's more important to face my demons."

"Your . . . demons."

"My demons . . . my fears. If I stay home, I'll just be hiding. Not wanting anyone to know it's Jodi Baxter who killed that boy. Not wanting to face the accusations against me."

Denny stared at me as if I were a stranger who'd crawled into bed with him. "But, Jodi. What if Jamal's family is there?"

I nodded slowly. "That, too. I . . . hope they are." The look on Denny's face was so odd, it was almost funny. But I didn't laugh. "Will you go with me?"

"Go with—?" Then he did laugh. "How else would you get there, you goose—hitchhike?"

THE HEARING WAS SCHEDULED for ten o'clock at the Second District Circuit Court of Cook County in Skokie. I'd been surprised it wasn't at the big county courthouse on the South Side, but Mr. Farrell had told us the Skokie court handled all the North Side Chicago cases.

Denny let me out as close as possible to the entry of the sprawling two-story red-brick building at nine-thirty then disappeared into the parking garage. The courthouse was surrounded by one of the local forest preserves, almost parklike . . . except for the police cars driving in and out. I wondered how I was going to get through the revolving door with my crutches, but a security guard on the inside waved me over to a regular glass door marked with the blue handicapped logo.

As soon as Denny came through the revolving door, we got in line to go through security, but I set off the metal detector when I hobbled through it, and a security guard made me pass through again. The third time he made me hand over the crutches and I hopped through. The alarm still went off.

Exasperated, Denny barely kept his cool. "Look, she broke her leg, and it's got a metal rod in it. Can't you just wand her and let her go?" Which they did, but they made Denny empty his pockets *and* pull off his belt. They kept his penknife and said he could pick it up on the way out.

We finally headed up the escalator to the second floor and found Courtroom 206 about ten minutes to ten.

I don't know what I expected, but the beige-colored room wasn't that large. The judge, a balding black man with grandfatherly jowls who amply filled out his black robe, was already hearing a case. Our lawyer, William Farrell, was sitting in the empty, cushioned, jury seats, waiting our turn, I supposed. His sunburned face, topped with a thick head of auburn hair, looked up, surprised, and he hustled our way as Denny and I slid into the first of three pewlike benches at the back of the room. "Denny. Jodi," he murmured, shaking our hands. "You didn't have to come, you know. I was going to ask for a continuance, citing recovery time for your injuries, Jodi."

"I know." How could I explain that I needed to do this—now?

Two cases were dispatched in fairly quick order as we waited— one involving a man in drab, Department of Corrections garb, flanked by two Chicago police officers, who pled guilty to abuse of a controlled substance. The judge gave him a one-year sentence on the spot, minus thirty-three days he'd already served.

I stared at the man's back as the police officers led him out, suddenly feeling claustrophobic, like I might never leave this room a free person. I grabbed Denny's hand and held on tight.

A door marked "Conference Room" opened along the right side of the room, and a middle-aged white man in a rumpled tan suit came in followed by an African-American woman with close-cropped hair, small glasses, and gold hoop earrings framing a thin, tense face. She was accompanied by two boys—one nine or ten, the other an older teen—wearing T-shirts, baggy jeans with crotches to their knees, and big gym shoes with floppy laces, who stared at me as they sat at the far end of the pews. Mr. Farrell murmured something to Denny, who turned to me. "That's the assistant state's attorney," he whispered.

Must be Jamal's mother with him, I thought, looking straight ahead. *Are those his brothers?* My hands felt clammy. *Why did I think I was brave enough to do this?*

Someone slipped into the row behind us. I turned slightly. Avis! What was she doing here?

She leaned forward. "Thought you weren't coming," she murmured.

"So why are *you* here?" I whispered back.

"*Somebody* needs to pray over this hearing."

I faced forward again, but at that moment, my heart ached with love for Avis, who came all by herself just to pray, not even knowing we were going to be there.

God, when I "grow up," I want to think like Avis . . . be obedient like Avis . . . pray like Avis.

I cringed when the clerk read, "In the matter of the State of Illinois versus Jodi Baxter . . ." Mr. Farrell motioned for me to join him at the defense attorney's desk, which I did, feeling like every eye in the room was boring a hole in my back as I awkwardly made my way around chairs and railings. I tried to listen as the indictment was read but was distracted by the assistant state's attorney whispering to an aide, who hustled quickly out of the room. But all I heard was, " . . . resulting in the death of Jamal Wilkins, male, age thirteen" and "vehicular manslaughter."

"Mr. Prendergast. Are you ready to present the state's evidence?" The judge peered over the top of his glasses at the prosecuting attorney. The man shuffled some papers then made his way to one of the two podiums facing the judge.

"Uh, my witness has not arrived yet."

The judge raised his eyebrows. "Your *witness* has not arrived yet? Witness . . . singular?"

"Yes sir."

The judge paged through the papers in front of him. "It was my understanding, Mr. Prendergast, that the court would hear three witnesses at this preliminary hearing—two young men who were with the victim at the time of the accident, and a bystander, with sufficient evidence to take this case to trial."

"That's true, Your Honor. But . . . ah . . . the bystander is now uncertain she can verify the information she first gave to the police, and one of the boys with Jamal that day has declined to testify. I did not have time to serve a subpoena before this morning."

I heard William Farrell snort beside me, scribbling something with his pen.

The judge made his fingers into a tent, tapping his lips with the tips. "And your other witness?"

"Uh, we're waiting for him to arrive, sir."

The judge shook his head. "Counsel, approach the bench."

William Farrell patted my shoulder and joined the assistant state's attorney before the judge's bench. They bent their heads together, but I was close enough to hear the other attorney say something about "running a red light . . . exceeding the speed limit . . . talking on a cell phone."

I bit my lip to keep it from trembling. Running a red light? Exceeding the speed limit? I didn't . . . I hadn't . . . had I? But how could we ever prove it? It was going to be their word against mine. But the cell phone—that I *knew* wasn't true!

I glanced toward Denny. Behind him I could see Avis's eyes closed, her mouth moving . . . she was praying.

William Farrell was leaning on the front of the judge's bench, looking completely relaxed. He had told us that only the state's evidence would be presented at the "pre-lim"; the defense could cross-examine their witnesses, but any defense witnesses did not have to appear until trial. *What witnesses?* Just me?

The other attorney pointed toward Jamal Wilkins's family, obviously asking for more time for his witness to arrive. My heart was pounding in my ears. Would there be a continuance after all? We'd come today for nothing?

But the judged eyed the clock, leaned back in his chair, and shook his head. The two attorneys returned to their seats.

"Ms. Wilkins, I presume?" The judge addressed the woman sitting behind the prosecuting attorney. She gave a slight nod, her thin face a mask of controlled emotion. "I am deeply sorry for your loss, Ms. Wilkins. It is a terrible thing to lose a child in an accident such as this, and we do not want to discount the pain that you and your family are going through. But . . ." The tented fingers tapped his lips again. ". . . without witnesses, the state has failed to show any evidence that would sustain taking this case to trial. I have no option here but to drop the charges against Mrs. Baxter." He banged his gavel. "Case dismissed . . . Next case."

Denny was out of his seat in half a second. "Thank you!" I heard him say to Mr. Farrell, pumping his hand. "Thank you!" Then, "That's it? It's over?"

"Yes—though the state's attorney could subpoena the witnesses and ask for a grand jury indictment. But don't worry—even if it went to trial, Jodi would walk . . ."

Even as Mr. Farrell started bragging about the defense witnesses he'd lined up, I could see Jamal Wilkins's mother sitting perfectly still on the other side of the room, staring straight ahead. Mr. Farrell's voice sounded far away, as if I had water in my ears . . .

"The driver of the car that slammed into your minivan is prepared to testify that you both had the green light . . . evidence technicians who examined the skid marks at the scene of the accident found nothing consistent with excessive speed . . . not to mention that no cell phone was found in the minivan at the time of the accident . . ."

Taking my crutches, I hobbled toward the other mother. Swallowing past the huge lump forming in my throat, I spoke.

"Ms. Wilkins? I'm Jodi Baxter. It was . . . my car that struck your son."

The woman's face turned slightly, her eyes cold. "I know."

"I just want to say how terribly sorry I am. I can only imagine the pain you must be going through. I would . . . give anything if it hadn't happened. Even exchange my life for Jamal's—if I could."

Jamal's mother just stared at me for what seemed like an

eternity. Then she stood abruptly, gripping her purse with both hands. "But you can't . . . can you?" She pushed past me and strode out the door of the room, the two sullen boys trailing behind her.

I watched her go. I could hardly forgive myself. Did I really expect that she could forgive me?

Avis came over and gave me a long hug, saying nothing.

Denny and Mr. Farrell joined us. The lawyer held out his hand. "Well, Jodi Baxter, you can go home a free woman. What happened today took me by surprise, but even if we had gone to trial, we could easily have proven you were not guilty."

I shook his hand. "Not legally, anyway."

He looked at me strangely, but I just said, "Thank you, Mr. Farrell," and headed my crutches for the door of the courtroom.

DENNY WANTED TO TAKE AVIS AND ME OUT TO LUNCH to celebrate, but I shook my head, hoping Avis would understand. I just wanted to get home. I wanted to think . . . or pray . . . or something. But not talk.

Once we arrived home, Denny said he'd fix lunch while I got off my feet in the living room. The room was dim, air moving lazily through it from the window fan. I swung my crutches over to the front windows and, one after the other, opened the mini-blinds, letting in the bright daylight.

Stopping by the music cabinet, I shuffled through the CDs sitting in little stacks. I picked up one of the *Songs 4 Worship* albums and ran my finger down the list of songs till I found what I was looking for.

Putting the disc into the CD player, I punched the "forward" button until it came to the number of the song I wanted.

In Your presence, that's where I belong . . .

The music, slow and majestic, swelled until it seemed to take over my whole body.

Seeking Your face, touching Your grace . . .

In Your presence, O God . . .

Lifting my face and with awkward grace, on one leg and two crutches, I began to dance.

Windy City Stories

in the "Yada Yada Universe"
By Neta Jackson and Dave Jackson
www.daveneta.com

The Yada Yada Prayer Group series

The Yada Yada Prayer Group
The Yada Yada Prayer Group Gets Down
The Yada Yada Prayer Group Gets Real
The Yada Yada Prayer Group Gets Tough
The Yada Yada Prayer Group Gets Caught
The Yada Yada Prayer Group Gets Rolling
The Yada Yada Prayer Group Gets Decked Out

The Yada Yada House of Hope series

Where Do I Go?
Who Do I Talk To?
Who Do I Lean On?
Who Is My Shelter?
Harry Bentley's Second Chance
Harry Bentley's Second Sight
Lucy Come Home

SouledOut Sisters series

Stand By Me
Come to the Table

Windy City Neighbors series

Grounded
Derailed
Penny Wise (2014)
Pound Foolish (2014)

A Note from the Author

Dear Readers,

One of the greatest gifts God has given me here in Chicago is a prayer group of multi-cultural women, going on sixteen years now. God has used these amazing "sisters" to turn my life upside down—or maybe I should say "right side up"—taking me deeper in prayer and higher in praise.

Which is where the Yada Yada Prayer Group story begins . . .

As a writer, I wanted to share what God has been teaching me through this group, but you know the drill: "What happens with the sisters *stays* with the sisters!" So I had to create a fictional group. But what I naively thought would be just one novel became a series of *seven* novels! I learned that you can't put twelve feisty women in a novel and expect them to meekly stay there. They *all* wanted their stories to be told.

The whole Yada Yada journey has been full of surprises. First were the reader letters:

- "I laughed. I cried. It's been a long time —if ever—that a work of fiction touched me spiritually like this series did. I have begun to think of my prayer life in a whole new way."
- "Your [novel] has reawakened my desire to have that kind of relationship with God, where praise and thanksgiving are a natural part of my life."

- "Your thoughtful way of making prayer and praise seem possible is inspiring. The diversity [in your characters] keeps me hopeful."
- "These books made me want to start a Yada Yada Prayer Group"

This was the second surprise: Yada Yada Prayer Groups began springing up all over the globe. What a thrill—to think that God was using this series to bring women together *to pray*. Totally knocked my socks off.

And now . . . the Yada Yada sisters are about to be reborn! Thomas Nelson Publishers has repackaged the series with new covers and is sending them out to a new generation of readers. Wahoo! (Wait . . . new covers? Replace the crazy socks? So when I saw the new covers, I showed them to the toughest critic of all—my almost-grown, very with-it granddaughter, who said, "I love these covers! I'd buy a book with a cover like that." So there you go.)

I'm excited to introduce the Yada Yada sisters to you. While the novels are *fiction*, the stories and characters were inspired by many real people and events God has used to encourage me and show me the gift of the beautiful diversity within the body of Christ. And the fact that we *need* each other (see 1 Cor. 12:21–26).

If you join me on this journey, I'd love to hear from you!

Neta

DaveNeta@daveneta.com

Reading Group Guide

1. Which character in this novel do you identify with most? Why?

2. Why do you think it was important for the women in The Yada Yada Prayer Group to get off the Internet and into each other's homes?

3. What was the common denominator that kept the women in Yada Yada hanging in there with each other?

4. Jodi, a longtime Christian, experienced what it truly meant to be "just a sinner, saved by grace" for the first time. Does admitting you're *still* "just a sinner" like everyone else feel like blame or freedom? How have you experienced "God's grace" up close and personal?

5. What "religious clichés" have basically lost their meaning for you? Brainstorm new ways to communicate old truths.

6. What particular barriers tend to divide people, even those who share the same faith, where *you* live? (Cultural or ethnic differences? Racial tensions? Doctrine or worship styles?) Brain-

storm ways you could be intentional about "breaking down the walls."

7. What obstacles have you experienced in making friends—*real* friends—"across the color line"? (Be honest!)

8. Share instances when a cross-cultural relationship has been a gift for you. Or ask yourself: *How might an interracial or cross-cultural friendship enrich my life?* What would you be able to bring to such a relationship? What challenges might you face?

9. Do you have a group of friends that "yada" you—i.e., know you deeply, inspire you to praise ("yadah")? If you were to form a "Yada Yada Prayer Group," who would you invite? (Pick up the phone!)

10. What would you still like to know about the characters after reading this novel? What do you think is going to happen to The Yada Yada Prayer Group in Book Two?

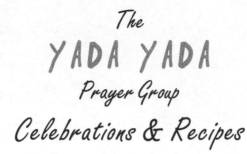

The
YADA YADA
Prayer Group
Celebrations & Recipes

Starting a *YADA YADA* Prayer Group

*I*s God tugging at your heart to start a prayer group? But you feel totally inadequate? God will give you wisdom, sister! (Read James 1:5 and *ask*!) There is no one-size-fits-all formula for putting together a prayer group, but here are a few things to consider:

Prepare yourself . . .

First of all, bring your desire to God and pray about it! (Funny how often we skip this step.)

Ask another sister to pray with you. "If two of you agree . . . about anything, it will be done for them" (Matthew 18:19).

Read *The Power of Praying Together* by Stormie Omartian (Harvest House). This sister knows what she's talking about!

Then . . .

Share with your pastor what you want to do. Choose a time for your prayer group to meet that does not conflict with other church meetings or responsibilities.

Who needs it? A prayer group for women in your church is perfectly legitimate. (Many "church" women are lonely or alone.) OR maybe God is calling you to reach beyond your circle of friends—to neighbors, co-workers, another parent at your child's school, across cultural or racial boundaries. This takes prayer and intentionality.

Personally invite other sisters to join you. If two of you are in agreement about starting a prayer group, each of you could invite one more. That's four. Then those four each invite one. That's eight. A good beginning!

Meet in your home—or ask another sister to host. Or share hosting among all the members of the prayer group. Meeting in homes helps create a circle of intimacy. Also, women who are not members of your church may feel more comfortable coming to a home meeting. (But if God directs you to meet at the office, at the park, at a coffee shop, at the jail, or at the church—do it!)

Size? Don't let the group get too big. Twelve is usually a maximum for a small group. Eight to ten is a good number. (If lots of women want to become a part, you may need to divide into two groups! What a wonderful "problem" to have.)

Leaders: Be sure one or two of the sisters who are well grounded in the Word of God are willing to function as leaders/facilitators.

The meeting itself . . .

Fellowship. Allow at least fifteen minutes for women to arrive, get snacks or drinks, and "unwind."

Begin with worship—a Scripture, a song, prayers of praise—to get your focus where it needs to be, on God alone.

Study the Word. Spend time in the Word. This can either be a Bible study using a study guide, a Bible book study using only the gospel of John, the book of James, etc., or a short devotion from the Word taught by someone in the group. But you will need someone to facilitate so you *do* leave time to . . .

PRAY! Share brief prayer requests. This is not the time for lengthy sharing or advice giving. Don't just talk about what needs prayer. *Pray* for one another!

Respect! Agree together that personal things shared in the group are to remain in the group—and not used as fodder for gossip. (However, if things come up that are too big to handle in the group, the leaders may need to seek outside counsel.)

Last but not least . . .

Pray during the week for the women who attend the group. Call to check on anyone who is missing, and pray for them over the phone.

Be expectant that God can do great things in you and through you as you pray.

So, Celebrate!

*I*n *The Yada Yada Prayer Group*, the sisters celebrated a major milestone for Florida: "Five years saved and five years sober!"

Well, why not? At birthdays and anniversaries, we celebrate those milestones in a person's life, to honor that person or marriage, to reflect on God's goodness in the past and look forward to the future.

Why not other milestones? Children and adults need encouragement, and celebrations are a great way to encourage someone. Like Samen . . .

Samen's Story

Several years ago, our family took in a Cambodian foster daughter. Samen Sang had been born in a refugee camp. When her family finally arrived in the U.S., Samen was nine years old but had never attended school. Tiny and petite, she looked six, so she fit right into the first grade. No problem . . . until her middle school teachers found out she was fifteen, going into seventh grade. *No way!* they said—and bumped her up into high school. Of course, she wasn't prepared, had no idea what was going on in her classes, so she started skipping school and hanging out on the street. Her mother, who spoke little English and didn't understand how to navigate American culture, was tearing her hair out and ready to marry her off.

Long story short, Samen came to live with us the middle of her freshman year. Her schooling was a mess, but we started with the first requirement for living with us: go to school every day. No skipping. It was a struggle. Temptation to skip was great. But Samen wanted to live with us, so she was in school every day. Her grades were terrible. But on the last day of school, she had *perfect attendance* for the second semester. So . . .

We celebrated! We took her out to dinner. We gave her flowers. We told her we were proud of her. We bragged on her to our church. And when she walked across the platform three years later to get her high school diploma, we were there cheering for her.

So, Celebrate!

It may seem a little silly to have "graduations" from kindergarten, but even small events and milestones may be worth celebrating—especially if a celebration honors someone who might otherwise be overlooked. Some events worth celebrating:

- A surprise Appreciation Party for the janitor at your child's school
- Balloons and snacks for the garbage truck guys—anytime, or near Labor Day
- A Thank You Celebration for the nurses who took care of you in your last hospitalization
- A one-year "You Did It!" party for someone who quit smoking
- The One-Year Anniversary of anything!—keeping a job,

your new prayer group, beating cancer, losing excess weight
and keeping it off
- Completing a marathon
- A backyard (or back porch) barbecue for the New Neighbor
- A school drop-out who finally gets his or her G.E.D.
. . . Or, as Yo-Yo might say, "Who needs an excuse to party?"

Make the Celebration Appropriate to the Occasion

Don't give your kids a blow-out party for every minor achieve-
ment. A simple, "I'm proud of you," might be all that's needed.
But don't take everything for granted, either. Pulling that D up to
an A-minus is a big deal and took hard work. So, celebrate!

Flowers, an inexpensive gift, even a card are wonderful ways to
say, "Thank you!"

Food . . . Did we mention food? Take a milestone in someone's
life, invite friends, *add food*, and *voila!* Instant party!

Speaking of Food . . .

Hey! If you're going to have a celebration—or even if you aren't—
it's time to introduce the Yada Yada Prayer Group's *Signature
Recipes.*

The YADA YADAS' Signature Recipes

*P*ut twelve feisty women in one prayer group, ranging in age from twenty to fifty-something, add a variety of skin colors, cultural backgrounds, ethnic upbringings, and years of church potlucks, and what do you get?

Food!

To introduce our cast of Yada Yada characters in another way, here are some "signature recipes" from each Yada Yada. "Signature?" you ask. Yep. Just another way of saying, if you see *that* on the potluck table, you know who made it without even seeing the name taped to the bowl (or pot, or plate, or whatever).

Jodi's No-Fail Chicken-and-Rice Casserole

Jodi's favorite when it comes to throwing stuff together for a church potluck or when she can't think of anything else to make for supper. No fail, too—IF she remembers to turn on the oven. Don't be a Jodi when it comes to little details like that.

Full recipe serves 6–8 (half recipe serves 3–4).

1 chicken, cut up, or 8–10 pieces with skin on
3 cups rice
2 (10.5-oz.) cans cream of mushroom soup
3 soup cans water (or use part white wine)
2 packages dry onion soup mix

Preheat oven to 350 degrees. Prepare 6-quart casserole by spraying with baking spray.

Mix cream of mushroom soup, water, and dry onion soup mix together. Pour a small amount in bottom of baking dish.

Measure raw rice into bottom of baking dish. Add half of soup & water mixture and moisten rice thoroughly. Arrange chicken pieces on top. Pour remaining soup & water mixture on top.

Cover. Place on middle rack in 350 degree oven for 1½ hours.

Or bake at 325 degrees for 2½ to 3 hours.

The secret to this tasty casserole is cooking it long enough so that the rice is tender, but not letting it dry out. It helps if you remember to turn on the oven—but we already said that.

Stu's Ramen Noodle Salad

What Stu brought to the Mother's Day Potluck at Uptown Community Church. (Good thing, since Jodi forgot to put her "no-fail" chicken-and-rice casserole into the oven.) Stu keeps stuff like dark sesame oil (has a lovely oriental nutty flavor), rice vinegar, and fresh gingerroot on hand, which might seem a bit much for the average household-with-kids, but she swears they make a world of difference for anything oriental—and salads.

1 (4-oz.) package ramen noodles (or use 4-oz. spaghetti, broken)
3 Tbsp. oil
3 Tbsp. honey
1 Tbsp. soy sauce
1 Tbsp. dark sesame oil
1 Tbsp. rice vinegar
1½ tsp. grated gingerroot
1 tsp. crushed red pepper flakes
3 cups cooked chicken, chilled and shredded
1 cup red cabbage, finely shredded
4 green onions, thinly sliced
2 large carrots, shredded
1 red bell pepper, sliced into thin strips or chopped
½ cup dry-roasted peanuts

Cook the ramen noodles as directed on the package. (Or cook spaghetti *al dente*.)

For dressing: Combine oil, honey, soy sauce, dark sesame oil, rice vinegar, gingerroot, and red pepper flakes in a small bowl and whisk thoroughly.

Shred chicken and chop vegetables; set aside.

Drain noodles and rinse with cold water. Then, in a large bowl, combine noodles, chicken, and vegetables. Toss with dressing. Top with peanuts (or pass separately).

Avis's Deluxe Macaroni and Cheese

Avis modestly says mac-and-cheese is one of the few things she can cook. "Everything else turns out raw or charred." Only later did the Yada Yadas discover this is actually true! As far as they're concerned, she can stick with the mac-and-cheese. It's good!

Preheat oven to 305 degrees. Recipe serves 6, more or less.

2 cups elbow macaroni, cooked and drained according to package directions
¼ cup butter or margarine
¼ cup flour
1 tsp. powdered mustard
2½ cups milk
3 cups sharp cheddar cheese, coarsely shredded
¼ tsp. salt
¼ tsp. fresh ground pepper
1 Tbsp. Worcestershire sauce
Tabasco sauce to taste (3 good shots)
Paprika as desired

While macaroni is cooking, melt butter in saucepan over moderate heat. Blend in flour and dry mustard. Slowly whisk in milk. Cook, whisking, until thickened. Mix in 2 cups of cheese and remaining ingredients *except* macaroni. Cook and stir until cheese melts.

Remove cheese mixture from heat; mix in macaroni. Turn mixture into a buttered 2-qt. casserole dish. Sprinkle with remaining 1 cup of cheese. Sprinkle with paprika as desired. Bake, uncovered, for 30 minutes until bubbly and lightly browned.

Florida's Quick Catfish Dinner

Who has time to spend an hour in the kitchen? Not Florida! When she gets home from work, not only are the husband and kids clamoring for supper, her own stomach is growling. Good thing about catfish—it cooks up in a jiffy. Tasty, too.

Total prep time: 20 minutes. Serves 4.

4 catfish fillets, about 2 lbs.
½ cup Italian-seasoned bread crumbs
2 Tbsp. flour
½ tsp. seasoned salt
4 Tbsp. butter or corn oil
Louisiana or Tabasco hot sauce

Also . . .
1½ cups white rice
1 package frozen green peas

Put rice, 3 cups of water, and 1 tsp. salt in a saucepan, cover, and bring to boil, then turn heat down to a low simmer for 12 minutes. Throw frozen peas in a saucepan with 1 cup of water and bring to a slow boil.

While rice and peas are cooking, heat butter or oil in a skillet large enough to accommodate the catfish fillets. Put the bread crumbs, flour, and seasoning in a paper bag, lunch size. Drop in fillets and shake two or three times until each fillet is coated. (Too much shaking will break up fillets.) Place the fillets in the hot skillet and cook on a medium-high heat for about 5–7 minutes per side until golden brown.

Serve with rice and peas, which should be done about the time the fillets are golden brown. Provide hot sauce for those who want it.

Chanda's Jamaican Rice and Peas

"Why you need a recipe?" Chanda scoffs, when asked about her favorite recipe for Jamaican Rice and Peas. "Just cook up some of dem red peas, t'row in de spices and coconut milk and some rice. What's so 'ard about dat?" Well, fine. But just in case you need a little help, here are a few tips from Chanda.

Dried red beans are the "peas" in Jamaican Rice and Peas, though fresh Pigeon peas (Gungo peas) are used in season. **Cooking dried beans:** Soak beans overnight in plenty of water, *or* (quick method) put dried beans in a pot, add water (about 2 inches above beans), bring to a boil for one minute, turn off stove, cover pot, and let sit for one hour. Then gently simmer soaked beans until tender.

1½ cups *cooked* red kidney beans, reserving cooking liquid
1 cloves garlic, chopped
1¼ cups unsweetened coconut milk, *plus* . . .
Reserved bean liquid and enough water to make 2¼ cups combined liquid
1 cup rice
2 green onions, chopped (*or* 1 med. onion, chopped)
1 or 2 sprigs fresh thyme (or ½ tsp. dried thyme)
Salt and pepper to taste

Put *cooked* red beans into a large pot. Add garlic. Measure all liquids (coconut milk, reserved bean liquid, and water) to make 2¼ cups, and add to the pot. Add rice, onion, and seasonings.

Bring to a boil, reduce heat, cover, and simmer for 20 to 30 minutes or until all liquid is absorbed.

If using canned beans, drain, but save liquid to add to the coconut milk and water. Then simply add the canned beans to the pot with the rice.

Ruth's Cheese Blintzes

Cheese blintzes are traditional fare for Shavuot—the Jewish Feast of Weeks, known as Pentecost to Christians. The first time Ruth made these yummy delicacies for her Yada Yada sisters, Yo-Yo piped up, "Why don't they just call 'em cottage cheese pancakes and be done with it?" . . . which earned her a whole string of Yiddishisms we can't repeat here.

Makes 16–18 blintzes.

Batter:
4 eggs
1 cup milk (or ½ cup milk and ½ cup water)
1 cup flour
¼ cup sugar
⅛ tsp. salt
2 Tbsp. oil or melted butter

Filling:
1 pound cottage cheese (dry type, or strained)
2 beaten eggs
2 Tbsp. flour
2 Tbsp. sugar
1 tsp. vanilla

Topping:
2 cups sour cream (can use half yogurt)
6 eggs

1 tsp. vanilla
1 tsp. cornstarch
¼ tsp. salt

Plus...
¼ cup melted butter (or oil) for frying blintzes

Step 1—Making the Crepes: Combine batter ingredients until smooth (use mixer, blender, or food processor). Heat a small frying pan (about 7 inches)—non-stick or a heavy, seasoned pan works best—with a small amount of oil or spray with cooking spray. Pour ⅓ cup batter into hot pan and tip frying pan to spread batter around evenly. Cook briefly until small air bubbles form; bottom should be golden brown. Turn over and allow to cook another 5 seconds. Remove crepe to a plate. Repeat with remaining batter, adding small amount of oil or cooking spray as needed. Stack warm crepes between sheets of wax paper so they don't stick. Makes 16–18 crepes.

Step 2—Filling the Crepes: Combine ingredients for filling; mix well. Place a heaping tablespoon of filling along one side of each crepe. Fold over once to cover filling, then tuck in sides and finish rolling. Set aside until all crepes are filled. Now they're blintzes!

Step 3—Frying the Blintzes: Melt 1 Tbsp. butter in frying pan, add three blintzes at a time, turning once until both sides are golden brown and crisp. Repeat until all blintzes have been fried.

(Recipe continues on next page.)

Step 4—Baking the Blintzes: Preheat oven to 350 degrees. Lightly grease a 9 x 13-inch pan and line up the blintzes. Prepare topping: Beat sour cream and eggs together until thick and creamy; add remaining ingredients and beat well. Pour topping over the blintzes and bake 1 hour.

Step 5—Serving the Blintzes: Serve hot with fresh cut-up fruit, such as peaches, strawberries, blueberries, etc. Or puree frozen berries and serve as a sauce. Allow 2–3 blintzes per serving. (Go ahead, *nosh* away!)

Yo-Yo's Brother's PB&Js

"Cook?" Yo-Yo says. "What for? Don't matter what I make; my brothers just want peanut butter and jelly. So, hey, I let 'em make their own PB&Js. It's food, ain't it?"

2 slices white bread (preferably cheap kind that wads into
   a ball instead of crumbles)
Brand-name creamy peanut butter (forget "natural"
   peanut butter)
Jar of strawberry jam

Teen male version: Dig knife into peanut butter; swab one slice of bread with thick layer of peanut butter. Dig same knife into jar of strawberry jam; swab the other slice of bread with thick layer of jam. Slap the two slices of bread together (peanut butter and jam on the *inside*). Tell someone you're going "out" while your mouth is full of PB&J. Leave jars of peanut butter and jam open on counter, along with gooey knife for someone else to clean up.

Adele's Foot-Stompin' Greens

Why "foot-stompin'"? Because when you take a forkful of Adele's greens, you want to stomp your feet and shout, "Hallelujah!" But you can't shout, because your mouth is full, so . . . foot stompin' will have to do to show just how mm-mm good these greens are.

Note: Greens are easy to grow. Even a small patch in your yard will provide enough for you and your kin. Started early, they will be ready by late June, even in Chicago, and produce sometimes into December, tasting even better after the first freeze if it's not too hard.

Serves 6–8.

2–3 lbs. collard greens (may substitute mustard or turnip greens)
1 pound smoked neck bone, ham hocks, or in a pinch ½ pound bacon fried not too crispy
2 medium onions, chopped
5 cloves of garlic, minced
1 tsp. crushed red pepper flakes
2 Tbsp. chicken bouillon
2 Tbsp. brown sugar

Wash the greens and slice out the stem and central rib. Stack several leaves on top of each other and roll them into a tube, then slice the roll to create ½ inch strips. Put 1 inch of water in the bottom of a 6–8 qt. kettle and add all ingredients. Cover and bring to a boil. Simmer 1–2 hours or until the meat falls off the bones and the greens are tender, checking periodically that the liquid does not boil away, adding more if necessary. (Depending on how fresh the greens, they will contribute liquid, but you don't want there to be so much "pot likker" that the greens are floating in soup.)

Good any ol' time—but absolutely kickin' when served with corn-bread, black eyed peas, and fried chicken!

Delores's Mexicali Soup

Delores calls this soup "Mexicali," because it's a blend of Mexico and California. (The Enriquez kids, however, call it "Taco Soup"!)

1 pound lean ground beef
1 onion, chopped
3 garlic cloves, chopped or minced
1 package taco seasoning
1 (14.5-oz.) can corn
1 (14.5-oz.) can pinto beans, drained
1 (14.5-oz.) can black beans, drained
1 (6-oz.) can chopped green chiles (mild or hot, depending on taste)
2 (14.5-oz.) cans diced tomatoes—or 1 (28-oz.) can
2 (14.5-oz.) cans chicken broth (or equivalent water & chicken bouillion)
½ cup cilantro, chopped
3 limes, squeezed

Garnish: Shredded cheese; corn chips; sour cream

Fry together in large soup pot: ground beef, onion, and garlic until beef is no longer pink. Add taco seasoning; stir until well blended. Add cans: corn, pinto beans, black beans, green chilles, diced tomatoes, and broth. Bring to a boil, reduce heat, cover, and simmer for 10–15 minutes. When ready to serve, stir in lime juice and cilantro. Ladle into bowls. Let your *niños* choose their garnish.

Edesa's Mama's Mango Salsa

Say "salsa" . . . think "tomato-salsa-in-a-jar"? Not if you drop by Edesa's apartment for a snack! Hondurans make good use of luscious mangoes growing everywhere in their country. Fortunately for us gringos, mangoes are becoming more common in the fruit and produce section of many grocery stores.

1 mango, peeled and diced
2 avocados, peeled and chopped
1 tomato, diced
¼ cup red onion, diced
1 red pepper, diced
1 garlic clove, minced
Juice of 1 lime

Peel, chop, and dice away! Combine all ingredients in a bowl, let it sit for 20 minutes to mingle flavors (*or* cover with plastic wrap and refrigerate overnight to preserve flavor). Serve with tortilla chips—and you better double the recipe next time!

Nony's Swazi Butternut Soup

If you're lucky enough to get invited to the Sisulu–Smith household for dinner, don't be surprised if you're served this rich, golden, satisfying soup for the first course, a favorite South African starter to a meal of roast beef or lamb. But why wait for an invitation? Make this for your own family—and be prepared to offer seconds.

2 medium onions, chopped
4 Tbsp. butter or margarine
2 medium butternut squash, peeled, de-seeded, and cut into cubes
1 large apple, peeled, cored, and chopped
1¼ tsp. curry powder
4 Tbsp. flour
½ tsp. ground nutmeg
3 cups chicken stock (homemade, canned, or water
   & chicken bouillion)
2 cups milk
1½ tsp. salt

Garnish: Parsley (chopped), sour cream

In a large saucepan or soup pot, sauté the chopped onions in the butter or margarine. Add chopped butternut, apple, and curry powder; continue to sauté gently. Add flour and nutmeg; stir until blended.

Now add chicken stock, milk, and salt to the vegetable mixture. Cover, bring to a boil, and continue cooking over medium heat until butternut pieces are soft, stirring occasionally. Puree entire mixture (you may have to do 4 cups at a time) in a blender or food processor until soup is smooth and creamy. Reheat and serve hot with a dollop of sour cream and sprinkles of chopped parsley.

Hoshi's Japanese Spring Rolls

Any kind of Asian cooking calls for some special ingredients, but you can often find them in the produce section or specialty aisle at your grocery store. If not, locate the closest Asian market. It's worth it—spring rolls are fun to make! (Shh, don't tell Hoshi, but when Jodi tried this recipe, she substituted regular ol' white button mushrooms for the shiitake mushrooms, and the spring rolls were still good, if not exactly authentic.)

4–5 dried shiitake mushrooms
1 oz. *harusame* (bean starch noodles), or cellophane noodles
⅓ pound ground pork
1 cup bean sprouts
1 can bamboo shoots, chopped
1 tsp. ginger, grated
1 Tbsp. vegetable oil
1 Tbsp. cornstarch
⅔ cup chicken broth
1½ Tbsp. soy sauce
1 tsp. sugar
1 tsp. sesame oil
2 Tbsp. sake rice wine (or 2 Tbsp. rice vinegar with a little sugar)
1 Tbsp. water mixed with 1 Tbsp. cornstarch
10 to 20 egg roll wrappers
1 tsp. flour mixed with 1 Tbsp. water
Vegetable oil for frying

Advance preparation: Soak shiitake mushrooms in water for 30 minutes to soften. Sprinkle cornstarch over ground pork and stir in well. Drop *harusame* or cellophane noodles in a pan of boiling water for 1 minute, then drain and cut into 3-inch lengths. Drain mushrooms and cut into thin strips.

Prepare filling: Heat oil in large frying pan, add grated ginger and sauté briefly. Add ground pork and fry until it loses its pink color; add mushrooms and bean sprouts and sauté. Then add chicken broth, sugar, soy sauce, sesame oil, sake (or rice vinegar-plus-sugar), and noodles to the pan. Heat through until mixture simmers; then add mixture of water and cornstarch. Stir well. Scoop filling into a bowl and cool.

Wrapping the rolls: Spoon 1–2 Tbsp. filling on egg roll wrapper. Fold one side of wrapper over filling to cover; then tuck both sides of the wrapper inward and finish rolling. Seal the edge with the mixture of water and flour.

Frying the spring rolls: Heat oil in a deep frying pan to 360 degrees F. Fry spring rolls, turning until all sides are golden brown. Drain and serve with soy sauce mixed with chili oil for dipping.

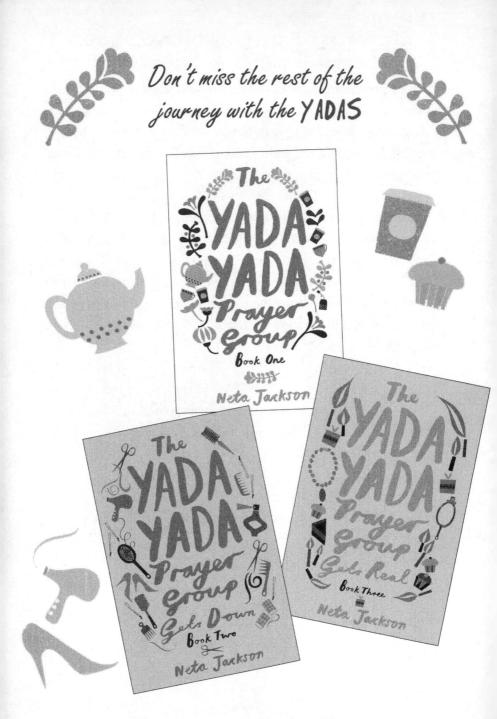

Don't miss the rest of the journey with the YADAS

AVAILABLE IN PRINT AND E-BOOK

About the Author

*N*eta Jackson's award-winning Yada books have sold more than 500,000 copies and are spawning prayer groups across the country. She and her husband, Dave, are also an award-winning writing team, best known for the Trailblazer Books—a 40-volume series of historical fiction about great Christian heroes with 1.5 million in sales—and *Hero Tales: A Family Treasury of True Stories from the Lives of Christian Heroes* (vols 1–4). They live in the Chicago area, where the Yada stories are set.

Visit them at daveneta.com

Challenges. Prayer. Friendship. Hope.
All come together in this inspiring
series from Neta Jackson.

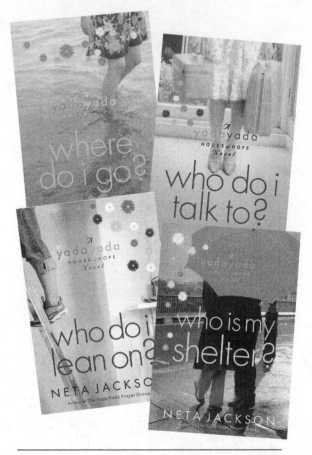

the HOUSE *of* HOPE SERIES

Available in Print and E-book

Visit DaveNeta.com